*Women's Struggle for Higher Education in Russia, 1855–1900*

In nineteenth-century Russia, women had greater access to medical and higher education than anywhere else in contemporary Europe. This book explores the remarkable expansion and upgrading of women's education during those turbulent decades following the Crimean War. Focusing on the relationship between developments in women's education and the domestic politics of the post-war era, the author reveals how the peculiar nature of autocratic rule under Alexander II facilitated the establishment of university-level courses for women. She also demonstrates that those women who co-operated with the government to increase their educational opportunities far outnumbered the more publicized female revolutionists who sought to overthrow it. Although Russian radicalism gave enormous encouragement to women's pursuit of university study, it was the support of reform-minded academics and government officials that made possible the creation of advanced educational facilities for women.

The author highlights ministerial disputes and public debate over women's education. She also examines the social and economic circumstances that promoted women's struggle for higher education. Special attention is given to female physicians, whose medical skills and commitment to social service were tested in the Russo-Turkish War and the tradition-bound peasant village. Women's advanced educational facilities fell victim to the conservative reaction following the assassination of Alexander II: most were shut down. They did not reopen until the last Romanov tsar, Nicholas II, allowed the second burgeoning of educational opportunities for Russian women.

Christine Johanson teaches in the Department of History, Queen's University.

# Women's Struggle for Higher Education in Russia, 1855–1900

## CHRISTINE JOHANSON

McGill-Queen's University Press
Kingston and Montreal

© McGill-Queen's University Press 1987
ISBN 0-7735-0565-2

Legal deposit first quarter 1987
Bibliothèque nationale du Québec

Printed in Canada

This book has been published with the help of a grant from
the Social Science Federation of Canada, using funds
provided by the Social Sciences and Humanities Research
Council of Canada.

Printed on acid-free paper

---

**Canadian Cataloguing in Publication Data**

Johanson, Christine, 1944-
    Women's struggle for higher education in Russia,
    1855-1900
    Bibliography: p.
    Includes index.
    ISBN 0-7735-0565-2
    1. Higher education of women – Soviet Union –
    History.    I. Title.
    LC2166.J64 1987    376'.65'0947    c86-094867-6

---

*To my mother and to the memory of my father*

# Contents

# Tables

# *Preface*

Russian women began their struggle for higher education during that turbulent period of reform following the Crimean War of 1853–6. The result was remarkable: by the late 1870s, they had greater access to physicians' training and university-level courses than women anywhere else in Europe.

This particular episode in the history of Russian women has not received much sympathetic attention from contemporary scholars. Most often, both Western and Soviet historians have focused on the female heroes of the Russian radical movement. That is not surprising: the exploits of some radical women are the stuff of epic drama. The majority of female activists in nineteenth-century Russia, however, did not join the revolutionary underground. Those women who co-operated with the government in order to increase their educational opportunities far outnumbered the female revolutionists who sought to overthrow it. Their quest for higher learning, a traditional male monopoly, also represents a significant development in Russian history. In pursuing university study and medical degrees, these women not only challenged time-honoured notions about the alleged intellectual inferiority of the female sex. They also defied custom and law, which had long prescribed women's subordination to the family. Advanced education, most believed, would enable them to contribute to the nation's welfare, in addition to promoting their own self-development. For their quiet rejection of women's traditionally subservient role, they, too, suffered public censure and material hardship. Indeed, women of extraordinary courage, determination, and talent figured prominently in the movement for higher education. But they were not its sole protagonists: professors and statesmen played major roles as well.

This book presents a brief history of the struggle to expand women's educational opportunities in Russia. Its main focus is on the relationship between developments in women's education and the domestic politics of the post-Crimean War era. Considerable attention is also given to the social and economic circumstances that encouraged women to step outside the family sphere and to embark on the quest for higher learning.

Several individuals and institutions have contributed to the making of this book. Charles Ruud first encouraged me to become a historian and, for more than a decade, has provided moral support and sensible advice. His comments on the manuscript were invaluable in helping to improve the final version. Ruth Dudgeon was particularly generous in sharing with me her ideas about the Russian women's movement. Her critical reading of the manuscript compelled me to see weaknesses that I otherwise might not have seen and to correct misstatements before they appeared in print. James McClelland, Richard Pierce, Robert Malcolmson, and Klaus Hansen also read an earlier version of the manuscript, and I wish to thank them, as well as my publisher's readers, for their helpful comments and criticisms. The usual disclaimer is, of course, in order: any errors, whether of fact or interpretation, are exclusively my own.

For financial support, I am beholden to the Canada Council, which provided much-needed fellowships during the early stages of my research. The Canada-USSR Exchange Program also funded and facilitated my work in the Soviet Union in 1975–6. For timely grants and fellowships, I am grateful to the University of California at Santa Barbara and the Advisory Research Committee of Queen's University. I have also incurred a debt to the librarians and archivists at the institutions where I did my research: the Library of Congress, the University of California at Santa Barbara, the University of Illinois Russian and East European Center, the Columbia University Archive of Russian and East European History and Culture, the Hoover Institution, Harvard University, the Lenin Library in Moscow, Saltykov-Shchedrin Library in Leningrad, the Leningrad State Historical Archive, and the Central State Historical Archive in Leningrad. I wish to pay special tribute here to the late Serefima Grigorevna Sakharova, former archivist at the Central State Historical Archive. She showed much kindness, skill, and industry in obtaining material for me. It is also a pleasure to express my appreciation to Karen Donnelly who typed more than one version of the manuscript with accuracy, speed, and good humour.

Finally, I must thank family and friends who provided moral support when I needed it most.

N.I. Pirogov,
surgeon and pedagogue

E.M. Bakunina,
Sister of Mercy

From *Nikolai Ivanovich Pirogov i ego nasledie. Pirogovskie s'ezdy. Iubileinoe izdanie*, ed. M.M. Gran, Z.G. Frenkel', A.I. Shingarev (St Petersburg, 1911).

A.S. Norov,
minister of education (1854-8)

K.D. Ushinskii,
pedagogue

A.V. Golovnin,
minister of education (1861-6)

D.A. Tolstoi,
minister of education
(1866-80);
minister of internal affairs
(1882-9)

I.D. Delianov,
minister of education
(1882-97)

From N.V. Chekhov, *Narodnoe obrazovanie v Rossii s 60-kh godov* XIX *veka*
(Moscow, 1912).

Nadezhda P. Suslova,
doctor of medicine

Mariia A. Bokova,
doctor of medicine

Sofiia V. Kovalevskaia,
mathematician

From L.A. Vorontsova, *Sof'ia Kovalevskaia* (Moscow, 1959).

Founders of the Bestuzhevskie Courses:
O.A. Mordvinova, A.N. Beketov,
A.P. Filosofova, P.S. Stasova,
N.A. Belozerskaia, V.P. Tarnovskaia,
N.V. Stasova, M.A. Menzhinskaia
(portraits in background of
M.V. Trubnikova and E.I. Konradi)

Anna P. Filosofova, leader of the
St Petersburg women's movement

From *Sbornik pamiati Anny Pavlovny Filosofovoi*, 2 vols (Petrograd, 1915).

Mariia V. Trubnikova, leader of the St Petersburg women's
movement

I.M. Sechenov,
physiologist

N.I. Kostomarov,
historian

D.I. Mendeleev,
chemist

A.P. Borodin,
chemist and composer

V.O. Kliuchevskii,
historian

From Inocento Serisev, *Album of Great, Outstanding and Eminent Personalities of Russia*, 2 parts (Sydney, Australia, 1945-6).

*Women's Struggle for Higher Education in Russia, 1855–1900*

# *Transliteration and Dating*

Transliteration follows the modified version of
the Library of Congress system. In the case of
pre-1918 orthography, the spelling has not been
modernized, except that the final hard sign ['']
has been omitted. All dates are given according
to the Julian calendar in use in Russia at the
time. It ran twelve days behind the Gregorian
calendar in the nineteenth century and thirteen
days behind in the twentieth century.

# Introduction

Long on hair, short on brains

TRADITIONAL RUSSIAN SAYING[1]

"Hitherto, our vast system of public education has had in view only half the population – the male sex."[2] So wrote Minister of Education A.S. Norov to the new tsar, Alexander II, in March 1856. The minister had scarcely exaggerated: at the time, one-tenth of 1 percent of the female population attended primary school.[3] Boys in the elementary system, in contrast, represented 1.3 percent of the male population and outnumbered the girls by more than eleven to one. Even fewer girls had access to secondary education. The very wealthy nobility sometimes employed foreign tutors to instruct their children,.but it was much more typical for well-to-do gentry and officials to send their daughters to elite boarding schools, the only girls' institutions beyond the primary level. Private *pansiony*, which were modelled on the French *pensionnat* and operated by foreigners, accommodated some privileged families. Most, however, preferred the august institutes of the Fourth Department, that section of the Imperial Chancellery which managed the charitable and educational institutions established in the name of the Dowager Empress Mariia Fedorovna. In the mid-nineteenth century, the twenty-five institutes of the Fourth Department represented the most advanced educational facilities available to Russian girls.

These preserves of the privileged cultivated the social arts deemed most appropriate to future wives and mothers of aristocratic households. Conversational French and music, therefore, dominated the six-year course of study, whereas daily routine emphasized deportment and obedience, presumably the cardinal virtues of well-born ladies.[4] A host of rules and regulations stressing the proper forms of behaviour governed the lives of pupils who resided in the institute from the age of ten to sixteen. During these formative years, strict supervision and rigid discipline encouraged the development of those submissive attitudes traditionally demanded of women. In Russia, as in Europe, the hierarchical family had long assigned its female members a subordinate role. The empire's legal code, moreover, specifically prescribed a woman's subservience to her spouse: "A woman must obey her husband as the head of the family, reside with him in love, respect, and unlimited obedience, and offer him every pleasantness and affection as master of the household."[5] Russian law also gave the husband the means to control his wife's movements. No married woman could obtain an internal passport, necessary for travel or city residence, without his permission. Fathers exercised similar control over unmarried daughters: a single woman under twenty-one was recorded on her father's passport. Sons, however, received their own passports at age seventeen.[6] Both law and custom, then, enshrined the notion of male supremacy; and girls' boarding schools were designed to uphold the status quo.

According to the memoirs of former pupils, the oppressive regime of institute life left little room for academic pursuits. Vera N. Figner lamented: "Reading was not encouraged at the Institute, and during all those years no one ever breathed a word of its necessity." She recalled leaving the institute with a "cultivated manner," but "almost nothing" in terms of "scientific knowledge" or "intellectual training."[7] Another graduate, Elizaveta N. Vo-dovozova, complained that its cloistered atmosphere and extreme regimentation not only militated against intellectual development, but also promoted artifice and sham in personal relations: "Gradually, losing all natural feelings, *institutki* invented artificial love, a parody, a caricature of genuine love, in which there was not a trace of true feelings."[8] Those girls who attended *pansiony* fared little better. Striving to emulate the more prestigious institute, the *pansion* also trained its charges to be as non-functional as upper-class women were expected to be. Indeed, the empty-headed boarding-school graduate was immortalized by the great Russian satirist, N.V. Gogol. In his novel, *Dead Souls*, the pathetically frivolous Mrs Manilov is the natural product of her education. The institute had taught her the three fundamentals of "all human virtue": conversing in French, playing the piano, and the "knitting of purses and other surprises."[9] Contemporary girls' schools were no laughing matter for N.I. Pirogov, the renowned surgeon and pedagogue. He was unmistakably serious when he charged that these schools offered no meaningful preparation for life, but transformed a young woman into a "doll."[10]

Education, however, seldom has the same effect on all its recipients. And as Aimé Martin commented in the early nineteenth century: "It is in spite of our stupid systems of education that women have an idea, a mind and a soul."[11] The Russian boarding school failed to dull the intellect or break the spirit of all its pupils. Figner, for example, surreptitiously read novels while pretending to do evening devotions in the lamplight of a holy icon.[12] She was not the only *institutka* to rebel against the sterile school environment. In both the institute and *pansion*, moreover, young women acquired at least fluency in French and a good command of Russian. During vacation and upon graduation, then, they were able to read the contemporary journals that loomed so large in the intellectual life of the nation. These journals would have a significant impact on young women's attitudes, particularly after the Crimean War when the periodical press became a forum for discussing the country's social problems.

It was during those turbulent post-war years that boarding school "dolls" gave way to women doctors. The reign of Alexander II (1855–81) witnessed an extraordinary expansion and upgrading of educational facilities for Russian women. In St Petersburg, Moscow, Kiev, and Kazan, professors organized women's higher courses. Boasting a curriculum and teaching staff drawn largely from the local university, these courses would admit thousands of women to advanced study in the sciences and humanities.[13] In addition, women's medical courses in St Petersburg offered a five-year program equivalent to that of male medical schools. By 1882, these courses would train over 200 female physicians, a contingent of women doctors far outnumbering that of any contemporary European state.[14] In that year, there were twenty-six women doctors in England and seven in France. Both Germany and the Austro-Hungarian Empire refused to admit women to advanced medical training and practice until the late 1890s.

The burgeoning of educational opportunities for Russian women is the subject of the present volume. Women's struggle for higher education not only achieved spectacular results during the reign of Alexander II; it also overshadowed all other aspects of the Russian women's movement until the early twentieth century. In striking contrast to Western feminists who campaigned on a variety of social and political issues, Russian women concentrated almost exclusively on education and employment. That they avoided appeals for political rights is not surprising: agitation for such rights was illegal in nineteenth-century Russia and carried the penalty of imprisonment or exile. For the most part, Russian women also remained silent on questions of family reform and sexual ethics that figured so prominently in feminist campaigns in the West. So few items on the Western agenda were championed by Russian women in the nineteenth century that it is difficult to draw parallels between the two movements. It must not be inferred, however, that they emerged in isolation from each other. On the contrary, contact with foreign feminists inspired and encouraged Russian women. Mariia V. Trubnikova, a leader of the St Petersburg women's movement, corresponded with French feminist Jenny d'Héricourt, as well as Josephine Butler, the English crusader against legalized prostitution. John Stuart Mill, England's outspoken advocate of women's rights, also wrote to Trubnikova, congratulating Russian women on their educational achievements. So too did Léonie

Bréa, the French novelist who published under the pseudonym Andrée Léo.[15] Since the late 1850s, moreover, Russian journalists had kept abreast of the feminist debate in Europe.

But the origins and development of the Russian women's movement for higher education owed much more to circumstances at home than to feminism abroad. This book investigates those circumstances. Considerable attention is given to the socio-economic conditions of the post-Crimean War era that fostered women's pursuit of university study. My main concern, however, is with the political culture that facilitated the rapid expansion and upgrading of women's education during Alexander II's reign. Since Elena I. Likhacheva published her *Materialy dlia istoriia zhenskago obrazovaniia v Rossii* at the turn of the century, no scholar has undertaken a systematic study of the relationship between the developments in women's higher education and the domestic politics of the reform era. Contemporary Soviet historians are prone to examining these developments from the vantage point of 1917, focusing on the Bestuzhevskie Courses of St Petersburg as a training ground for female revolutionists.[16] Western scholars tend to emphasize, on the one hand, the progressive involvement of educated women in revolutionary activity during the late nineteenth century and, on the other, the struggle for women's suffrage in the early twentieth century.[17] From these perspectives, recent research has contributed significantly to the social history of imperial Russia. At the same time, however, there has been a general underestimation of the significance of the political culture in which women's higher education flourished.

In an attempt to redress the balance, this study explores those distinguishing features of Russian domestic politics under Alexander II that promoted women's higher education. First, the preparation and implementation of the "Great Reforms" generated an emancipatory spirit never before equalled in Russian history. For many, the first flush of freedom came in late 1857 when the autocrat pledged to reform serfdom, the country's most fundamental socio-economic institution. The following January, censorship of the press was relaxed, thereby encouraging public discussion of prospective reform. Three years later, serfdom was abolished and some twenty-four million male peasants owned by the gentry, state, or crown were legally emancipated. Subsequent legislation recast other traditional institutions or created new ones: the army was completely overhauled; the courts and administration of justice underwent radical reorganization; popularly elected organs of government were created at the district and local levels; and the universities received a new statute. Such massive reform fostered the vision of a new Russia, revitalized and transformed. Indeed, the very promise of such sweeping change stimulated dreams and hopes among all ranks of society, from the most humble peasant who hungered for land to the high-ranking official who yearned for his nation's rapid recovery from the humiliating defeat in the Crimea. It was this heady atmosphere of the early reform era that raised women's expectations and promoted their pursuit of higher education.

Second, public opinion emerged as a factor in Russian political life and confronted the autocracy on issues of educational reform. In these years of social and intellectual fermentation, a broad segment of literate society began to evince an independent judgment on the country's problems and future. Mitigation of the censorship precipitated a veritable explosion in Russian journalism and allowed the publication of views untutored by the government. Meanwhile, the loosening of state control over the universities led to an unprecedented degree of experimentation in higher education. It also facilitated the development of the university into a vigorous cultural centre, with a restive student community and a professoriate committed to academic freedom. These scholars and journalists became leading spokesmen of emergent public opinion. The most reform-minded among them also championed women's higher education.

Finally, the manner in which Alexander II exercised sovereign power over the government administration permitted his ministers to implement competing policies on women's education. The tsar created no institution to co-ordinate the various branches of the bureaucracy, but granted his most trusted officials considerable authority within their respective realms of the administration. Such officials were much more than obedient servitors of the crown: they were policy-makers who proposed and implemented significant reform. Dedicated support of Russian autocracy united these statesmen. Disagreement over how state interests would best be served, however, often made them bitter rivals. The individual minister, moreover, enjoyed the greatest latitude in matters about which the emperor had few convictions or was simply undecided. Women's education was one of those issues on which Alexander II failed to take a stand, and thus it remained a source of contention in high government circles throughout his reign.

In this volume, then, ministerial in-fighting merits far more attention than revolutionary conspiracy; public debate plays a much larger role than underground propaganda; and reformists who co-operated with the autocracy overshadow the revolutionists who sought to destroy it. The Russian radical movement, however, is not completely ignored: its impact on the attitudes and policies of contemporary statesmen is examined in detail. With few exceptions, the chief protagonists in this particular episode of Russian history are from privileged society. The wives and daughters of gentry and officials spearheaded the movement for women's higher education. Their menfolk made up the cadres of the autocratic government, and along with other members of the educated elite – academics, publicists, and literati – participated in the political culture of the reform era. Those who had access to the new women's courses, however, included a sizeable minority of urban women of the lower social strata. For the peasant majority of the female population, the expansion of women's educational opportunities had little relevance. In the tradition-bound village, poverty, illiteracy, and the brute form of male domination forced most women, in the words of the poet Nekrasov, "to be enslaved to a slave to the grave."[18]

The organization of this book closely follows the chronological development of women's higher education. The first part provides the socio-political context of the "thaw" in educational affairs. Beginning with the accession of Alexander II and ending with the promulgation of the University Statute of 1863, chapter I investigates the conditions that encouraged public debate over women's education and permitted the temporary admission of female auditors to Russian universities. The second part (chapters 2 and 3) examines the joint efforts of academics and women to organize advanced educational facilities in Moscow and St Petersburg, as well as the exodus of Russian women to Zurich University. Spanning the period when Minister of Education D.A. Tolstoi and Chief of Gendarmes P.A. Shuvalov exerted considerable influence on court politics, this section also analyses their attempts to frustrate women's educational ambitions without provoking an adverse public reaction. The third part (chapters 4 and 5) traces the evolution of women's higher courses and medical courses during the last decade of Alexander II's reign. Here, much emphasis is placed on high-level government debate over women's medical education, particularly the controversy between Tolstoi and D.A. Miliutin, the minister of war. The final section of this part also assesses the significance of the women's medical courses in relation to the health needs of the Russian population at large. In conclusion, chapter 6 focuses on the conservative reaction that forced the closure of most women's courses after the regicide of 1881, and outlines that second burgeoning of women's educational opportunities under the last Romanov tsar, Nicholas II.

### CHAPTER ONE

# The "Thaw": Women in the Popular Press and University Corridors, 1855–63

Beginning in 1855, one sensed a thaw; the doors of the prison began to open; fresh air produced a giddiness among people unaccustomed to it.

S.M. SOLOV'EV (n.d.)[1]

*Nauka* [learning], citizens, has always been for us one of the most important needs, *but now it is the first.* If our enemies have a superiority over us, it is solely due to knowledge.

A.S. NOROV (1855)[2]

Women's higher education first emerged as an issue of public debate in Russia during the "thaw" following the Crimean War. Military defeat had convinced statesmen that educational reform was indispensable to the restoration of Russia's great-power status: the production of able soldiers, administrators, and technicians demanded the massive overhaul of the school system.[3] In order to secure the co-operation of academics and educational administrators in the preparation and implementation of reform, however, the government invited them to propose changes in education.[4] At the same time, relaxation of the censorship encouraged discussion of school reform in the contemporary press. The removal of former restrictions on new periodicals also expanded the forum for public discourse: within five years of the Crimean War, the total number of journals and newspapers more than doubled, increasing from 104 in 1855 to 230 in 1860.[5] In the most tangible sense, then, literate society now enjoyed abundant opportunity to publicize its views on education. By allowing popular debate of impending reform, however, the government inadvertently fostered the development of a public opinion highly critical of official educational policy and contemporary schools.

Central to this public opinion were reform-minded educators and journalists. Appalled by the paucity of girls' schools and complete absence of women's higher educational facilities, they called for drastic reform and expansion of women's education. Such demands would have implications far beyond the ordinary sphere of pedagogy. They would not only promote women's pursuit of university study, but become entangled in disputes over the role and status of women in society. Controversy over women's higher education would be further complicated during the last years of the "thaw" when burgeoning student radicalism and the emergence of a liberal professoriate increased tensions between the government and the university community. The troubled relationship of academics and state officials would influence, in no small degree, the future development of women's higher education.

I

The man most responsible for focusing public attention on girls' schools was N.I. Pirogov, the famous surgeon who won national acclaim for saving hundreds of lives during the seige of Sevastopol. In 1856, while the country fêted his wartime service, Pirogov published his provocative article, "Questions of Life." Exploring the problems of modern education, he complained that contemporary institutes trained young women not to think, but to perform like puppets on a string. If a woman is to fulfil her familial responsibilities, Pirogov insisted, then education must promote her intellectual development: a woman required knowledge in order to participate in man's "struggle," "an independent will" to make the "necessary sacrifices," and she must be able to think to educate her children. Despite the heroic terms used to describe woman's role, however, Pirogov prescribed limits to the scope of her education: "Let many things remain unknown to her. She must be proud that she does not know a lot of things. Not everyone is a doctor. Not everyone must needlessly gaze on the sores of society."[6]

Pirogov's counsel echoed his society's traditional concern for feminine modesty and innocence. It is somewhat surprising, nevertheless, that such advice came from the individual who introduced Russian women to wartime medical service. During the Crimean War, Pirogov had trained and supervised Russia's first order of nurses – the Sisters of Mercy of the Exaltation of the Cross.[7] These women, unlike their English counterparts who remained at the base hospital, served at the more hazardous aid stations and field hospitals near the front. Here they confronted first hand the horrors of war. For their skill and valour, the Sisters earned the tsar's commendation as well as Pirogov's praise. It is highly unlikely, then, that Pirogov had any doubts about women's ability to know "many things" or to practise medicine. His insistence on shielding women from the more brutal aspects of life may have emanated, at least in part, from the same humanitarian spirit that underlay his struggle against the use of corporal punishment in schools.[8] Yet, it must be conceded that Pirogov's protective attitude toward women also demonstrates the persistence of Russia's traditionally paternalistic culture among the most humane reformers.

Pirogov did not advocate any transformation of woman's role in society, rather he called only for improved education so as to enhance her duties as teacher and guardian of children: "Not the position of woman in society – but her education, which contains the education of all humanity – that is what needs to be changed."[9] Such reform, he implied, would have no ramifications on women's status or the family structure. Like several reform-minded educators during the "thaw," Pirogov viewed an expanded education system primarily as a means of strengthening the social order. He argued that a reformed school system, accessible to both sexes and all classes (*sosloviia*), would promote national revitalization. Pirogov expressed no fear that extensive educational reform might jeopardize the stability of a society ruled by an autocrat, legally divided by class, and traditionally committed to sexual discrimination. Such optimistic faith in the rejuvenating power of education inspired government officials, as well as intellectuals, in the immediate aftermath of the Crimean War. Wounded national pride took comfort in the belief that educational reform would ensure Russia's recovery as a great power. This faith, particularly in government circles, would be increasingly challenged as the 1860s progressed. Student radicalism and isolated acts of violence would convince several statesmen that the dangers of educational reform outweighed any potential benefits.

"Questions of Life" ignored the risks that massive educational reform entailed. Nor did Pirogov offer any specific recommendations for the development of girls' schools. Nevertheless, serious reflections on women's education by a leading member of the intellectual community provoked excitement in academic and literary circles. Following the publication of Pirogov's article, the question of women's education became one of the most widely debated issues in university corridors and the periodical press.

K.D. Ushinskii, an influential educator and disciple of Pirogov, proposed more fundamental reform than his mentor. He advocated equal educational opportunities for women and men. During his brief tenure as inspector of Smolny Institute (1859–62), Ushinskii attempted to prepare young women for university study.[10] He revamped the curriculum, upgrading the academic program and introducing the study of natural science. He also publicly encouraged *institutki* to challenge the male monopoly of higher education. In a speech celebrating the emancipation of serfs in 1861, he exhorted young women: "You are obliged to be imbued with the yearning for the conquest of the right to higher education, to make it the goal of your life, to instil that aspiration in the hearts of your sisters, and to attempt to secure the achievement of that goal as long as the doors of the universities, academic and other higher schools are not thrown open before you as hospitably as before men."[11] Before his Smolny audience, Ushinskii had exalted women's higher education as a goal independent of, if not superior to, the fulfilment of woman's familial responsibilities. Ushinskii's ideas, not to mention his educational reforms, provoked strong opposition from the more traditionalist administrators of Smolny. In 1862, he was forced to resign as inspector, but not without some honour: the Fourth Department immediately sent him on an extended foreign tour to study women's education in Europe.

Honourable exile abroad did not alter Ushinskii's views. He continued to insist that education be geared not only to women's familial role but, more importantly, to her development as "a person with basic human needs."[12] Ushinskii's demand militated against the state's service-oriented view of education. Traditionally, the needs of the state, not individual pupils, had determined the development of the school system. Under Nicholas I, its main function was to train competent personnel for civil and military service. Accordingly, educational achievement was rewarded by advancement in the Table of Ranks, the hierarchy of government service positions created by Peter the Great. This functional educational system had always excluded women. Thus Ushinskii was suggesting the abandonment of traditional educational priorities in order to accommodate that segment of the population which the government considered unfit for state service.

Appeals to reform women's education were an integral part of the much larger and more volatile *zhenskii vopros* or woman question, the controversy over the role and status of women in Russian society. The man who most stimulated public interest in the woman question was M.L. Mikhailov, a minor poet and radical journalist.[13] In a series of articles between 1858 and 1861, Mikhailov established *zhenskii vopros* as one of the hottest issues in the periodical press. Like Ushinskii, he, too, emphasized the need for woman's development as an individual as well as wife and mother. Education was the key to this development. Mikhailov, however, envisioned far greater change than contemporary pedagogues: he saw educational reform as a means to social emancipation. Inspired by Western feminists, particularly Jenny d'Héricourt, Mikhailov proposed that a woman's ability alone should determine her role in society. In essence, he was suggesting nothing less than the transformation of the traditional family structure and social order.

Mikhailov's exposition of the revolutionary implications of the woman question fit the controversial tenor of the popular press during the "thaw." Recently released from the most rigid strictures of Nicholas I's censorship, the Russian press revelled in its new freedom. Extremist demands from radical journalists provoked equally uncompromising rebuttals from conservative publicists. In this spirited atmosphere, the woman question could hardly serve as a topic of reasoned public discussion; instead, *zhenskii vopros* was embroiled in journalistic warfare. As a result, demands for women's higher education became intimately associated with social radicalism, and particularly with nihilism. This post-war ideology, which exalted science

as the sure and single arbiter of truth and justice, applauded the overthrow
of traditional values and norms.

Demands for women's higher education did in fact challenge Russian
tradition. Both law and custom had long relegated women to the domestic
sphere under the authority of parent or husband. By contemporary standards,
then, the woman who sought to improve her position, to become more than
an obedient wife or daughter, could be labelled "radical." At the same time,
however, the majority of women who pursued university study during Alexander II's reign were not committed to radical politics in the broader sense.
Very few called for the transformation of the political structure or class
system. Indeed, most eschewed any contact with revolutionary groups. They
worked within the existing system to expand women's educational and
employment opportunities. Moreover, their methods were essentially traditional: solicitous appeals to state authorities and educational personnel.
That is not to deny that these women received encouragement, moral support,
and publicity for their cause from politically radical journalists. Loud advocacy of women's rights by leftist writers, however, would also exacerbate
fears of educated women in more conservative social circles.

Polemics over the woman question punctuated the press. D.I. Pisarev, a
leading spokesman of radical journalism, gave unconditional support to the
emancipation of women: "In the first place ... I absolutely justify women
in all things; in the second place ... I regard the present situation of women
extremely miserable and distressing."[14] Pisarev's peremptory declaration
succinctly expressed the radicals' stance on the woman question. His colleague, N.G. Chernyshevskii, described the plight of Russian women and
their path to emancipation in laborious detail. His novel, *What Is To Be
Done? Tales About New People*, surpassed other contemporary writings in
its exposure of the problems impeding women's liberation and its eulogy
to the female sex.[15] And, although devoid of artistic merit, this book captured
the imagination of Russian youth.

Undoubtedly, Chernyshevskii's stature as a radical publicist, as well as
the circumstances under which *What Is To Be Done?* was written and published, contributed to the popularity of the novel. As a literary critic, essayist,
and editor of the progressive journal *Sovremennik*, Chernyshevskii probably
did more than anyone else during the "thaw" to acquaint the Russian reading
public with the Western doctrines of rationalism, positivism, and utilitar-
ianism. He was also a leading spokesman of revolutionary populism, a
radical brand of agrarian socialism.[16] Even his arrest and subsequent confinement in the fortress of Peter-and-Paul in 1862–4 did not force him to
renounce his convictions or abandon his literary activities. It was during his
first year in prison that Chernyshevskii wrote *What Is To Be Done?* Lack
of co-ordination between prison authorities and the censors allowed the novel
to be published in early 1863. The following year, Chernyshevskii was

sentenced to hard labour in Siberia where he remained for almost two decades. The solemn celebrity of the martyred journalist could not but enhance the appeal of his tendentious novel.

Chernyshevskii based the account of his heroine's emancipation on the actual experiences of a contemporary gentry woman, Mariia A. Obrucheva.[17] When her parents rejected her appeals to study at the university, Mariia escaped parental control by marrying P.I. Bokov, a medical student who sympathized with her educational ambitions. According to Russian law, marriage transferred supreme authority over a woman from her father to her husband. Bokov, however, had no intention of using his new legal powers to restrict his wife's activities. Nor did the young couple plan to observe the traditional social norms of married life. They wed so that Mariia would be free to pursue advanced education. This so-called "fictitious marriage" subsequently allowed her to audit classes in St Petersburg's Medical-Surgical Academy. Here, Mariia fell in love with the eminent physiologist I.M. Sechenov, and became his common-law wife. As Chernyshevskii hoped, but could not possibly foresee, this love match did not thwart Mariia Bokova's educational ambitions: in 1871, she received the degree of Doctor of Medicine from Zurich University.

Similarly, Chernyshevskii's fictional heroine, Vera Pavlovna, escaped parental domination and gained access to higher education by marrying a sympathetic student. For Vera, marriage was neither a permanent nor patriarchal institution, but a union of equals who respected each other's independence and right to terminate the relationship if either party so desired. Her first marriage was Platonic: its raison d'être was to free her from parental tyranny. Mutual respect and a modern conception of human behaviour as totally rational forbade sexual intimacy between the partners of this "fictitious marriage." Neither passion nor possessiveness hindered their separation when the heroine discovered she loved another. This chaste and dégagé union would provide a model escape route for young women fleeing parental control during the reform era.

Vera's second marriage was no less remarkable. Although the heroine bore a daughter, neither child care nor household chores hindered her pursuit of university study and a medical career. At this point in the novel, Vera's exploits begin to diverge radically from the actual experiences of Mariia Bokova. Whereas devotion to Sechenov and medical science largely defined the contours of Bokova's life, the woman of fiction was a *nigilistka* par excellence: Vera not only rebelled against parental authority and prevailing social mores, but also established a new type of economic relations – an artel for seamstresses. Her co-operative workshop became a model of socialist organization: each member worked according to her abilities, participated in the shop's management, and shared the profits of the business. New economic relations, in turn, gave rise to new forms of social organization. After benefiting from the co-operative work experience, most members entered a communal household where they shared food, lodging, and other domestic provisions. In Vera Pavlovna's society, there was little room for private property and no place for the hierarchical family structure.

Education played a crucial role in the development of the new people in Chernyshevskii's novel. Radical journalists, in general, extolled education as a liberating force and mechanism of social change. In particular, they applauded women's pursuit of university study as the first step toward the emancipation of women and the equality of the sexes.

This was exactly what conservative publicists feared. Warning that women's higher education endangered the family and entire social order, the conservative press conjured up the spectre of studious *nigilistki* contaminating the moral and physical health of the nation:

... they dress with no taste and in impossibly filthy fashion, rarely wash their hands, never clean their nails, often wear glasses, always cut their hair, and sometimes even shave it off ... They read Feuerbach and Büchner almost exclusively, despise art, use *ty* [the familiar form of address] with several young men, light their cigarettes, not from a candle, but from men who smoke, are uninhibited in their choice of expressions, live either alone or in phalansteries, and talk most of all about the exploitation of labour, the silliness of marriage and the family and about anatomy.[18]

Allegations of the *nigilistki*'s hygenic and moral laxity excited the public imagination. Scandalous rumours spread among even the most cultured circles of society. V.F. Odoevskii, a contemporary writer and senator, recorded the following conversation with the wife of the vice-governor of Tver: "She told me ... that one of the rules of the nihilists was not to be clean. What filth, especially if they live with men in carnal relations; they must have an intolerable stench."[19] Exaggerated fears of the social implications of educating women would haunt the conservative press throughout the reform era. In the early 1870s, *Grazhdanin*, the conservative paper of Prince V.P. Meshcherskii, went so far as to claim that higher education transformed women into a "third sex."[20] Meshcherskii's allegations, however, would carry far more weight in the following decade when his former confidant, the tsarevich Alexander, became emperor.

Hysterical reactions to educated women were, by no means, peculiar to Russia. The West experienced them as well. The notion that education worked a strange sort of sexual metamorphosis in women was particularly prevalent among England's professional classes. In 1869, for example, a history professor at Oxford warned that the university-educated woman was a "hybrid," a new breed of "man-woman."[21] Such ideas died hard. During the later 1870s, a leading medical man in London characterized women pursuing medical degrees as "intellectual hermaphrodites."[22] Doubtless the scholar and physician in England feared more than the destruction of traditional femininity: educated women threatened male domination of the professions.

Writers of the Russian classics relegated the woman question to the periphery of their work. Nevertheless, both F.M. Dostoevskii and I.S. Turgenev created indelible caricatures of *nigilistki*, who grovel in the shadow of the spiritual or emotional intensity of their tragic heroines. Kukshina, the so-called emancipée in *Fathers and Sons*, frolics in silliness and superficiality. Mrs Varents, the false progressive in *Crime and Punishment*, wallows in self-indulgence and deceit.[23] Although only secondary characters, the pseudo-emancipées of the great novels contributed to the negative stereotype of the liberated woman.

Press polemics over the woman question created a bizarre, if not threatening, image of the woman who sought higher education. At the same time, however, the physical appearance of the journalist's *nigilistka* did bear some resemblance to a few studious young women of the "sixties," as the period from 1855 to 1866 has come to be known in Russian historiography.[24] Because conventional social morality declared femininity incompatible with serious study, a number of women discarded the traditional trappings of their sex. Drab clothes, cropped hair, large glasses, cigarettes, and awkward manners demonstrated their rejection of sexually defined roles.[25] "To be called '*nigilist*,' '*nigilistka*' during the 60s was an honour," wrote Elena A. Stackenschneider, a contemporary advocate of women's higher education.[26]

Not all studious women of the period agreed. Ekaterina F. Iunge, a gentry teenager who sought higher education in St Petersburg, found the *nigilistka* repulsive: "Nihilism in its crude form made a grim impression on me ... I could not understand why Russian women who are studying must be dirty and carelessly dressed."[27] The *nigilistka*'s flagrant defiance of social convention undoubtedly provoked similar reactions from many contemporary women. Years of training in deportment and social propriety, at home or in the institute, militated against public display. Even more important, the very pursuit of advanced education constituted a bold new venture that generated considerable opposition. To create a public spectacle would increase antagonism and further jeopardize women's educational ambitions. Consequently, most studious women went out of their way to avoid, rather than capture, public attention. The behaviour of these women, however, would exert far less influence on government officials than polemical journalism.

II

Public debate over the woman question also raised the expectations of women, particularly those from the privileged classes, and encouraged their struggle for higher education. Not unlike other members of literate society during the "thaw," they, too, experienced a new sense of freedom and optimism. Ekaterina Iunge described the buoyant confidence of her generation: "The greatest happiness for us, the people of the 'sixties,' lay in our confidence: we had no agonizing doubts and hesitations ... Everything was clear to us ... Russia will enter a new era, will go hand in hand with the rest of the world along the road of human progress and happiness. And we saw our ardent desires coming true, our dreams becoming a reality."[28] While the emancipatory spirit of those years nurtured women's desire for advanced education, the loosening of state control over educational affairs permitted women's admission to the university.

Almost immediately on his accession, Alexander II abolished the most oppressive educational restrictions imposed by Nicholas I. In early December 1855, the autocrat removed limitations on the number of students admitted to university study.[29] Three years later, an unrestricted number of external auditors (*vol'noslushateli*) who lacked the academic qualifications for admission as degree students also gained access to university courses. Between 1855 and 1859, the total enrolment in the empire's six universities increased from 3659 to 5555.[30] Moreover, official recognition of the need for reform, coupled with the lack of any overall plan for higher education, induced the government to grant educational personnel an unprecedented degree of autonomy at the district and local levels. Caught up in the reformist spirit of the times and enjoying their new freedom, various administrators and professors embarked upon a series of liberal experiments in higher education. In St Petersburg, Kiev, and Kharkov, the state-appointed district curators allowed the local professoriate to regulate admissions to the university. Numerous professors opened their lectures and laboratories to women. Because girls' secondary education did not satisfy student entrance requirements, women enrolled as external auditors.

St Petersburg University was the first higher educational institution to admit women. In the fall of 1859, K.D. Kavelin, the distinguished jurist and historian, welcomed the first female auditor, Natalia I. Korsini, to his lectures.[31] Kavelin was no stranger to innovation. He had already made substantial contributions to scholarship, as well as to the political philosophy of Russian intellectuals. While a professor at Moscow University during the 1840s, he played a major role in establishing the foundations of modern Russian historiography. He was also one of the nation's original "Westernizers" and a founder of Russian liberalism. This liberalism was far less bold than the European variety: its adherents advocated orderly, gradual change within the autocratic system. After the Crimean War, Kavelin had abundant opportunity to test his liberal views in the realm of practical politics: he participated in the planning of the "Great Reforms," including the emancipation of serfs. The parallels between the subjugation of peasants and the subordination of women escaped few intellectuals during the "thaw." For Kavelin and several like-minded scholars of the northern capital, liberal reform began in their own classrooms as well as on distant estates. Historian N.I. Kostomarov, whose sympathy for federalist politics and Ukrainian nationalism had landed him in jail during Nicholas' reign, now called for the democratization of higher educational institutions. He advocated opening the universities to "all who wished to attend."[32] Russian women were quick to test professorial commitment to such egalitarian views. During the academic year 1860–1, it was not unusual to find as many women as men in the classrooms of several professors. Women gravitated to the lectures of Kostomarov, N.I. Utin, V.D. Spasovich, M.M. Stasiulevich, and N.N. Sokolev.[33] Reminiscing about Kostomarov's lectures, Iunge recalled the warm reception accorded women by male students: "The students were very polite to the ladies. In the big overflowing auditoriums ... we kept the best places. With former strangers, we met as with brothers."[34]

Not all members of St Petersburg's academic community proved so receptive to women's pursuit of university study. According to a contemporary report, one professor resorted to "cynical expressions (sweetened with a cynical smile)" in order to evict a young woman from his classroom. Others rejected women's admission as "incompatible with the dignity of the educational institution." Yet another representative of the academic community expressed his opposition with the classic remark: "We know why you must go to the university. You are looking for fiancés!"[35]

Following the lead of St Petersburg, the universities of Kiev and Kharkov opened their lecture halls to women. The adoption of regulations governing female auditors suggests that both provincial universities considered the admission of women a permanent feature of the reformed university system. St Vladimir's University in Kiev admitted women under the newly formulated regulations governing male auditors. The individual professor, in consultation with the university rector, determined the number of auditors allowed in his classes. As was the case in St Petersburg, each professor decided whether women could audit his lectures. At Kharkov University, a special set of regulations, similar to those for male auditors, governed the admission of women.[36] Kharkov professors, moreover, appeared willing to grant women the same rights as male students. They petitioned the Medical Council, Russia's supreme medical authority, to admit Liudmila A. Ozhigina to the degree program in Kharkov's medical faculty. In May 1861, the Medical Council approved the petition.[37] Before Ozhigina had the opportunity to enrol in the fall term, however, the goverment would ban women from the universities.

No women entered Kazan University during the "thaw." The women of Kazan apparently failed to exploit the recent liberalization of the university system.[38] According to one source, both the local academic community and district curator would have welcomed women to the university. Kazan students even attempted to persuade women of the importance of higher education, but none responded to their appeals.[39] Undoubtedly, inadequate academic preparation contributed significantly to women's absence from Russia's most easternly university. The women of Kazan had even fewer opportunities for secondary education than their sisters in the more central regions of the empire.

Women's admission to Moscow University was cut short by district curator N.A. Isakov. When two young women appeared in the lecture halls, Isakov threatened to expel their brother if they continued to audit classes. Claiming that these women attended lectures only to tease the students, Isakov then banned all women from the university. Unlike the more liberal administrators of St Petersburg, Kiev, and Kharkov, the Moscow curator used the power of his district office to control admissions to university classrooms.[40]

Women also studied in Russia's most prestigious medical school – the Medical-Surgical Academy of the War Ministry. Although the academy statute did not authorize the admission of women, several scientists, including I.M. Sechenov, opened their laboratories to women. Among the most promising female auditors were Mariia Bokova and Nadezhda P. Suslova. Their academic accomplishments would inspire a generation of women to seek medical careers. In particular, Suslova's achievement of a doctor's degree encouraged the first migration of Russian women to foreign medical schools. In 1867, Zurich University awarded her the degree of Doctor of Medicine, the first such degree granted a woman by a European university. Suslova's career, however, represents more than a brilliant page in the history of women's education. It also illustrates one of the many strange paradoxes of nineteenth-century Russia: the first Russian woman to receive her doctor's degree was the daughter of a former serf![41] Suslova's achievements testify to her remarkable talent and determination. Yet, Sechenov also deserves some credit for assisting her medical research in Russia and abroad.[42] Such support and encouragement from professors would prove crucial to Russian women seeking higher education, particularly after their expulsion from Russian universities in the fall of 1861.

III

The phenomenon that more than anything else prompted the government to expel women from the universities was the emergence of the Russian radical student movement. Since the late 1850s, student disorders had disrupted university life. The absence of any clearly formulated university policy, coupled with the repudiation of Nicholaian controls, had led to congested lecture halls of unruly students and auditors. At the same time, surging confidence in the power of knowledge had given the student an exalted sense of self-importance. One distinguished group of Moscow professors described the prevailing attitude toward students during the "thaw": "In our time every Russian man senses a profound need for education as the only way out of the social evils that bear heavily on our people ... It is for this reason that young men are fully conscious of their great historical role. A student in Russia is not a person who studies but a person who teaches, and our society looks on him with pride and respect. In the eyes of many, the student represents the future hope of Russia."[43] Emboldened by the sense of historical mission, the student community organized extra-legal organizations, boycotted derelict professors, and demanded a larger role in both the academic and administrative affairs of the university.

Student activism provoked no concerted reaction from the government during the first half-decade of the reform era because statesmen were preoccupied with the emancipation settlement. Only after the Emancipation Proclamation of 19 February 1861 did the government focus attention on the universities. By that time, student protests had acquired a blatantly political character. Student participation in the memorial services for Poles killed by Russian troops in Warsaw and for the peasants killed at Bezdna demonstrated the emergence of a politically volatile student community.[44]

Hopes in the future utility of Russia's educated youth now gave way to fears of impending student rebellion: the government tightened its grip over educational institutions. Military and security personnel assumed command of university affairs. In spring 1861, Alexander II entrusted the formulation of more stringent university regulations to Count S.G. Stroganov, a cavalry general, V.N. Panin, the minister of justice, and Prince V.A. Dolgorukov who headed the Third Department, the centrally organized gendarmerie of His Majesty's Own Chancellery. A few months later, Admiral E.V. Putiatin was appointed minister of education.[45]

Primarily concerned with transforming student activists into obedient subjects fit for government service, these officials quickly dismissed the question of women's admission to the university. From the point of view of Russia's great-power status, women's education was irrelevant. Moreover, in the context of the public debate over the woman question and in the wake of student disorders, women's appearance in lectures and laboratories was construed as contributing to the rebelliousness of the university community. The restoration of order, therefore, demanded their expulsion.

Restrictions on regular students generated much more controversy than the ban on women. In September 1861, Putiatin prohibited all corporate student activities, and reduced fee exemptions, which formerly had benefited over 50 percent of Russia's university youth, to two incoming students per province.[46] Putiatin's crackdown provoked massive student demonstrations in St Petersburg and Moscow. By winter, riots erupted in the provincial universities of Kazan, Kharkov, and Kiev.[47] Women played a minimal role in the disorders. Only one woman, who spoke at a student rally in St Petersburg, attracted memorable attention.[48] This woman, according to one source, persuaded the students to refrain from violence.[49] Much more notable was the defiant reaction of a liberal contingent of St Petersburg professors. Kavelin resigned in protest in October; Utin, Spasovich, Stasiulevich, and A.N. Pypin soon followed suit.[50] The relative freedom of the past six years had so strengthened professorial commitment to academic autonomy that these scholars refused to compromise their liberal educational ideals when the government attempted to resume total control over university affairs.

Indeed, in the aftermath of the Crimean War, the academic intelligentsia had come of age. This independent-minded community of scholars had developed its own ideology of *nauka* that rejected state interference in higher education. They insisted that *nauka* be pursued for its own sake and be subject to no utilitarian goal. Commitment to learning for learning's sake, however, did not imply that professors divorced university research from problems of contemporary life. On the contrary, they were convinced that the disinterested pursuit of *nauka* would inevitably lead to social and economic progress.[51] Their boundless confidence in the progressive power of autonomous learning has been dubbed the "mystique of *nauka*."[52] Yet, this new ideology had a much more practical function that the term "mystique" implies: it constituted their main defence of university autonomy. In advocating the supremacy of *nauka*, professors were demanding nothing less than complete academic freedom. To admit that *nauka* could serve some external goal would justify outside interference in university affairs and thus jeopardize the independence of scholars. In self-defence, then, the academic intelligentsia argued that *nauka* could flourish only in the autonomous university, outside the arena of power and politics. The new ideology, moreover, elicited much more than lip-service from its adherents, as the resignation of several St Petersburg professors clearly demonstrates.

Professorial disaffection, appended to student revolts, renewed the urgency of university reform and prompted Putiatin to invite professors and district curators to participate in the preparation of the new University Statute.[53] Later, it would become clear that Putiatin's gesture was also a ploy to quiet rebellious academics and to ease the transfer of authority from local personnel to the central administration. At the time, however, co-operation of the academic community in the reform plans encouraged discussion of women's university education in high government circles. Particularly significant in the thirty-month debate over the new University Statute was the poll of the university councils on the question of admitting female auditors.[54] The voting members of each council, which was formally subordinate to the curator, included only senior faculty members: emeritus (*zasluzhennye*) and regular (*ordinarnye*) professors. Docents and other junior members of the teaching staff who possessed a doctor's or master's degree had no voting rights, but were only allowed to express their views on academic issues. Although it might be assumed that older, well-established professors would be more reluctant than their junior colleagues to advocate radical change in the composition of the student body, this was not the case in St Petersburg, Kiev, Kharkov, and Kazan. At all four universities, the majority of professors approved much more than the admission of female auditors: they also recommended granting women academic degrees.[55]

Only Moscow and Dorpat opposed women's admission to higher educational institutions. The vote of Moscow University Council was overwhelmingly negative: twenty-three against two.[56] Like the district curator, the council claimed that women's admission would have a "harmful influence" on students. Although it is possible that Isakov used his office to exert pressure on some council members, it is doubtful that most voting professors of Russia's oldest university needed any prodding by a state official to reject female auditors. At least, after Isakov relinquished his administrative post in 1863, very few established professors in Moscow actively supported women's struggle for higher education. Moreover, during the 1870s, when the government allowed the creation of women's higher courses in university towns, most members of Moscow University Council failed to participate in them. Instead, junior faculty, docents, and gymnasium instructors dominated the teaching staff of women's courses in Moscow. At Dorpat University, which primarily served Baltic Germans, the council of professors also voted against female auditors. Here, however, curator E.F. von Bradke composed the council's report that emphasized his own notions about woman's alleged infirmities. Reiterating the traditional pseudo-scientific arguments against women's higher education, the curator insisted that "the female sex, according to the pecularities of its design and its intellectual and emotional faculties," was incapable of pursuing university study.[57] Although it is difficult to determine the extent to which Dorpat professors shared von Bradke's views, it is evident that local academics in general had little sympathy for women's educational ambitions. Throughout the reform era, and under different curators, Dorpat's academic community made no effort to expand women's educational opportunities.

Nevertheless, the results of the poll revealed that the majority of university councils advocated women's admission to the university. Top government officials decided otherwise: women would have no place in the reformed university system. This, however, was not clear at the outset. Just as the debate over university reform seemed to indicate that the opinions of local educational personnel would be taken into account, so too did the much publicized text of the University Statute of 1863 suggest that the question of women's admission would be left to the discretion of the local university and district curator. Article 42:B-8v and Article 90, which governed the admission of auditors, granted the local university the right to formulate admission regulations with the approval of the district curator.[58] Neither article made any reference to women.

This apparent concession to local university autonomy proved little more than the government's ingenuity in coping with public opinion aroused by the debate over educational reform. Given the state's growing distrust of students, which had been exacerbated by the St Petersburg fires of 1862 and the Polish revolt of 1863, it was hardly prepared to grant the local university control over admissions. Within a month of the promulgation of the University Statute, the Ministry of Education issued a directive to all university councils clarifying admission regulations and specifically banning women from the university.[59] The introduction of these restrictions in a ministerial circular, rather than in the much more publicized University Statute, helped to maintain, at least publicly, the aura of compromise and concession surrounding the university reform of 1863.

The university councils officially expelled women during the winter of 1863.[60] Although most had recently recommended opening the universities to women, professors complied with the ministerial circular because they now had too much to lose by antagonizing the government over the issue of female auditors: the new University Statute had granted them a substantial degree of self-government, and they were unwilling to risk their new freedom for the sake of women. Their failure to protest the ban on female auditors certainly deserves no applause, but it is understandable given the power of the Russian government over the university system. At that time, moreover, all major Western universities, including those not subject to direct state control, excluded women. Higher educational institutions in the most democratic countries were slow to accept female students.[61] Oxford and Cambridge opened their colleges to women only in the 1870s, but refused to award them academic degrees. In the United States, the beginning of university education for women can be traced to the founding of Oberlin College in 1833. Nevertheless, American women would wait more than forty years before gaining access to the nation's leading universities – and then they were taught in separate facilities. Cornell established Sage College for women in 1874 and five years later, the Harvard Annex was opened. In the context of contemporary Western developments, then, the reluctance of Russian professors to champion women's admission to the university in 1863 was not unusual. Furthermore, the new statute had granted such freedom in other areas of university life that professors were in no mood to contest the government's restrictions on auditors.

Recognition of the university's value as a research institution, as well as an educational centre for service personnel, had induced the government to allow considerable university autonomy. The new statute authorized the local university council to elect its own rectors and deans, and to appoint and dismiss instructional staff.[62] Each council was also entrusted with establishing research and teaching programs, course curricula, and examinations. In addition, it elected a university court to deal with student grievances and discipline. University autonomy, however, was both limited and tenuous. The state-appointed curator retained broad powers, including the final say in the appointment and dismissal of teaching and administrative personnel. During times of crisis or when the government perceived potentially dangerous situations in higher education, the curator could assert his authority over university affairs. As one astute historian has pointed out, the maintenance of university autonomy depended less on the exact wording of the new statute than on the degree of "mutual self-restraint" exercised by the university and the government.[63]

In the following decades, professors would show much more restraint than either statesmen or students. Conscious of the university's vulnerability to bureaucratic onslaught, they shunned any drastic measures that might jeopardize the precarious autonomy of the university. After the promulgation of the new University Statute, professors confronted the autocracy on issues of educational reform in a legal, non-violent manner. In the periodical press and meetings with state officials, they defended academic freedom in the name of *nauka*. University councils also petitioned the government to provide educational opportunities for those not accommodated by the existing school system. In private educational ventures, often organized by professors, many taught for little remuneration. In sum, they relied on patient petitioning and private initiative to prod the autocracy on the road to reform. These tactics would characterize Russian liberalism throughout the reign of Alexander II.

A similar strategy would be pursued by reform-minded gentry on the zemstvos, the organs of local self-government created by the Statute of 1864. Elected on a weighted franchise that favoured large landowners, and entrusted with the promotion of education, health care, and various social services in the countryside, the zemstvo served as a local welfare agency dominated by the gentry. Like the professoriate, zemstvo reformers understood that their relative autonomy and scope of activity depended upon the good will of the government. Consequently, they avoided conflict and presented modest proposals in the form of loyal appeals to the tsar.[64] The "small deeds" reformism of the zemstvo, one Western specialist has argued, "tended to be cautious to the point of timidity."[65] Yet caution was warranted. The realities of Russian politics – the arbitrary power of autocracy and the institutional weakness of Russian liberalism – demanded extreme moderation. The strategy of zemstvo reformers and university professors, moreover, would in fact promote considerable social reform during the reign of Alexander II. "Small deeds" and persistent petitioning would foster the expansion of education and health care in the countryside, and the creation of advanced courses for women in university towns.

The future of women's higher education, however, appeared bleak during the early 1860s. Although Putiatin was replaced by the more liberal A.V. Golovnin in late December 1861, it was Golovnin's ministry which had directed the universities to ban women in 1863. The following year, the Medical-Surgical Academy of the War Ministry also expelled female auditors. The driving force behind their expulsion was P.A. Dubovitskii, the president of the academy and, during the last year of his life, chief war-medical inspector (1867–8). Like most conservative officials, Dubovitskii contended that women's admission contributed to student disorders. But academic tranquillity was not his only concern. The training of women doctors, Dubovitskii feared, would advance the cause of socialism: "The question of the introduction of female physicians is, in my opinion, the first step in accomplishing the so-called emancipation of women which has its origin and foundation in the communistic theories of Saint Simon and others."[66] Dubovitskii's distrust of women doctors was, by no means, shared by War Minister D.A. Miliutin (1861–81). During the 1870s, Miliutin would actively promote the expansion of women's medical education. Earlier, however, the new war minister could ill-afford to oppose the president who had transformed the academy into one of the leading medical schools in Europe.[67] Consequently, in 1864, the War Ministry announced that the academy would no longer admit women.[68]

Only one woman was permitted to remain in the academy until the completion of her medical training: Varvara A. Kashevarova. Her agreement to treat Bashkir women, whose religion forbade the attendance of male physicians, had earned Kashevarova the sponsorship of the military governor of Orenburg and special consideration by the War Ministry. As a result, Kashevarova was the first woman awarded a medical degree in Russia. In 1868, the Medical-Surgical Academy granted her the diploma of physician (*lekar'*).[69]

This pioneer in women's medical education had also overcome considerable social, as well as sexual, prejudice. An orphan of Jewish descent, Kashevarova had earned her keep as a child by doing housework. At fifteen, she married a prosperous St Petersburg merchant who promised to further her education. When he later opposed her plans to seek a medical career, the marriage collapsed. Determined to become a physician, Kashevarova accepted the stipend from Orenburg and subsequently audited lectures in the Medical-Surgical Academy. Here, like Bokova, she, too, won the affections of a local scientist: pathologist M.M. Rudnev became her husband after the official dissolution of her first marriage in 1870. Regrettably, Kashevarova-Rudneva would never fulfil her obligations to the Bashkir women of Orenburg. Unlike the male physician whose diploma automatically conferred status in the Table of Ranks, she was denied this right. Without rank, she was barred from all positions in state medical institutions, including the military hospitals of Orenburg. The autocracy would collapse before admitting female physicians to the Table of Ranks. Kashevarova-Rudneva continued her formal education until 1878 when she received her doctorate from the academy. Still unable to secure a salaried post in a state hospital, she spent the rest of her life in private practice.

Nevertheless, Kashevarova-Rudneva had occupied an unusually privileged position among women of the mid 1860s. Even with the support of Sechenov, neither Bokova nor Suslova could secure special permission to continue medical training in St Petersburg. Both women had petitioned the government, volunteering to serve on the steppe if allowed to remain in the academy. They received no reply.[70] As a result, their medical careers were interrupted, but only temporarily.

Expulsion from the academy and universities failed to halt women's quest for higher education. Brief admission to lectures and laboratories had bolstered women's confidence and strengthened their resolve. After the abolition of serfdom, moreover, economic pressures increased women's demand for advanced education. The emancipation settlement had deprived the gentry of bonded labour and much land. Deeply in debt and accustomed to living off the resources of their serfs, most gentry landowners could not compete in the emergent market economy.[71] As a result, it became more difficult for the gentry family to provide economic security for unmarried female relatives. Traditionally, a daughter lived with her parents until she married, and a single woman, no matter her age, was usually supported by relatives. For the less fortunate woman with kin of limited means, the only acceptable form of gainful employment was a position as governess in a more prosperous household. Increased financial restraints after the emancipation, however, also reduced the number of gentry families who could afford to hire governesses. The repercussions of the emancipation thus deprived some gentry women of their normal means of support. In order to survive, they had to abandon their traditional lifestyle. In the words of a contemporary: "The economic conditions of Russian life and the social upheaval created by [the settlement of] 19 February 1861 summoned woman to the struggle for existence and demanded her indispensable contribution to labour."[72] Aristocratic disdain for manual work, however, forbade gentry women from toiling in factory or field.[73] University study, they hoped, would allow them to earn a living by using their heads rather than their hands. Such aspirations would garner the support of numerous academics. Although the state prohibited women in the academy and universities, scholars and teachers from St Petersburg to Kazan would demonstrate their more progressive philosophy of education by sponsoring advanced courses and medical training for women.

By the early 1870s, ministerial in-fighting would also complicate the struggle for women's higher education. In particular, controversy over women's medical training would compound the rivalry of two leading statesmen: War Minister Miliutin and D.A. Tolstoi, the new minister of education (1866–80).[74] Whereas Tolstoi would oppose the development of advanced medical education for women, Miliutin would sponsor women's medical courses in the Medical-Surgical Academy. The jealous nature of autocratic rule under Alexander II allowed these ministers to develop contradictory policies governing women's medical education. In order to guard his autocratic power, Alexander II created no central agency to co-ordinate the tsarist administration. Instead, the emperor divided authority among favoured statesmen who enjoyed almost exclusive command of their respective spheres of government service, but little influence in any other area of the administration.[75] This compartmentalized administration demanded constant intervention by the tsar to maintain the functioning of the government and thus prevented any individual from acquiring extensive power. At the same time, however, lack of co-ordination in the bureaucracy also enabled ministers to pursue divergent policies in their respective spheres of influence and thus imparted a somewhat erratic quality to Alexander II's rule. This erraticism became particularly evident in the educational policy of the 1870s. Fragmentation of the administration and autocratic intervention on behalf of favoured statesmen, but only within their restricted realms of authority, would permit the introduction of Tolstoi's classical system of education, despite the protests of Miliutin and the majority of the State Council.[76] Similarly, women's medical courses would be established in the Medical-Surgical Academy, despite the offical ban on women in university medical faculties and considerable high-level opposition.

Expulsion from higher educational institutions, therefore, did not entirely frustrate the educational ambitions of Russian women. Instead, it inaugurated three new phases in women's higher education. First, it fostered an alliance between women and several members of the academic intelligentsia. This alliance would eventually succeed in establishing women's higher courses in four university towns. Second, it precipitated an exodus of women to Zurich University where they continued their education. Finally, the War Ministry under Miliutin would open advanced medical courses for women in the Medical-Surgical Academy.

# The Politics of Minimal Concessions: Women's Courses in St Petersburg and Moscow

What an uproar, what joyful excitement followed the first publication announcing the permission of the minister of education to open women's courses! That was the first women's holiday in Moscow, that was the joyful reception of a new dawn, a new life. Each woman sincerely, frankly welcomed this dawn. At that time, it seemed to her that finally she would meet a new liberator, one more trustworthy than all others! And this liberator in which she believed was knowledge.

EKATERINA NEKRASOVA (1880)[1]

Six years after the university councils banned female auditors, the minister of education finally approved the creation of women's advanced courses in Moscow. Seven months later, in December 1869, public lectures for both sexes were also allowed in St Petersburg. Russian women now rejoiced, although many had not patiently suffered the state's long delay in expanding their educational opportunities: an adventurous few had migrated to Zurich University, which began to admit women as degree candidates in 1867;[2] others had attended the so-called "flying universities" or unauthorized lectures that moved from one private home to another.[3] Although they were offered by scholars from the university and Medical-Surgical Academy, these irregular lectures could not serve as a forum for systematic study or accommodate a large audience. Undoubtedly, their unofficial status also deterred the more cautious. Women's general inexperience in organizing activities outside the domestic sphere had also postponed improvement in the situation. Fearful respect of state officials, as well as disagreements over the type of educational facilities women required, further hampered collective action. Nekrasova recalled how a meeting of Moscow women became so rowdy that the police intervened, thus frightening several women into withdrawing their names from a petition for a women's university. She suggested that the sight of a "police overcoat" was enough to intimidate these women.[4] Only in the late 1860s were Russian women sufficiently organized to garner the support of local academics for their educational projects.

By that time, two other contemporary developments had begun to exert considerable influence on women's struggle for higher education. On the one hand, the reform of girls' secondary schools would provide more young women with more adequate academic preparation, thereby increasing demands for university study. On the other, the emergence of a powerful conservative faction in top government circles would pose a serious obstacle to women's academic pursuits.

I

Girls' secondary education underwent drastic expansion and upgrading during the reform years.[5] In 1856, not a single secondary school for girls existed under the jurisdiction of the Ministry of Education. Two years later, Norov launched the creation of a network of two types or orders of girls' secondary institutions, which, by 1868, boasted 125 schools with an enrolment exceeding 10,000.[6] These new day schools were officially open to girls of all social classes. Thus, fourteen years before England had opened its public schools and almost thirty years before France had established the lycées de demoiselles, autocratic Russia had founded a system of non-exclusive girls' secondary institutions.[7]

In practice, however, enrolment in the new Russian schools remained far from representative of the nation's social estates. Financial restraints hindered the development of non-exclusive education. The costly Crimean War and impending overhaul of the agricultural and military systems left the government with few resources to devote to girls' schools that, by tradition, were considered unworthy of state funding. Local society, therefore, had to finance them.[8] As a result, girls' secondary institutions were established primarily in the capitals and provincial towns with a sufficiently large and prosperous population. Their location severely curtailed access by peasant girls, whereas the tuition fees required to maintain the schools discriminated against rural and urban poor alike. Consequently, girls' secondary institutions remained largely the preserve of the gentry and moderately wealthy urban families.

Nevertheless, the ministry's schools provided more substantial education to more young women than had the pre-reform institutes.[9] Schools of the first order originally offered a six-year course of study in the Russian language, religion, arithmetic, penmanship, needlework, and "a little" (*nekotoroe svedenie*) science. After a decade, the general program was upgraded and expanded to seven years. A supplementary year of pedagogical training was also added. Graduates of the full eight-year course received the title of domestic teacher (*uchitel'nitsa*) or domestic tutor (*nastavnitsa*), and the right to teach in elementary schools, private homes, and the four lower classes of girls' secondary institutions. The three-year schools of the second order offered a similar academic program but excluded science. Those who completed the course were authorized to teach in elementary schools. In 1870, the Ministry of Education renamed the schools of the first and second order gymnasia and progymnasia respectively, and awarded them a combined annual grant of 150,000 rubles.[10]

The first minister of education to subsidize girls' schools was none other than D.A. Tolstoi, the statesman who, for more than a decade, would block women's access to universities and higher academic degrees. Indeed, Tolstoi's restrictive policies governing higher education in general alienated much of literate society, and not only the academic community. In populist circles, he was dubbed "Minister of Public Darkness" (*promrachenie*).[11] Contemporary radicals and liberals, however, often failed to recognize the "enlightened grain" among the "reactionary chaff"[12] in Tolstoi's policies. Although it cannot be denied that student unrest had convinced Tolstoi of the potential threat of higher education to autocracy and thus shored up his faith in repression, he also recognized that the existing regime could not survive in a rapidly modernizing world without a literate population. And this devoted supporter of autocracy worked with a will throughout his ministry to raise the educational level of the population. The massive expansion of secondary education for both sexes is testimony to his industry and achievement. Admittedly, Tolstoi's policies were designed to promote no fundamental change in the status quo. In fact, he attempted to discourage the lower social orders from pursuing higher education by making the classical gymnasium, which emphasized the study of ancient languages and literatures, the only avenue to the university.[13] Poor pupils, he calculated, would be attracted to the more practically oriented *real* gymnasium or municipal school. Such goals notwithstanding, Tolstoi made no attempt to enforce social discrimination in secondary education. He neither established enrolment quotas on a class basis nor ordered gymnasium directors to impose prohibitive admission fees.

Tolstoi's administration of girls' schools, moreover, indicates that he attempted to prevent them from becoming even more exclusive. When problems of local funding threatened their closure, he opposed any increase in pupils' fees on the grounds that such a measure would reduce the number of admissions and transform girls' gymnasia into "privileged institutions accessible only to children of rich families."[14] The minister's subsidy prevented the fee increase, but it was not enough to reduce fees or to lessen significantly the schools' dependence upon local financing. In 1871, for example, the ministerial grant covered only 8 percent of the total operating costs of the school network, whereas fees and the contributions of various zemstvo and urban organizations constituted 34 and 41 percent respec-

TABLE 1
Growth of girls' gymnasia and progymnasia, 1865–93

| Year | Girls' gymnasia | | Girls' progymnasia | |
| | Number of schools | Number of pupils | Number of schools | Number of pupils |
| --- | --- | --- | --- | --- |
| 1865 | 29 | 3440 | 75 | 4326 |
| 1873 | 55 | 8713 | 116 | 13940 |
| 1883 | 100 | 29748 | 185 | 22392 |
| 1893 | 143 | 40309 | 177 | 22007 |

*Source*: Dneprov, "Zhenskoe obrazovanie," 22.

TABLE 2
Social origins of pupils in girls' gymnasia and progymnasia in 1865 and 1898

| Social origins | Girls' gymnasia | | Girls' progymnasia | |
| | 1865 | 1898 | 1865 | 1898 |
| --- | --- | --- | --- | --- |
| | % | % | % | % |
| Gentry and officials | 61.7 | 45.1 | 19.9 | 17.0 |
| Clergy | 5.9 | 3.3 | 5.5 | 7.3 |
| Townspeople | 28.2 | 43.4 | 66.9 | 56.9 |
| Peasantry | 2.3 | 5.3 | 7.4 | 16.1 |
| Others | 1.9 | 2.9 | 0.3 | 2.7 |

*Source*: Dneprov, "Zhenskoe obrazovanie," 23.

tively.[15] Local funding sponsored the burgeoning of girls' secondary schools: between 1865 and 1893, the gymnasia increased fivefold and the number of progymnasia more than doubled (see table 1).

Enrolment patterns during this period reveal that girls' gymnasia remained far more exclusive than progymnasia. The seven-year program ensured the preponderance of young women from prosperous families. At the same time, however, the progressive increase in the number of non-gentry pupils also reflects the changing socio-economic conditions of the empire. The more affluent sectors of the urban middle class were making significant gains in girls' secondary education at the expense of the formerly dominant landed estate. By the late nineteenth century, the percentage of non-noble urban girls rose by more than one-third, while pupils from the gentry and officialdom declined by at least one-quarter (see table 2). Daughters of well-to-do townspeople also dominated the progymnasia. Because these schools required only three years' freedom from labour, they also attracted a larger number of peasants. By 1898, peasant girls constituted slightly more than

16 percent of the total enrolment. Much more striking, however, was the emergence of townspeople as the main beneficiaries of girls' secondary education.

Admittedly, urban girls did not gain a majority in the much smaller and more prestigious school system of the Fourth Department, although it, too, was reformed during the "thaw." In 1858, the Fourth Department officially "democratized" its institutes and also opened its own non-exclusive girls' gymnasia, the so-called Mariinskie schools.[16] Both offered programs and teaching rights comparable to girls' gymnasia of the Ministry of Education. Unlike the ministry, however, the Fourth Department financed almost the entire operation of its schools. Nevertheless, the seven-year course, as well as the imposition of tuition fees, restricted enrolment. The Fourth Department's century-old sponsorship of institutes for noble girls also increased the appeal of its schools to the most privileged families. As late as 1880, gentry girls and daughters of officials constituted over 88 percent of *institutki*, and more than 53 percent of the pupils in Mariinskie schools. The social composition of these schools by no means suggests that girls' secondary education continued to favour only the most privileged classes. Fourth Department schools experienced little expansion during the nineteenth century: the institute network included only thirty schools in 1864 when the last institute was established, and Mariinskie schools never exceeded thirty.[17] In 1894, enrolment in Fourth Department schools totalled 17,700, whereas over 40,000 girls attended the gymnasia of the Ministry of Education during the previous year. Another 22,000 were enrolled in progymnasia (see table 1).

This dramatic expansion of girls' secondary education could not have occurred without the support of local society. By the 1870s, zemstvo and urban organizations were leading the government in promoting girls' schools. This, however, had not been the case when Norov first established these secondary institutions: townspeople had then resented financing girls' education, whereas the gentry had opposed funding non-exclusive schools.[18] Indeed, given the initial resistance of local society, the government must be credited with providing the original impetus for the development of a public school system for girls. Widespread publicity of the inadequacy of girls' education during the "thaw" convinced statesmen that better schools would benefit the nation's future wives and mothers. As Pirogov had suggested, they attempted to create an education system that would enhance, not transform, women's social role. The new girls' schools of the Ministry of Education had one specific aim: "to impart to pupils that religious, moral, and intellectual education which is expected of every woman, especially the future mother of a family."[19] Accordingly, these schools were terminal institutions that prepared women for the traditional female vocation of teacher of small children, not public service or professional careers. Furthermore, although Tolstoi opposed the development of exclusive ministerial schools, tuition fees and location discouraged the enrolment of peasants, thereby preventing significant social dislocation.

Statesmen had not anticipated that more substantial secondary education would also generate ambitions for more advanced study. The first graduates of reformed girls' schools swelled the ranks of women seeking university education during the late 1860s. Their timing was hardly propitious. On 4 April 1866, attempted regicide by a former university student propelled conservative statesmen into power. Convinced of the revolutionary potential of higher education, they would do their utmost to frustrate the development of women's advanced educational facilities.

II

D.V. Karakozov's attempt to kill the tsar precipitated a shift to the right in educational policy. Within ten days of the assassination attempt, Alexander II dismissed Golovnin, and entrusted Tolstoi with the administration of educational affairs. Reformist elements within the bureaucracy shuddered at Tolstoi's appointment. War Minister Miliutin, who became Tolstoi's main critic and rival within the government, complained: "It would have been impossible to make a better choice for the post of Minister of Education, if his main task had been conceived of as the suppression and smothering of every rudiment of vital strength of the younger generation."[20] The new minister asserted strict control over the student community and attempted to strip the university of the relative autonomy granted by the Statute of 1863. The restoration of order and discipline in higher education precluded any possibility of lifting the ban on women. Emphasizing the "dreadful consequences" of women's admission to university lectures during the "thaw," the *Journal of the Ministry of Education* alleged that female auditors had "threatened to disturb the seriousness of university teaching and to lower the intellectual and moral level of these higher educational institutions."[21]

Tolstoi's plan to strengthen ministerial control over the universities included restraints on the activities of professors as well as students. Rather than allow the professoriate to participate in the formulation of educational policy, Tolstoi relied on his bureaucratic underlings to implement his programs. One individual outside his ministry, however, played a significantly large role in the preparation of educational reforms: M.N. Katkov, the conservative publicist and editor of *Moskovskie vedomosti*, served as the "troubadour" and guide of educational policy throughout Tolstoi's fourteen-year ministry.[22] While his journal prescribed classicism and the repeal of the new University Statute as antidotes to student radicalism, the Moscow editor privately composed plans for educational reform that made their way into the Classical Gymnasium Statute of 1871 and the University Statute of 1884. Similarly, Katkov's diatribes against university study for women

evoked a sympathetic response in most ministerial corridors. He claimed
that the so-called struggle for women's higher education, like the "false
woman question," did not exist in its own right, but was only a manifestation
of that same "nihilism" that erupted in university disorders during the early
1860s.[23]

While Katkov orchestrated educational affairs from his home base in
Moscow, his trusted supporter, A.I. Georgievskii, served as his minion
within the Ministry of Education. At the beginning of Tolstoi's administration, Georgievskii became editor of the *Journal of the Ministry of Education*,
and later assumed the chairmanship of the Academic Committee of the
ministry. These positions enabled him not only to promote Katkov's projects,
but also to provide his mentor with official documents and off-the-record
information concerning high-level government debates. As Tolstoi once
remarked to Georgievskii: "Vous êtes une âme damnée de Kathow."[24] Indeed, this able bureaucrat would remain the faithful disciple of Katkov long
after the editor's death. During the second half of the nineteenth century,
the Ministry of Education did not harbour a more consistent and uncompromising opponent of women's higher education.

Such opposition garnered the support of the newly appointed guardians
of state security. In 1866, Count P.A. Shuvalov, a boyhood friend of the
emperor, became the head of the Third Department and the chief of gendarmes (1866–74). This aristocrat, whose strong personality was enhanced
by good looks and an elegant manner, rapidly emerged as one of the country's
most influential statesmen.[25] Shuvalov's dedication to the existing regime,
however, was not so disinterested as Tolstoi's devotion to autocracy: the
chief of gendarmes wanted the tsar to delegate more power to the nobility,
the traditional bulwark of autocratic rule. Nevertheless, there was still much
to draw these two statesmen together. Shuvalov also opposed any fundamental reform of the status quo and advocated increased state control, rather
than concession, as the solution to domestic unrest. Fear that advanced
education would undermine the stability of the family made him a committed
foe of the studious women. As a favourite of the emperor, Shuvalov would
exploit his court connections to block the expansion of women's educational
facilities. At the same time, command of the gendarmerie would facilitate
his investigation and "exposure" of the dangers of women's pursuit of university study. He also acquired a reliable ally when he secured the appointment of A.E. Timashev as minister of internal affairs (1868–78).[26] Timashev
was a wealthy landowner and former military man with simple political
views: opposition to all reform and faith in the efficacy of administrative
and police power. Although lacking both the vision and talent to formulate
or introduce policies on his own, he could be counted on to give unques-
tioning support to Shuvalov's projects. By the late 1860s, then, Tolstoi,
Shuvalov, and Timashev had formed a powerful coalition against women

seeking higher education. Their obstructionist efforts would guarantee that any advanced women's courses would remain private, non-degree institutions outside the regular education system.

III

St Petersburg boasted the first organized movement to expand women's educational opportunities. The individual who launched this movement was Evgeniia I. Konradi, the married daughter of a wealthy Tula landowner and co-editor of the journal *Nedelia*.[27] In January 1868, Konradi appealed to the First Congress of Natural Scientists in St Petersburg to petition the government for women's higher educational facilities. Reiterating the traditionalist arguments that had won official approval for the reform of girls' secondary schools, Konradi insisted that women required more extensive education in order to fulfil their familial responsibilities. She also reminded the delegates that the main purpose of the congress was the propagation of knowledge. The scientific community applauded the sentiment of Konradi's speech, but declared that the congress lacked the facilities to sponsor women's education.[28] Several local university professors, however, agreed that advanced courses should be established for women.

Rumours of professorial support galvanized a number of high-society women into action. Mariia V. Trubnikova, Anna P. Filosofova, and Nadezhda V. Stasova spearheaded the movement to establish university courses for women. These activists were considerably older than most contemporary women seeking higher education and all came from notable Russian families. Stasova, the eldest member of the triumvirate, was born at Tsarskoe Selo in 1822.[29] The daughter of a court architect and godchild of Alexander I, Stasova was reared amidst the high culture of the St Petersburg nobility. Her brother was the eminent music critic, V.V. Stasov. Luxurious surroundings, however, did not shield Stasova from much anguish during young womanhood. She suffered an emotional breakdown after her fiancé deserted her for another woman. No less painful was the death of her only sister some years later. Undoubtedly, these personal losses contributed to Stasova's growing sense of self-sacrifice and concern for the misfortune of others. In 1859, only a year after the death of her sister, she began to dedicate her life to improving the lot of women. At that time, she was introduced to the philanthropic circle of Mariia Trubnikova.

Thirteen years younger than Stasova, Trubnikova was the daughter of V.P. Ivashev, one of the exiled Decembrists who had participated in an abortive gentry rebellion at the outset of Nicholas I's reign. The death of both parents in early childhood left Mariia in the care of a wealthy aunt who provided her niece with an excellent education. Mariia was fluent in several languages and well-versed in Western and Russian literature when she married K.V. Trubnikov at age nineteen. During the first decade of her marriage, she became the happy mother of four daughters, but relations with her husband were strained. Trubnikov was not so progressive as Mariia earlier believed, and had also lost his wife's inheritance, which she had entrusted to him, through a series of poor investments.[30] Mariia's increasing involvement in the charity work and educational projects of St Petersburg women was probably an additional cause, as well as a consequence, of marital discord. In 1859, she launched the establishment of a philanthropic society to provide inexpensive lodging for working women. During the next two decades, the society opened dormitories, cafeterias, schools, and child-care centres for the capital's poor.[31] Among the leading members of this charitable organization was Anna Filosofova.

Filosofova was born into the old Muscovite family of the Diagilevs in 1835, the same year as Trubnikova's birth. At twenty, she wed V.D. Filosofov, the high-ranking official who worked closely with Miliutin in reforming the War Ministry. The marriage was happy and their children were numerous by the time of Anna's involvement in the struggle for women's higher education. Like Stasova, she, too, was drawn into organized philanthropy by Trubnikova. These three women helped establish a clothing workshop to provide employment for needy women, as well as a women's publishing artel, a co-operative enterprise that printed, bound, and sold books.[32] In these philanthropic ventures, the triumvirate developed the skills needed to organize the women's movement in St Petersburg.

Also important to the success of the movement were the court connections of Stasova and Filosofova. Few government officials were likely to dismiss offhand an appeal from the godchild of a former tsar. Nor would Filosofova allow them to ignore questions of women's education. She was not averse to badgering Tolstoi at official functions and regal balls. Indeed, her aggressive advocacy of women's higher education helped label her a "red" in high government circles, although her propensity to blush may have contributed to this epithet. The Minister of Education viewed Filosofova's "politics" with wry amusement: at a ball in the Winter Palace, he presented her with a portrait of Madame Roland, which she accepted as a "symbolic compliment" and then hung in her boudoir.[33] All symbols aside, Filosofova's "politics" were far from revolutionary.

Trubnikova could not be classified as radical either, although her daughters seem to have inherited the rebellious streak of their maternal grandfather. They hosted meetings of political suspects and hid illegal literature in the family home.[34] Trubnikova's tolerance of her daughters' activities, however, did not signify any political commitment, but expressed maternal devotion. In terms of ideology and tactics, none of the leaders of the St Petersburg women's movement belonged to the radical political camp. Like zemstvo liberals and the academic intelligentsia, they eschewed violent confrontation and tried to win concessions through personal appeals and patient petitioning.[35]

Such tactics would facilitate the expansion of women's educational opportunities. Filosofova, Stasova, and Trubnikova also demonstrated considerable skill in rallying popular support. Within four months of Konradi's speech, 178 St Petersburg women had signed their appeal for women's university courses. On 11 May 1868, they submitted the collective petition to K.F. Kessler, the rector of St Petersburg University. Drafted to mollify any potential opponents of the proposed courses, it emphasized the social utility of women's higher education: "The opening of your auditoriums to them [women] will be a veritable blessing which, subsequently, will enrich our society with many useful members and our families with more competent mothers and teachers."[36] An explanatory note, dated 13 May, however, revealed that these women had career ambitions outside their traditional nurturing role: "Our aim: to raise the level of women's education in general and, at the same time, to give several capable persons the opportunity to acquire the level of erudition necessary for the occupation of the position of teacher in women's higher educational institutions."[37] By the end of May, four hundred women had endorsed the petition. Prominent among the numerous signatures of teachers, midwives, translators, and wives of doctors and students were those of such high-society women as Princess Eristova, Baroness Korf, Countess A.I. Tolstaia, the aunt of author Leo Tolstoi, and Natalia M. Miliutin, the wife of the War Minister. The proposal to open university courses for women also marshalled support outside the northern capital: sixty-three Smolensk women submitted a similar appeal in June 1868.[38]

Kessler forwarded the petition to a special commission of university professors that immediately approved the establishment of advanced courses for women, stipulating that they must be regular, serious courses and not public lectures. Professors agreed to teach the courses and prepare the academic program. Several reputable scholars, including Sechenov, botanist A.N. Beketov, historian K.N. Bestuzhev-Riumin, and chemist D.I. Mendeleev, also volunteered to teach without remuneration during the first year. On 26 November 1868, Beketov accompanied the women's delegation, composed of Filosofova, Stasova, and E.N. Voronina, the wife of a university student, to their first formal negotiations with Tolstoi.[39]

Tolstoi was well-groomed for the encounter. Immediately on their arrival, he announced: "You've come at last: everywhere I keep hearing that a women's educational institution is being opened, even the Emperor has asked me: 'Are you opening a women's university?'" Tolstoi questioned both the ability of women to finance the courses and the motives of those who had petitioned for their establishment. He insisted that women did not need university courses, but would get married and forget about education completely. When the delegates responded by pointing to the 400 signatures on the petition, Tolstoi scoffed: "Indeed, they are all sheep! You are the leaders, but it's all the same to them what or where to go – it's fashionable, that's all."[40] In more select company, the minister would reveal that Shuvalov considered a good number of these "sheep" politically suspect: "All these four hundred women are four hundred sheep, and half of them are registered in the Third Department."[41] When Tolstoi concluded the meeting, he warned the delegates that they could hope for no more than public lectures.

Tolstoi officially rejected the appeal for women's university courses on 21 December 1868.[42] Alleging sympathy for women's pursuit of advanced education, however, he indicated his willingness to allow public lectures for both sexes. As Tolstoi was well aware that some professors had specifically opposed public lectures, his "sympathetic" response represented little more than a shrewd attempt to undermine professorial support for the St Petersburg women.

Tolstoi's strategy failed. Most women and professors became resigned to lectures rather than courses. Now acquainted with the minister's obstructionist tactics, the organizers of the women's petition decided to ask Miliutin, rather than Tolstoi, to house the lectures. The War Minister immediately volunteered the facilities of the Medical-Surgical Academy. Contemporary memoirs suggest that Miliutin's wife and daughter, as well as Filosofova, had convinced him to promote the expansion of women's education.[43] At the same time, however, Miliutin's sponsorship of extensive reform within the War Ministry indicates that Miliutin, unlike Russia's more conservative statesmen, was extremely receptive to change. The basic philosophical differences separating Miliutin from the more cautious Tolstoi are particularly evident in the controversy over educational reform. Whereas Tolstoi had responded to Karakozov's shot with demands for more rigid control over the student community, Miliutin had recommended freedom and opportunity, rather than discipline and oppression, as the solution to youthful dissidence.[44] Later, Miliutin described his anomalous position among Russia's leading statesmen: "It was not for nothing that long ago they repeatedly told the emperor that I am a liberal, a democrat, a red, and an altogether dangerous fellow."[45] Miliutin's offer to house the public lectures, then, would hardly be welcomed by the more conservative minister of education.

Tolstoi refused to allow university professors, who were under the jurisdiction of the Ministry of Education, to teach in the Medical-Surgical Academy. Instead, he offered to accommodate the lectures in his own quarters, which were located in the building of the Ministry of Internal Affairs.[46] A recent historical study has argued that this gesture illustrates Tolstoi's sympathy for women's demand for higher educational facilities.[47] Given his attempts to sabotage them, however, it is more likely that caution prompted the minister's offer. Since he could not openly prohibit the lectures without risking a public outcry, their establishment in his quarters would at least enable him to check their development.

Shuvalov remained more adamant than Tolstoi in his opposition to public lectures. In June 1869, the chief of gendarmes complained that many signatories on the women's petition had aroused the suspicions of the state police, and warned that the opening of public lectures might spark a new wave of university disorders.[48] Convinced that the shortage of university teachers had contributed to recent student disturbances, Shuvalov feared that those professors who agreed to give lectures would be unable to fulfil their obligations at the university, thereby precipitating further student unrest. His concerns about university teaching personnel were not unfounded. Negligent and incompetent professors had been the targets of student boycotts during the "thaw." In those turbulent years, many university chairs were empty, and the situation had not improved after the university reform of 1863. A statistical survey compiled in 1868 revealed that 50 percent of the positions of professors and docents were vacant.[49]

Nevertheless, the Third Department grudgingly approved the establishment of public lectures in October 1869. Increased awareness of the power of public opinion had prompted a change of tactics. Rumours about the prospective lectures had spread rapidly throughout St Petersburg: more than a thousand people awaited their establishment. Under these circumstances, official prohibition of the lectures was likely to generate public discontent. Rather than take this risk, Shuvalov, in co-operation with Timashev and Tolstoi, adopted a somewhat shrewder strategy. In order to prevent women from financing the lectures, they prohibited any announcements or publications soliciting funds for the lectures until they were established on a regular basis.[50] On these conditions, Tolstoi authorized the establishment of the St Petersburg Public Lectures on 29 November 1869.

Despite the ban on advance publicity, private donations and the early payment of admission fees allowed their opening on 20 January 1870. The lecture series initially included six subjects: botany by Beketov, chemistry by Mendeleev, Russian history by Bestuzhev-Riumin, anatomy by F.V. Ovsiannikov, zoology by N.P. Wagner, and Russian literature by O.F. Miller.[51] Lectures were held in the evenings, four times a week. As the only admission requirement was a fee of 25 rubles per semester or 25 kopeks for a single lecture, they attracted a large and diverse audience.[52] Over 900 persons, including 767 women, attended the lectures on their opening. Along with serious women were ladies who came out of idle curiosity and young girls who lacked a sufficient background to comprehend the lectures. The much smaller male contingent revealed a similar diversity: some came in pursuit of knowledge; others attended with hopes of gazing at pretty faces or dreams of romantic intrigues with *nigilistki*. As Tolstoi had calculated, public lectures did not promote serious or systematic study.

Bureaucratic obstructionism also hampered the successful operation of the lectures. Shuvalov continued his search for signs of political deviance and often disrupted the lecture program.[53] As each lecture series required preliminary approval by the Third Department, over-zealousness on the part of the gendarmes sometimes delayed the reading of lectures by months. Their diligence notwithstanding, Shuvalov's aids "uncovered" no evidence to justify closure of the lectures. Similarly, Timashev resorted to delaying tactics. On 30 May 1870, Tolstoi solicited the views of Timashev and Shuvalov concerning the introduction of new lecture topics and the resumption of lectures by previously approved professors. In early November, the minister of education still awaited their reply.[54]

Frequent transfer of the lectures to different locations created additional problems. During the first four years, the lectures moved three times. They were expelled from Tolstoi's quarters in early 1871 because the government now needed these accommodations for a special commission on Poland.[55] Maintaining stability on the Western borderlands was far more crucial to national security than keeping close watch over studious women. When the lectures moved into the small gymnasium of the Historical-Philological Institute, however, the local police increased surveillance over them. In March 1871, F.F. Trepov, the governor and police chief of St Petersburg, launched an official protest against the public lectures. Beginning with an attack on the teaching staff, Trepov charged the new instructors in government and criminal law with disseminating politically dangerous ideas: "Professors [A.D.] Gradovskii and [N.S.] Tagantsev do their utmost in these lectures to popularize those scientific truths which can be considered questionable and related to the liberal utopias of a certain party of scholars." Equally dangerous, the governor claimed, was the type of women attracted to the lectures. He alleged that most female auditors belonged to the "St Petersburg society of *nigilistki*." Suggesting that the lectures promoted immoral behaviour, Trepov argued that inadequate supervision allowed young men and women to stroll "down the very long corridors of the philological institute, in complete darkness." In conclusion, he advised the immediate closure or total reorganization of the public lectures.[56]

Trepov's protest attracted the attention of Alexander II. On 5 April 1871, the emperor ordered an investigation of the governor's allegations by a special review board staffed by Tolstoi, Shuvalov, Timashev, and P.I. Liven, the St Petersburg curator.[57] Although these officials harboured no particular sympathy for the public lectures, they dismissed Trepov's charges. Unlike the local governor, Shuvalov, Timashev, and Tolstoi had become increasingly adept in coping with issues of public debate. For them, the continued operation of public lectures represented only a minimal concession to the growing demands for women's higher education.

During the previous year, numerous requests for increased employment opportunities for women, not to mention the public debate over women's work and education, had prompted Shuvalov to insist that the Council of Ministers clarify the government's position on the employment of women. Warning that the expansion of women's career opportunities would have "harmful and disastrous consequences" for women and their families, Shuvalov recommended that women be confined largely to their traditional vocations as teachers and midwives.[58] He did, however, suggest that the government expand women's midwifery training and encourage women to become teachers in elementary schools and in the lower classes of girls' gymnasia. Concerning their more recent employment as clerks, stenographers, and telegraphists, the chief of gendarmes stipulated that the number of women admitted to these occupations should be limited. Less than a month later, Shuvalov's recommendations were inscribed in the Imperial Order of 14 January 1871.[59] Shuvalov's almost complete authorship of state policy governing women's employment demonstrates his extensive influence in court circles. The very formulation of this official policy statement, moreover, reveals that the government was now forced to acknowledge women's increased participation in economic activities outside the domestic sphere.

At the same time, Tolstoi was more confident than ever that public lectures would never provide women access to Russian universities. In June 1871, the emperor approved Tolstoi's gymnasium reform, which restricted university admission to graduates of the classical male gymnasium.[60] The new Gymnasium Statute, promulgated the following month, standardized university entrance requirements and thus guaranteed women's exclusion. It also marked a personal victory for Tolstoi over his adversaries in court: Miliutin, in particular, had vigorously opposed the minister's reform plan, and the majority of the State Council rejected it. The tsar, however, decided to make it law.

Now that Tolstoi had succeeded in tightening control over university admissions, he adopted a more conciliatory policy concerning the public lectures. When they were transferred to Vladimirskii district school in 1872, the minister of education allocated over 1000 rubles for the renovation of the new facilities.[61] At that time, he began to subsidize the Vladimirskie Courses, as the lectures were popularly known, with an annual grant of 1000 rubles. Although the ministerial subsidy constituted only a negligible part of the operating costs of the lectures, it represented a significant departure from Tolstoi's early obstructionist efforts. Two years later, when the minister authorized their transfer to Vasiliostrovskii Girls' Gymnasium, he also allowed their transformation into courses exclusively for women.

I.T. Osinin, the director of the St Petersburg Girls' Gymnasia of the Fourth Department, had agreed to house the courses on the condition that admission be restricted to women.[62] Undoubtedly, the "safer" location in a girls' school influenced Tolstoi's decision to accept Osinin's offer. The minister's recent promotion of non-exclusive girls' gymnasia indicates that he considered such institutions no threat to the established order. In 1869, he had also approved the opening of advanced secondary courses for women. They were called the Alarchinskie Courses after their location near Alarchin bridge.

Division within the St Petersburg women's movement led to the founding of the Alarchinskie Courses. Controversy over whether university lectures or university-preparatory courses would be most useful prompted a small number of women to separate from the main group of activists. Led by Ekaterina A. Solodovnikova, they appealed to I.I. Paulson, a professor of pedagogy at the university, to teach women's courses in the subjects of the male gymnasium.[63] Paulson agreed, and so, too, did other local academics. The director of a local boys' gymnasium also offered classroom facilities free of charge in the evening. In February 1869, Paulson petitioned the Ministry of Education on Solodovnikova's behalf. Within five weeks, Tolstoi, Shuvalov, and Timashev agreed to allow the courses.[64] Their co-operation is not that surprising: the courses did not encroach upon the male monopoly of higher education and, as a privately funded institution, would not burden the state treasury.

On their opening in April 1869, the Alarchinskie Courses admitted over 100 women to classes in physics, chemistry, mathematics, the Russian language, and pedagogy. Enrolment soon tripled, thus assuring their continued operation. Tuition fees and the proceeds from banquets organized by Solodovnikova financed the courses until their voluntary closure in 1875.

Preparation for university study was the main preoccupation of most *kursistki*, as pupils in women's courses were known in popular parlance. Enrolment in the courses, however, also increased their opportunities to meet other young people and discuss current social and political issues. Shortly after the courses opened, women's discussion groups and circles of *kursistki* and students mushroomed in the northern capital. *Zhenskii vopros* dominated the debates of most women. But such was not the case of the Chaikovskii Circle. This socialist organization concluded that the most pressing problem was not women's emancipation, but the liberation of Russian society as a whole.[65] Formed in 1871 by the merger of a student commune and small group of Alarchinskie pupils, the Chaikovskii Circle conducted socialist propaganda among workers and peasants. Its most famous female member was Sofiia L. Perovskaia, the revolutionary who would later be hanged for her role in the regicide of 1881. Other Chaikovtsy from the Alarchinskie Courses included Elizaveta Koval'skaia, Olga Schleissner, and two Kornilova sisters, Liubov and Aleksandra. Indeed, there is a certain irony in the fact that while most state officials eagerly combatted the allegedly revolutionary struggle for women's higher education, they failed to notice that these advanced secondary courses harboured some of Russia's most committed socialists.

Why these particular *kursistki* became involved in radical politics requires detailed investigation of their personal histories beyond the scope of this study.[66] Nevertheless, there can be little doubt that these women were attracted by the egalitarian principles espoused by the men of the Chaikovskii Circle and embodied in its organization. Here they found immediate sexual equality and the blueprint for a future society that promised freedom for all men and women. The illegal and violent means required to accomplish this goal, however, appealed to only a few women in the Alarchinskie Courses. The overwhelming majority of women pursuing advanced education in the capital favoured peaceful, moderate measures. In most cases, they avoided contact with radical circles for fear of jeopardizing their recent gains.

Their achievements, nevertheless, were too meagre to satisfy the educational ambitions of most women. Whereas the Alarchinskie Courses offered only preparatory classes, those in Vasiliostrovskii Girls' Gymnasium consisted of a series of lecture presentations that allowed for little interaction between pupil and professor. Consequently, the early 1870s also witnessed the increased migration of Russian women to Zurich University. This, in turn, would generate suspicions about women imbibing revolutionary ideas abroad. To counter this threat, the government would promise the creation of women's higher courses in Russian university towns. It is not surprising, then, that in 1875, St Petersburg women turned their attention to the prospective higher courses and abandoned, without reluctance, both the lectures and the Alarchinskie Courses.

IV

Considerable controversy surrounds the early efforts of Moscow women to expand their educational opportunities. According to three contemporary proponents of women's higher education, Moscow University Council in 1868 refused to endorse their appeal for university courses.[67] This is in keeping with the council's earlier rejection of female auditors; and, it is possible that the boisterous meetings of local women, which had attracted police attention, hardened the opposition of Moscow professors. Regrettably, these sources provide few details concerning the council's discussions, nor do they reproduce the women's petition. A fourth account makes no reference to this particular petition, but suggests that women appealed directly to Tolstoi for access to university lectures.[68] It also specifies that the minister refused on the grounds that women lacked the necessary academic preparation for university study. A similar interpretation appeared in the *Journal of the Ministry of Education* in 1912.[69] The problem here, however, is that the contemporary press never mentioned this appeal to Tolstoi, whereas it recorded all other women's petitions, even those the minister rejected. No reference to this appeal, moreover, has been found in the archives of the Ministry of Education.[70] Whether Moscow women made a concerted effort to establish university-level courses at this time, then, remains unclear. There is no doubt, however, that by early 1869, they had turned their attention to preparatory classes. F.V. Korolev, the director of Moscow's Second Boys' Gymnasium, had agreed to organize advanced secondary courses for women.

In April, Korolev solicited Tolstoi's permission to create women's courses in all subjects of the male gymnasium. His petition won almost immediate ministerial approval. By the end of May, Tolstoi, Shuvalov, and Timashev had authorized their establishment as a private institution. Korolev's specific request for courses in Latin and Greek particularly appealed to Tolstoi who considered the classics fundamental to secondary education. Not only did the study of the classics require intellectual discipline, but the culture and complex grammars of antiquity might distract pupils from contemporary intellectual and social movements that criticized the existing order. Shuvalov, on the other hand, mistakenly assumed that the instructors of the courses would be drawn from local gymnasia rather than the understaffed university.[71]

Korolev opened the women's courses in October 1869. During the first year, the curriculum included all subjects offered in the male gymnasium, except Greek.[72] In 1870, however, when the courses moved to Moscow's Third Gymnasium on the Lubianka, the course program began to shift toward the sciences. Declining enrolment in the humanities classes, particularly after Professor V.I. Guerrier (Ger'e) established his own women's courses in 1872, forced their abandonment. During the academic year 1873–4, Latin and geography were discontinued in favour of new courses in botany and zoology. World history and the modern languages survived for a few more years, but by 1878 they had been replaced by additional courses in mathematics and science. By that year, the Lubianskie Courses, as they were popularly known, boasted a curriculum equivalent to the physical-mathematical faculty of Moscow University. Such dedicated scientists as physicist N.A. Umov and chemist V.V. Markovnikov lectured and supervised laboratories. Few of Moscow's established professors, however, were willing to participate in the women's courses. Instead, docents, assistant professors, and gymnasium instructors dominated the teaching staff.[73]

During the first semester, the Lubianskie Courses admitted 190 auditors (*slushatel'nitsy*) as the pupils in non-degree courses were officially designated. Enrolment declined considerably over the next nine years and dropped to eighty-six in 1878, when women's higher courses were established in St Petersburg.[74] During the following year, however, enrolment increased by almost 30 percent, and by the fall of 1885, 150 women attended the Lubianskie Courses. Admission

TABLE 3
Religious affiliation of auditors of the Lubianskie Courses, 1882–5

| Year | Orthodox | Jews | Roman Catholics | Lutherans | Other | Total |
|---|---|---|---|---|---|---|
| 1882 | 92 | 20 | 3 | 5 | 0 | 120 |
| 1883 | 80 | 22 | 5 | 2 | 1 | 110 |
| 1884 | 94 | 16 | 3 | 3 | 1 | 117 |
| 1885 | 111 | 23 | 5 | 5 | 6 | 150 |
| Total | 377 | 81 | 16 | 15 | 8 | 497 |
| Percentage | 75.9 | 16.3 | 3.2 | 3.0 | 1.6 | 100 |

*Source*: TSGIAL, f. 733, o. 191, d. 674, l. 40.

records for the early 1880s reveal that women of the Orthodox faith exceeded 75 percent of the total enrolment, whereas Jews represented 16 percent (see table 3). Moscow's other educational institutions admitted a far smaller contingent of Jews. For example, only 5 Jews numbered among the 169 women attending Guerrier's Courses in 1881–2.[75] In the boys' gymnasia of Moscow educational district, Jews constituted 5.5 percent of the student body in 1886.[76] The main attraction of the Lubianskie courses to women of Jewish culture was the science program:[77] because Jews were barred from pedagogical activity in the empire, they entered the Lubianskie Courses to prepare for medical careers.

Representation from the urban estates was also greater in the women's courses than in the male gymnasium. Non-noble urban women exceeded 46 percent of the total enrolment during the years 1882–5, whereas townsmen constituted only slightly more than 37 percent of the gymnasium population of Moscow district in 1886 (see table 4). The proportion of privileged society was high in both types of educational institutions: 42.7 percent of the Lubianskie auditors came from families of gentry and officials, compared to 49 percent of gymnasium pupils. At the same time, however, the gymnasium was also more accessible to the lowest social order: peasants accounted for 5 percent of gymnasium enrolment, but less than 2 percent of admissions to the Lubianskie Courses. Indeed, the *muzhik* had greater opportunity than his female counterpart to ascend the educational ladder. State scholarships and stipends also enabled several male peasants to enter the university where they represented 3.3 percent of the student body in 1880, and 7.1 percent in 1895 (see table 4). The government provided no financial aid to impoverished women seeking higher education.

Poverty was not the only factor limiting peasant enrolment in the Lubianskie Courses. Because peasant girls remained the smallest minority at the lower levels of the education system, few had the academic background to pursue advanced study. Even the expansion of rural schools during the reform era

TABLE 4
Social origins of auditors of the Lubianskie Courses, compared to students in male gymnasia of Moscow educational district and in Moscow University

| Social Origins | Lubianskie Courses | | | | | | Moscow Gymnasia | | Moscow University | | | |
| | 1882 | 1883 | 1884 | 1885 | Total | Percent | 1886 Total | Percent | 1880 Total | Percent | 1895 Total | Percent |
| --- | --- | --- | --- | --- | --- | --- | --- | --- | --- | --- | --- | --- |
| Gentry, officials | 50 | 41 | 51 | 70 | 212 | 42.7 | 4991 | 49.7 | 884 | 47.3 | 1753 | 40.8 |
| Clergy | 8 | 11 | 10 | 11 | 40 | 8.0 | 540 | 5.4 | 413 | 22.1 | 241 | 5.6 |
| Townspeople | 57 | 54 | 55 | 64 | 230 | 46.3 | 3731 | 37.2 | 398 | 21.3 | 1888 | 44.0 |
| Rural | 3 | 4 | 0 | 2 | 9 | 1.8 | 511 | 5.1 | 62 | 3.3 | 304 | 7.1 |
| Foreigners, others | 2 | 0 | 1 | 3 | 6 | 1.2 | 263 | 2.6 | 112 | 6.0 | 107 | 2.5 |
| Total | 120 | 110 | 117 | 150 | 497 | 100 | 10036 | 100 | 1869 | 100 | 4293 | 100 |

*Source:* TSGIAL, f. 733, o. 191, d. 674, l. 40. Figures for gymnasium enrolment are adapted from table 5 in Alston, *Education and the State*, 256; those for university students, from tables in Leikina-Svirskaia, *Intelligentsiia v Rossii*, 62–3.

failed to provide them with equal opportunities for primary education: the boys in these schools outnumbered the girls three to one.[78] Largely responsible for the poor attendance of girls was the *muzhik*'s reluctance to relinquish the labour services of daughters: "Why should we teach our girls, ask the peasants ... They're too busy to read books. On weekdays they work at heavy labor side by side with men, either in the fields, the woods or in the garden. They have an equal amount of work waiting for them at home, preparing meals for the family, tending the cattle, taking care of the family and sewing the clothing. On holidays they are busier than ever!"[79] Peasant women could ill afford the elementary education available in their districts, much less advanced study in Moscow.

Nor could the courses offer financial assistance to these disadvantaged women. Admission fees, which provided approximately 80 percent of the annual income, barely covered the salaries of instructors.[80] Additional operating costs consumed most of the proceeds from concerts and bazaars, as well as the donations of local society. Given the absence of state funding, it is highly unlikely that the courses could have survived without the free facilities of the boys' gymnasium. This location, as well as the orderly behaviour of auditors, apparently discouraged official surveillance: at least no state or local authority reported the transformation of the Lubianskie Courses into a self-governing women's university, albeit with no degree-granting powers.

After their transfer to Moscow's Third Gymnasium in 1870, the Lubianskie Courses developed an unusually democratic administration. A general assembly of auditors drew up the annual budget and regulations of the courses, and appointed supervisors from their own ranks.[81] More important, assembly delegates, in consultation with instructors, revised the curriculum and chose the teaching staff. Although the gymnasium director remained the official manager of the courses, his actual participation in their administration was negligible. He served as the treasurer, authorized the meetings of the general assembly, and approved its decisions.

Given Tolstoi's recent assault on the regular university system, the developments in the Lubianskie Courses testify to the government's inability to investigate and control fully the social movements that proliferated during the reform era. It must be conceded, however, that these *kursistki* avoided any activities that might arouse the suspicions of officialdom. In particular, they did not participate in the student demonstrations that attracted the attention of state security agents. Indeed, Moscow women had come a long way from the noisy discussions of the late 1860s: in the quiet corridors of a boys' gymnasium, they not only studied university science, but achieved self-government – the ultimate goal of the student protests that rocked higher educational institutions during the reign of Alexander II.

Women in Guerrier's Courses, on the contrary, played no role in their administration.[82] Nor did the teaching staff. Instead, Guerrier ruled almost single-handed. This historian, who was also Moscow's most outspoken defender of university autonomy during Tolstoi's ministry,[83] controlled both the academic and administrative affairs of the courses. That Tolstoi would allow such an individual to open women's courses can be explained in part by the moderate nature of Guerrier's proposal, which called for increased secondary education in the humanities. The professor's paternalistic attitude toward women may also have influenced the minister's decision. Long after Russian women had demonstrated their ability to master university-level courses, Guerrier continued to treat them as children in certain respects. Sophie Satina, who attended Guerrier's Courses after they reopened in the early twentieth century, recorded the following incident: when one woman complained that "we were no longer children, but students, who wanted to express our views, the Director interrupted her and taking her by the chin asked: 'Ducky, how old are you?'"[84] Such behaviour hardly endeared Guerrier to the auditors, but his domination of the courses provoked no opposition from his colleagues who taught them during the 1870s and early 1880s. Admittedly, most teachers were junior faculty members who ranked below Guerrier in the academic hierarchy of Moscow University. For example, the eminent historian V.O. Kliuchevskii was a docent when he participated in Guerrier's Courses. As the development of the Lubianskie Courses also indicates, the majority of Moscow's established professors failed to support the expansion of women's education. It appears that the only local professor eager to organize and administer women's courses was a somewhat authoritarian individual who did not trouble to conceal his paternalistic views. Nevertheless, the scholar in Guerrier ensured that the women in his courses received rigorous academic training. He also attempted to expand their employment opportunities in girls' schools.

When Guerrier requested Tolstoi's permission to open women's courses, he specified that their main objective was to provide women with more substantial secondary education, and thus create more qualified teachers.[85] As well as citing the recent imperial order endorsing women's pursuit of teaching careers, he emphasized that the courses would not cater to women's particular interests, but offer a strictly regulated two-year program in the humanities. Unlike the earlier appeals for women's courses, his petition stipulated that all auditors must fulfil academic entrance requirements, complete regular assignments, and sit for semester and final examinations. Later, the orderly operation of Guerrier's Courses would induce Tolstoi to acknowledge them as the model for women's higher courses that opened in the provinces during the late 1870s. When the minister initially approved Guerrier's petition in May 1872, however, he authorized their establishment only on a four-year experimental basis. He also refused to grant the prospective graduates the title of domestic tutor,[86] a teaching credential many prospective auditors already possessed. Throughout their sixteen-year existence, the Ministry of Education denied the courses any degree-granting rights or state subsidies.

Guerrier's Courses opened on 1 November 1872. Women who held a graduating or teaching certificate from a girls' gymnasium or institute, or who passed entrance examinations in the subjects of the girls' gymnasium qualified for enrolment.[87] An annual fee of 50 rubles or the payment of 10 rubles per subject admitted women to classes taught by scholars who would soon be ranked among the nation's finest: the history of art and civilization by Guerrier; Russian history by Kliuchevskii; philosophy by V.S. Solov'ev; world history by S.F. Fortunatov; Russian literature by N.S. Tikhonravov; and world literature by N.I. Storozhenko.[88] These instructors, moreover, not only presented lectures, but also conducted seminars and read assignments and examinations. Like the Lubianskie Courses, Guerrier's Courses developed into a much more advanced educational facility than originally proposed to the minister of education. In 1874, Guerrier expanded the courses into a three-year program of university study.

Similarly, instructors' fees constituted the major expense of the courses, and tuition payments provided the main source of income.[89] Local society offered little financial assistance, contributing only 7 percent of the total income during the first fourteen years. The Moscow Merchants' Association, which donated 500 rubles annually for stipends during the years 1875–82, however, benefited auditors from the merchant class. Fortunately, the steady increase in enrolment, which expanded from 66 in the first semester to 227 in 1886, allowed the courses to operate on a small profit margin.

Guerrier's Courses were far more exclusive than their counterpart on the Lubianka. Academic entrance requirements, as well as the humanities program, discouraged attendance by the less privileged. Enrolment information for the years 1882–6 reveals that almost 60 percent came from the gentry, and less than 30 percent from artisan and merchant families (see table 5). Only one peasant attended during this period. Religious conformity also characterized the auditors; only a few Jews and Protestants enrolled.[90] Neither the social background of the auditors nor the regular examinations and operation of Guerrier's Courses, however, could persuade Tolstoi to grant *kursistki* any teaching rights. Guerrier tried different methods to change the minister's mind. In 1876, he again petitioned Tolstoi, requesting that his graduates be permitted to teach the upper classes of girls' gymnasia.[91] The following year, he made a public appeal for expanding women's careers in *Vestnik evropy*. The growing number of unmarried women without relatives to support them, the Moscow professor insisted, made increased educational and employment opportunities for women an economic imperative.[92] Such practical arguments did not convince Tolstoi. But he was not the most intransigent minister Guerrier would confront. Tolstoi had, after all, approved the new three-year program and allowed the continued operation of the courses. His successor, I.D. Delianov, would shut them down.

That is not to suggest that Tolstoi had any qualms about thwarting women's

TABLE 5
Social origins of auditors of Guerrier's Courses, 1882–6

| Year | Course | Total | Gentry | Clergy | Mer-chant | Officials | Artisans | Peasants |
|---|---|---|---|---|---|---|---|---|
| 1882–3 | Iᵃ | 69 | 39 | 6 | 23 | 0 | 1 | 0 |
|  | part time | 43 | 29 | 3 | 8 | 0 | 3 | 0 |
| 1883–4 | I | 99 | 64 | 7 | 22 | 0 | 6 | 0 |
|  | part time | 29 | 18 | 3 | 3 | 2 | 3 | 0 |
| 1885–6 | I | 81 | 40 | 6 | 9 | 8 | 17 | 1 |
|  | II | 65 | 37 | 4 | 9 | 10 | 5 | 0 |
|  | III | 29 | 14 | 2 | 7 | 3 | 3 | 0 |
|  | part time | 52 | 37 | 3 | 9 | 0 | 3 | 0 |
| Total |  | 467 | 278 | 34 | 90 | 23 | 41 | 1 |
| Percentage |  | 100 | 59.5 | 7.3 | 19.3 | 4.9 | 8.8 | 0.2 |

a Indicates auditors enrolled in full first-year course.
*Source*: Bobrova, "Vysshie zhenskie kursy professora Ger'e," 258.

educational pursuits, particularly outside the capitals. During the early 1870s, he rejected two provincial appeals on the grounds that their demands were excessive: Kharkov women had petitioned for admission to the local university; Kazan professors had proposed a three-year course program for women.[93] Regardless of their content, Tolstoi could dismiss these appeals with relative ease, as both Kazan and Kharkov were far from the centre of political power. And unlike the sponsors of the St Petersburg Public Lectures, the provincial advocates of women's higher education included no wives or confidants of influential officials who frequented the social circles of Tolstoi. Only Moscow, the ancient capital and seat of Russia's most prestigious university, rivalled St Petersburg in its influence on court politics and educational policy. Here, however, no well-connected individuals had applied pressure on behalf of women's courses. No such pressure was needed to win ministerial approval of the Moscow courses because neither Korolev nor Guerrier had requested university-level education for women. They asked only to upgrade women's secondary education at the very time when Tolstoi was revamping the male gymnasium system and standardizing university entrance requirements.

Provincial university towns would remain without women's higher courses until the late 1870s. By that time, the exodus of Russian women to Zurich had convinced the government that local courses would provide a much safer and more controllable outlet for women's educational ambitions.

### CHAPTER THREE

# Russian Women in Zurich:
# Education and Revolution

On arriving in Zurich [in 1872], I was possessed by a single idea – to devote myself completely to the study of medicine – and I crossed the threshold of the university with reverence ... I was nineteen years old, but I intended to renounce all pleasures and amusements, even the most innocent ones, in order to lose not a minute of precious time, and I got down to the lectures, academic and practical assignments with an ardour that did not weaken for more than three years.

VERA N. FIGNER (1921)[1]

Women's struggle for higher education met strong opposition in all European countries during the early 1860s. In Germany, girls had no access to the gymnasium, much less the university. Traditional notions of woman's "divinely willed dependency" and the more recent overcrowding of the academic professions would conspire to frustrate women's educational ambitions in Germany until the 1890s, when the universities finally admitted female auditors.[2] France was somewhat more progressive: the Ministry of Education opened medical schools to women in the late 1860s, but most university faculties remained male preserves until after the founding of the Third Republic.[3] It was not a great European power, however, that first granted equal educational opportunities to women. Instead, a small Swiss canton broke the traditional male monopoly of higher academic degrees: in 1867, Zurich University awarded Nadezhda Suslova the degree of Doctor of Medicine, Surgery, and Midwifery. Suslova's dissertation on the physiology of the lymphatic system won immediate international recognition. As a result, the following year, the Russian Medical Council admitted her to colloquium examinations for foreign doctors, a procedure that conveniently avoided any reference to the candidate's sex, and granted her the right to medical practice in Russia.[4]

Encouraged by Suslova's achievements, over one hundred Russian women flocked to Zurich during the next five years. More than ninety arrived in

1872 and 1873.[5] They found few European women studying there: four
German women were enrolled at the university, whereas Switzerland, England, and Austria had two female representatives each.[6] One American
woman also completed her degree at Zurich in the fall of 1871. In the student
community, the Russians constituted the largest foreign element and, by
late 1873, the women outnumbered the men by two to one.[7] Female students
also represented approximately one-third of the entire Russian colony in the
Swiss canton. The majority of women came from European Russia, but a
few hailed from such distant regions as the Caucasus, Siberia, and the
Cossack hosts.[8] The expense of living and travelling abroad ensured that
most were daughters of relatively well-to-do gentry, officials, and merchants.
Several, however, had fled the less privileged classes of peasants, clerics,
and artisans. Religious diversity also characterized the female emigrants:
women of the Orthodox, Lutheran, and Roman Catholic faith, as well as
twenty Jews, studied in the lakeside town. The overwhelming majority were
young unmarried women. In their chosen field of study, they also revealed
considerable conformity: seventy-seven Russian women had enrolled in Zurich's medical faculty by 1873.[9]

Undoubtedly, Russian women's attraction to the medical profession was,
in part, a natural outgrowth of the traditional female role of healer and
comforter of the sick. Even more important, the intellectual atmosphere of
the post-Crimean era had imbued medicine with a special significance and
appeal. During this period when educated society in general looked to learning as the key to progress, the leading spokesmen of the younger generation
exalted the sciences as the true source of knowledge and the panacea of
Russia's social ills.[10] The revival of Western positivism and materialism
contributed to the development of this utilitarian creed; the reforming zeal
and sense of historic mission that characterized contemporary Russian youth,
however, informed it with an ethos of social service. Medical practice
represented the perfect embodiment of this new ideology. The study of
medicine would yield a body of scientific knowledge easily translated into
social service. And, in a country that suffered a chronic shortage of medical
personnel, the social utility of such education could not be overestimated.

Medical education beckoned Russian women to Zurich University, but
Swiss students did not welcome them there. The inequitable admissions
policy was a major cause of discontent: whereas residents of the Swiss
canton were required to pass entrance examinations, foreign students only
had to present a certificate of good behaviour. Because Russian women were
the chief beneficiaries of the disparate admission standards, they became
the main object of resentment. At the same time, however, Swiss men
showed considerable antagonism to other female students as well. Franziska
Tiburtius, the first German woman to enrol at Zurich, described how the
shouts of male students prevented her and a Russian woman from entering

a lecture hall and forced them to seek shelter in a nearby cloakroom.[11] Fortunately, most professors allowed no sexual discrimination in the classroom and such incidents were rare. It is also possible that some instructors may have fuelled the bitterness of male students by praising the outstanding work of some women in order to reproach the men. According to Peter Kropotkin, the Russian anarchist who visited the Swiss canton in 1872, "Zurich professors were never tired of showing the progress accomplished by women at the university, as an example to the male students."[12]

Russian women also did much to alienate the Swiss. Marie Voegtlin, the first Swiss woman to attend the university, found them self-centred and aggressive: "Russian women demanded not only the same rights, but special privileges, and everywhere put themselves in the foreground and occupied the best places [in university classrooms]."[13] Her compatriots agreed. The lifestyle of Russian women also set them apart from the native inhabitants of the old Zwinglian town. Most rented communal lodgings in special sections of Zurich that housed their countrymen and "where the Russian language prevailed over all others." Here, financial restraints often demanded the pooling of resources, and extreme frugality reigned. Daily fare usually consisted of bread and tea, supplemented by a little milk and a "thin slice of meat."[14] To the further dismay of the Swiss, Russian women also smoked cigarettes and walked about town unchaperoned. Such blatant disregard for decorum irritated native residents. They showed little concern, however, for the political developments within the Russian community as a whole. Indeed, in 1872–3, when the influx of Russian women was at its height, Zurich emerged as the centre of Russian revolutionary organizations abroad. Both the anarchist Michael Bakunin and the populist Peter Lavrov had established their headquarters there.[15] Still Swiss authorities did not interfere in the affairs of the Russian colony.

But the Russian government did. In May 1873, it ordered all Russian women to abandon their studies at Zurich. A special commission staffed by Tolstoi, Shuvalov, Timashev, and N.A. Shtorkh, the assistant head of the Four Department, had concluded that education alone had not drawn Russian women to the Swiss canton. Rather, their exodus abroad was intimately connected to social and political radicalism. Propaganda of the "so-called woman question," the commission argued, had promoted their migration to Zurich: "Under its cover, together with demands for sound, basic education for women and the expansion of their sphere of activities, are carried others [demands] which have a utopian, almost revolutionary character: equalization of the rights of a woman with the rights of a man, her participation in politics and even the right to free love, which destroys the very basis of the family and makes a principle of the extreme dissoluteness of morals."[16] As the conservative publicists had earlier warned, the commission "found" moral corruption rife among women engaged in university study. The fact that many of these young women had left their parental nests before marriage was itself an affront to social morality. Sofiia V. Kovalevskaia, the daughter of wealthy landowner Korvin-Krukovskii, described how her father responded to her elder sister's request to study in St Petersburg: "Father got angry at last and shouted at her as if she had been a child. 'If you don't understand that it is the duty of every respectable girl to live with her parents until she marries, I won't argue with a stupid, bad little girl.'"[17] What social morality prescribed, the legal code enforced. A single woman under twenty-one was registered on her father's passport and, therefore, required his permission to travel or reside elsewhere.[18]

Contemporary memoirs indicate that several women who lacked parental approval to study abroad entered a "fictitious marriage." As Chernyshevskii had described in *What Is To Be Done?*, a suitable bachelor would marry a woman to free her from parental control and, after the wedding, renounce his marital "rights." Such marriages often marked the termination of the relationship between the contracting parties. For Rosaliia Kh. Idel'son (née Iakershberg), a "fictitious marriage" gave her the freedom to travel abroad and join Lavrov's populist organization in Zurich.[19] In the case of Kovalevskaia, it led to advanced study in Germany and a brilliant career in mathematics.[20] She would also become the first female professor in nineteenth-century Europe. At least one such nominal union, however, developed into a love relationship: deep mutual affection bonded the partnership of Larissa V. Chemodanova and Sergei S. Sinegub in the Chaikovskii Circle.[21]

Contemporary memoirs also dispute the commission's charges of sexual promiscuity. The few that discuss the sexual life of Russian youth suggest that a somewhat puritanical code governed the behaviour of studious women as well as of female revolutionists. Within the student community and radical circles, the "right to free love" did not imply indiscriminate sexual liberty, but rather the freedom to enter a love relationship of one's own choosing rather than a marriage arranged by parents or sanctioned by the church.[22] For some, the struggle for reform or revolution became an all-consuming passion, which left no room for love or sexual relationships. When the attractive Mariia Kal'enkina was asked why she was indifferent to men, the young revolutionary replied, "I love the movement."[23] A number of women who participated in the peaceful struggle for increased educational and professional opportunities also claimed to relegate love relationships to the bottom of their scale of values. Kovalevskaia, for example, related how her young female friends were both disappointed and angered when a colleague "committed the crime of a love-marriage."[24]

Demands for personal sacrifice were even more pronounced among the radical women of the Fritschi Circle, so named after their Zurich landlady, Frau Fritsch.[25] For them, the renunciation of the smallest, most innocent pleasures assumed the gravity of a "categorical imperative."[26] When Sofiia

Bardina, the disaffected daughter of a Tambov noble and acknowledged leader of the Fritschi, admitted: "'I love raspberries and plums,'" her colleague, Vera Liubatovich, was appalled and considered Bardina "bourgeois."[27] This snap judgment was, of course, mistaken. After leaving Zurich, Bardina demonstrated her commitment to socialist principles by spreading revolutionary propaganda among Moscow factory workers. At the Trial of Fifty in 1877, her speech captured the sense of self-sacrifice and righteous defiance that motivated the Fritschi and other young defendants who stood with her in the dock: "Go on persecuting us, physical force is still on your side; but moral force and the force of historical progress is on ours; ours is the power of ideas, and ideas – you may regret it – cannot be impaled on the points of the bayonets."[28]

This trial also gave substance to the government's earlier charge that Russian women imbibed revolutionary ideas in the émigré circles of Zurich: eleven of the sixteen female defendants had studied in the Swiss canton. And five of the six women awarded the harshest sentences were Fritschi: Bardina and Olga Liubatovich were condemned to nine years hard labour; Vera Liubatovich received six years; Varvara Aleksandrova and Lidiia Figner, five years.[29] The appeals of their lawyers, however, succeeded in getting the sentences commuted to Siberian exile. Two other Fritschi, who had also been arrested and detained, never did stand trial: after a few months in prison, Betia Kaminskaia went insane; a year of pre-trial confinement also wrecked the health of Mariia Subbotina who was released when she appeared to be dying of tuberculosis.

Indeed, the lives of these radical women have the makings of high drama. It is no wonder that the Fritschi, rather than the less colourful female émigrés, captured the attention of scholars. As a result, the historical portrait of Russian women at Zurich remains somewhat distorted and one-sided. Recent research reveals that a number of women are listed in the biographical dictionary of Russian revolutionaries simply because they studied at the Swiss university during the years 1872–3.[30] The memoirs of Vera Figner also indicate that academic pursuits preoccupied most female colonists, and that the desire to serve society, through the study of medicine, was the primary motivation of the majority of women who migrated to Zurich: "Having set off for Zurich not for higher education in general, we sought special training and the majority became medical students in order to have in their hands *an instrument for social work*. The striving to be useful to society – that is the most appropriate formula for defining the mood of Zurich youth in 1872."[31]

At the same time, Figner also documents her own painful transformation from a serious student into a dedicated revolutionist. In the radical émigré circles of Zurich, she became convinced that the welfare of Russia demanded wholesale revolution, not simply improved medical care: "On the one hand

– a pitiful palliative, which does not eliminate the evil; on the other – a radical upheaval, the establishment of justice and, on the basis of economic equality and socialist brotherhood, the harmonious development of all spiritual and physical aspects of the human personality." Despite this conviction, Figner's decision to risk her medical career was a torturous one. She wanted the love and recognition she could earn as a physician. The very possession of a doctor's degree appealed to her. Moreover, she doubted her readiness to forgo the tastes and lifestyle that her gentry birth and education had conferred. The dilemma of medicine or revolution haunted her: "My soul was divided, my feelings in conflict."[32]

No such conflict tormented the majority of Russian women who avoided radical politics at Zurich. Those about to complete their medical degrees suffered a different kind of anxiety: fear of antagonizing their government and thus jeopardizing their educational pursuits. Even when the government publicly accused them of practicing "free love" and abortions, they opposed Figner and several younger women in the first- and second-year courses who planned to protest these allegations. These moderates, whom Figner castigated as "the complacent-liberal-bourgeois party," threatened to publish a counter-protest if anyone launched a public complaint.[33] The majority prevailed and all plans for protest were abandoned. Their silence, however, could hardly allay the government's suspicions that revolution, not education, had attracted women to the Swiss university.

Accusations of subversive activities notwithstanding, the expulsion of women from Zurich involved no arrests, trials, or criminal punishments. Public opinion and persistent demands for women's higher education convinced Russian statesmen to adopt measures of "a preventative rather than repressive character," and to explain their actions in a press release.[34] By the early 1870s, the movement for women's higher education had gained considerable momentum, particularly in the northern capital. Not only academics and high-society women continued to support the movement: the War Ministry now sponsored advanced midwifery courses for women in the Medical-Surgical Academy. The provinces also showed renewed interest in women's education: both Kharkov and Kazan had petitioned Tolstoi to expand women's educational opportunities. At the same time, the opening of women's courses in Moscow and St Petersburg, as well as the migration to Zurich University, generated further discussion of women's education in the press. Although conservative papers, like *Grazhdanin*, railed against women's pursuit of university study, the more widely read liberal journals, such as *Otechestvennye zapiski*, applauded women's educational achievements at home and abroad.[35] Aware of growing public sympathy for women's higher education, Russian statesmen prepared a carefully worded press release in order to discourage any adverse public reaction to the expulsion of women from Zurich.

On 21 May 1873, *Pravitel' stvennyi vestnik*, the official government news-paper, announced that those women who refused to leave Zurich by 1 January 1874 would be excluded from all educational and employment opportunities in state institutions. Not only aimed at expelling Russian women from the Swiss university, but also calculated to persuade readers of the justice of the government's actions, it accused these women of succumbing to "communistic theories of free love," and implied that they studied medicine in order to perform abortions on each other. Moreover, to assure the public that there was no need for women's migration to Zurich, the official news-paper pointed to the St Petersburg Public Lectures, Guerrier's Courses, and the recently established midwifery courses of the War Ministry as evidence of the government's willingness to accommodate women's demand for higher education. It also reported that the emperor had ordered preparations for the establishment of women's higher courses in university towns. Indeed, this official announcement revealed how well Russian statesmen had learned to use the press to shape public opinion favourable to the government.

Once again, the spectre of political and social radicalism had prompted the Russian government to forbid women from pursuing higher education through regular academic channels. The majority complied with the May decree and left Zurich before the new year.[36] None had yet completed their education. Only one Russian woman had repeated Suslova's achievement: Mariia Bokova, who graduated from Zurich's medical faculty before the massive influx of Russian women, returned to St Petersburg with a doctor's degree in 1871 and successfully passed the colloquium examinations for domestic medical practice.[37] Not all female émigrés, however, abandoned their studies and returned directly to Russia. A significant number continued their education at other European universities that had recently opened their doors to women.[38] The majority of those who remained abroad enrolled in the medical faculty of Bern University, which, by the summer of 1874, had admitted thirty-four Russian women. A much smaller contingent entered the judicial and natural science faculties at Geneva University. Only a few went to Paris where both the language of instruction and program of study differed from those of Zurich University.

At least one woman appealed for personal exemption from the May decree. In December 1873, Stephanie Wolicka, a history major at Zurich, solicited Tolstoi's permission to remain at the Swiss University until she completed her degree in August 1874. Wolicka's appeal proved futile. Similarly, her assumption that compliance with the May decree would absolve her from all punitive measures was mistaken. Almost three weeks before the expulsion deadline, Shuvalov had sent Tolstoi a confidential memorandum listing the names of forty-five Zurich women, including Wolicka, to be barred from pedagogical activities on their return to Russia. Tolstoi promptly dispatched a secret circular to the heads of all educational districts, instructing them to enforce Shuvalov's directive.[39] Contrary to the official press release, the unpublicized activities of these statesmen revealed a government bent on punishing several studious women whether or not they obeyed its commands.

Officialdom would prove no match for the likes of Vera Figner. The joint efforts of the Third Department and the Ministry of Education failed to thwart her career aspirations. When Figner returned to Russia, she found herself barred from the state examinations required for all foreign-trained medics seeking domestic midwifery practice.[40] Consequently, she decided to work with a local doctor in Iaroslav who, after a short six weeks, awarded her a graduating certificate from the local midwifery course. In her subsequent application for admission to the state examinations, Figner presented only the Iaroslav certificate and avoided any reference to her medical training abroad. The relative ease with which Figner escaped the penalties of the Shuvalov list demonstrates the ingenuity of this youthful revolutionist. It also illustrates the lack of co-ordination within the government administration. Admittedly, enforcement of Shuvalov's directive would have been easier had the Third Department been more discriminating in its choice of political suspects. Wolicka, for example, had not participated in the socialist circles of Zurich. Her Polish name, however, made her suspect. By including such politically innocuous women in their investigations, the security forces squandered resources needed to control the activities of the most deadly revolutionists. Less than a decade later, police inefficiency would also allow Figner and her associates in the People's Will to succeed in their seventh attempt to assassinate Alexander II.

The implications of the Zurich investigation, nevertheless, promoted the development of women's higher education in Russia proper. In an attempt to discourage women's flight to foreign universities, a special government commission was appointed in September 1873 to draft plans for women's higher courses in university towns. Domestic politics, to some degree, would also facilitate their establishment. In 1874, Shuvalov relinquished his leadership of the Third Department. Alexander II never hesitated to remove any official whom he suspected might threaten his personal authority. Thus, after Shuvalov presented the Council of Ministers with proposals to include representatives of the nobility and zemstvos in the legislative process, the tsar appointed him ambassador to London.[41] None of Shuvalov's short-term successors would exert similar influence in top government circles.[42] After Shuvalov's departure, then, not only did the gendarmerie lose its most powerful chief: so, too, did the conservative opponents of women's advanced education. But all was not lost. Tolstoi remained in office. And the career bureaucrat Georgievskii had honed his obstructionist skills. Together with Delianov, the assistant minister of education, Georgievskii would manage to steer the commission on women's higher courses away from its original purpose, thereby delaying the tsar's approval of such courses until 1876.

### CHAPTER FOUR

# Women's Higher Courses: A Domestic Safety Valve

The opening of women's higher courses should be recognized as a fatal accident. Originally, the question was raised about diverting our women from foreign universities, mainly from Zurich, but the matter was resolved with the decision to establish nothing similar here.

A.I. GEORGIEVSKII (1886)[1]

Tolstoi could not have chosen more reliable delegates to the commission on women's higher courses: Georgievskii manipulated its proceedings to preclude any discussion of university-level education; Delianov, the chairman, ensured that the commission's recommendations made no mention of higher courses.[2] Ministerial obstructionism, however, would precipitate strong opposition from unexpected quarters: Prince P.G. Ol'denburgskii, the head of the Fourth Department, who had previously remained on the sidelines of the debate over women's higher education, suddenly emerged as the champion of the courses. Although higher educational facilities did not fall within the traditional purview of the Fourth Department, reports of the corrupting influence of Zurich on Russian women had propelled Ol'denburgskii into the controversy. When the commission failed to plan for higher courses, the prince played a key role in persuading Tolstoi to allow their establishment. Had the minister been less agreeable, he would have risked the opening of such courses by the Fourth Department. Sharing jurisdiction over higher education with another state agency was one thing Tolstoi never learned to accept. If higher courses were to be established, he was determined to control them.

I

Conflict between the Fourth Department and Ministry of Education dominated the Delianov Commission, which included middle-level officials from both educational administrations.[3] The Fourth Department had welcomed the new opportunity to promote women's higher courses: two months before the commission met, it offered to assume jurisdiction over them.[4] Its most outspoken delegate, I.T. Osinin, also demonstrated his support by providing gymnasium facilities for the Vladimirskie Courses. From the outset, however, the ministerial faction dominated the proceedings. Rather than investigate the recently established women's courses in Moscow and St Petersburg, Delianov fed the commission data on girls' secondary education in Germany.[5] When Osinin protested and demanded consideration of higher courses, Georgievskii went so far as to challenge the Fourth Department's jurisdiction over its own school network. He called on Tolstoi to close its pedagogical classes on the grounds that they acquainted girls with an "anti-Christian way of thinking."[6] Osinin easily rebutted these charges. Even without this rejoinder, it was highly unlikely that Tolstoi would attempt such blatant interference in Fourth Department schools because the Ministry of Education had no legal authority over them. Georgievskii's accusations, nevertheless, produced the desired result: they directed attention to teachers' training in gymnasia, thereby facilitating the commission's transformation into a review board on girls' secondary education.

With Delianov as chairman, the ministerial faction had no difficulty railroading its report through the commission in February 1875.[7] Despite Osinin's objections, the report made no reference to higher courses, but focused on secondary education for women teachers and girls' vocational training. In particular, it recommended the study of Latin and increased pedagogical training in girls' gymnasia, as well as the creation of a women's pedagogical institute in which Latin would be the core subject. Promotion of the classics was in keeping with recent reforms in ministerial schools. In 1874, the revised statute of girls' gymnasia introduced Latin and Greek as optional subjects.[8] Three years earlier, Tolstoi's reform of boys' secondary schools had entrenched the system of classical gymnasia as the only avenue to university study. This strong preference for classical studies, however, also benefited one private girls' school: the report requested state funding for Sofiia Fisher's classical gymnasium. From its founding in 1872, Fisher's school had enjoyed the personal patronage of Georgievskii, Delianov, and Katkov. The journalist and assistant minister enrolled their daughters in its first classes, whereas both Katkov and Georgievskii personally conducted examinations of pupils in the classical languages.[9] In addition, the report reflected Delianov's special interest in primary education and basic vocational training: it called for the expansion of girls' elementary schools, as well as the development of handicraft, technical, and commercial courses for young women.[10]

This last proposal represented a much-needed change in educational priorities. The Russian education system was top-heavy. Peter the Great had established the pattern for future development by creating an Academy of Science before Russia had a functioning university or lower-school network.[11] Confronted, on the one hand, by an increasingly modernizing Europe and, on the other, by a huge illiterate population and a treasury exhausted by war, Russia's first emperor attempted to "catch up" with the West as quickly and cheaply as possible. Two hundred and fifty years later, the education system still lacked a broad, elementary foundation. During the first half of the nineteenth century, Peter's successors concentrated on the university network. The post-Crimean regime promoted secondary education, but allocated little funds to the primary sector. Although the zemstvos sponsored considerable expansion of elementary schools, as late as 1897, only 21.1 percent of the population were literate.[12] Peasant women suffered most from discriminatory education: fewer than 10 percent were literate. Among the male peasantry, on the other hand, 25 percent were literate.[13]

Widespread illiteracy was but one of the tragic consequences of an ill-balanced education system that also nurtured such distinguished scholars as chemist Mendeleev, historian Kliuchevskii, and physiologist I.P. Pavlov. No less anomalous was the unemployment of teachers in this largely illiterate country. The primary and secondary school network simply could not provide jobs for university and gymnasium graduates seeking teaching posts. During the period 1880–4, for example, over 1400 women failed in their attempts to secure positions as teachers and governesses in Moscow guberniia.[14] Undoubtedly, the influx of graduates from girls' secondary schools outside Moscow province contributed to such high unemployment. At the same time, however, the less urbanized outlying regions could not accommodate all the graduates of local girls' gymnasia and progymnasia who sought teaching posts: Bessarabia reported 67 unemployed domestic teachers and tutors; Perm, 48; and Simbirsk, 18. The Kazan governor also noted that 22 of the 54 women who applied for teaching positions in 1884 were unsuccessful, but he explained that the number of unemployed female teachers was probably much greater because local women were well aware of the scarcity of such positions and, therefore, did not bother to apply. This may have been the case in other provinces as well. In 1888, the Moscow curator also reported unemployment among classics students and university graduates who specialized in mathematics.[15]

Had Delianov's recommendations for elementary and vocational schools been implemented on a grand scale in the mid 1870s, the ranks of Russia's unemployed teachers, as well as the cultural gap separating the privileged minority from the illiterate peasantry, might have been diminished. As it happened, however, only after the country's polarities and tensions erupted in revolution in 1905, did the state make a concerted effort to educate the peasant village and expand the educational opportunities of all. That is not to suggest, however, that some thirty years earlier, Delianov had tried to undermine the fundamental elitist or sexist character of Russian education. Although he attempted to raise the general educational level of the population, he did so only to the extent considered appropriate to the beneficiary's sex and social station. This meant barring the lower orders from advanced academic or professional training, as well as scuttling plans for women's higher courses.

The commission's failure to recommend higher courses outraged the Fourth Department. Osinin refused to endorse the report and complained to both Tolstoi and Ol'denburgskii that the minister's underlings had subverted the very purpose of the commission.[16] In February 1876, the prince confronted Tolstoi with Osinin's charges.[17] He insisted that Russian women went to Zurich for university study, not the teachers' training recommended in the commission report. Thus, he proposed that higher courses be established in Russian university towns which had the necessary academic personnel. To the chagrin of Georgievskii and Delianov, Tolstoi agreed and solicited the emperor's approval to open such courses for women.

Political expediency had once again prompted a change in strategy. Shuvalov was no longer in a position to advise the imperial entourage of the folly of women's higher education and thus minimize Ol'denburgskii's influence at court. Had Tolstoi rejected the prince's proposal, there was a strong possibility that the Fourth Department would establish higher courses under its own administration. By petitioning the tsar himself, Tolstoi could be assured that his ministry would supervise their development. After the Zurich investigation, Tolstoi had no doubt that Russian women imbibed dangerous ideas abroad. And since women's demand for advanced education had not subsided during the 1870s, the opening of higher courses in Russia might serve as a safety valve for their educational ambitions, thereby curbing the flow of Russian women to foreign universities. Consequently, on Tolstoi's recommendation, Alexander II authorized the creation of women's higher courses in April 1876.

II

Official sanction of women's higher courses could not in itself guarantee their development. Because Tolstoi classified them as private courses, rather than regular academic institutions, they had no degree-granting powers nor any claim to state subsidies. Even the high-society women of St Petersburg could cajole only a small annual grant from the minister. On average, the ministerial grant covered less than 7 percent of the yearly expenditures of the courses during the first decade of their operation.[18] The courses in Moscow and the provinces received no government funding whatsoever. For the most part, Tolstoi reserved his generosity toward women's private educational ventures for Fisher's classical gymnasium. In November 1876, he awarded this school the same rights and privileges as girls' gymnasia of his ministry.[19] Three years later, Fisher's graduates received the *attestat zrelosti*, the certificate normally reserved for graduates of boys' gymnasia, as well as the right to teach in all classes of girl's secondary schools.[20] These young women, then, possessed more prestigious academic degrees and greater employment opportunities than the graduates of all other girls' secondary institutions. Thus, they had considerable advantage over other women seeking teaching posts. For many of Fisher's pupils, however, employment was not an economic necessity:[21] their wealthy or well-connected fathers could easily provide for them. But then, it was not the desire to expand women's employment that had prompted Katkov and Georgievskii to encourage the minister to accord Fisher's graduates special privileges. Rather, they wanted official recognition of the school that they patronized and which did in fact compare most favourably to the boys' classical gymnasium. Both individuals, moreover, had a long history of opposition to women's higher education and thus welcomed Tolstoi's niggardly treatment of the higher courses.

Without state funding, higher courses depended upon the ability and willingness of local society to finance them. Most relied almost exclusively on income from admission fees. Only the Bestuzhevskie Courses of St Petersburg could boast numerous benefactors. In comparison to sister institutions in Moscow, Kiev, and Kazan, the courses of the northern capital prospered. Not even the Bestuzhevskie Courses, however, enjoyed the financial security of state-funded schools. In all higher courses, economic restraint would test both the seriousness of women's pursuit of higher education and the commitment of male scholars to liberal academic ideals. Those who taught the courses received little remuneration; yet Russian academics generously donated research and leisure time to further women's education. Since the courses were housed in local educational institutions after regular classes were dismissed, most lectured or supervised laboratories in the late afternoons and evenings.

Enrolment in the higher courses also required no meagre sacrifice by Russian women. High tuition influenced both the composition and lifestyle of *kursistki*. An annual fee of 50 rubles, which was the same as regular university tuition, severely curtailed admissions from the lower social orders. It also imposed considerable hardship on women from Russia's traditional elite. Gentry status had long ceased to be a barometer of economic well-being, and noble daughters, unlike the sons who attended the university, had no access to government stipends. *Kursistki* relied on local patrons for financial assistance. In Kiev, for example, the proceeds from various social and cultural events enabled the Trustees Committee of the courses to offer individual grants of 25 rubles to 189 of the 708 auditors enrolled during the period 1878–82.[22] In St Petersburg, private donations financed the 50-ruble stipends given to 12 of the 793 women attending the Bestuzhevskie Courses in 1884–5.[23] By contrast, the local university in 1885 awarded over 7600 rubles in stipends and scholarships to 577 of its 2280 students. Moreover, 92 percent of Bestuzhevskie auditors paid full tuition fees, compared to 55 percent of St Petersburg University students. Despite these numerous fee waivers and stipends, poverty remained widespread in the student community. Much more severe were the problems confronting *kursistki*.

A few women made the ultimate sacrifice for higher education: at least one auditor in Kiev and two in St Petersburg died from hunger.[24] For most, enrolment in higher courses meant a constant battle against the elements, malnutrition, and fatigue. Mariia Tsebrikova, a sponsor of the Bestuzhevskie Courses, described the deprivations suffered by local auditors: "Those damp and crowded quarters where three or four women huddled together; frequently one bed on which three women slept by turns; that rug thrown over an unlined coat in the bitter cold; those meals in cheap cookshops, and often sausage, black bread and tea; those sleepless nights spent copying for kopeks instead of resting."[25] Finding employment to improve their living conditions was difficult. Traditionally, private lessons had offered the greatest opportunity for educated youth, but after the emancipation, positions for tutors and governesses became increasingly scarce. In addition, women lacked the academic credentials to compete successfully with local university students. During the academic year 1885–6, for example, only 29 of the 717 full-time auditors of the Bestuzhevskie Courses financed their studies by giving lessons.[26] Job scarcity and male competition, however, were not the only barriers to women's employment. Malicious gossip about the auditors also deterred parents from entrusting their child's education to *kursistki*.

Rumours about licentious behaviour among Bestuzhevskie auditors spread through St Petersburg after the courses opened in September 1878.[27] Later that year, the minister of education also received unsubstantiated reports of sexual promiscuity among Kiev *kursistki*: "For the intimacy of students and auditors, shortly after the courses opened, parties were organized where they and others got drunk, then paired off in rooms. A *studentsko-kursistkaia* commune has already been established where each room houses two *kursistki* and one student."[28] The Kiev curator, P.A. Antonovich, rushed to the defence of local auditors, assuring the minister that the accusations were totally groundless. But he could not prevent the die-hard opponents of women's higher education from concocting wild fabrications about auditors. Rumours of moral decadence ran rampant wherever the higher courses were located and, again in early 1879, prompted further investigation by the Ministry of Education.[29] These scandalous stories also owed much more to the imagination of antagonists of women's courses than to the actual behaviour of *kursistki*.

Indeed, enrolment in higher courses demanded moral courage as well as physical stamina. Russian women were not found lacking: almost 1300 attended the courses during the academic year 1878–9.[30] Whether compelled by economic necessity, the desire for a larger social role, or the belief that knowledge constituted a greater good, these women and hundreds more who audited the courses in subsequent years proved willing to suffer material hardship and public slander in order to find their "liberator" in education. Tolstoi made their struggle no easier, particularly in Kazan province.

The minister's obstruction of women's courses in Kazan dates back to 1874 when he rejected the local university's petition to open three-year courses for women. At the time, Tolstoi advised professors to sponsor public lectures or revise their proposal along the lines of Guerrier's Courses.[31] Although Kazan professors followed the latter suggestion and proposed a two-year humanities program with entrance requirements and regular examinations, the minister continued to withhold his approval. Only in May 1876, after his confrontation with Ol'denburgskii, did Tolstoi authorize women's courses in Kazan.

Five months later, local professors opened higher courses. Taught at Kazan University in the evenings, the women's courses originally offered fifteen class hours each week in six compulsory subjects: Russian literature, world literature, Russian history, world history, the history of art, and physics. Optional subjects included foreign languages, mathematics, and hygiene.[32] By 1878, the sciences received more emphasis: classes in arithmetic and geometry, as well as geography, were now obligatory, whereas the history of art became an option. Like Guerrier's Courses, entrance requirements permitted only those who had completed the girls' gymnasium or its equivalent or who passed entrance examinations to enrol as regular auditors.[33] Women who lacked these qualifications were admitted as *volnye slushatel'nitsy* or external auditors. They were excluded from course examinations and, if they did not take the full program, paid a biannual fee of three rubles for each subject.

Academic admission requirements had a far greater impact on enrolment in Kazan than in Moscow. Because Kazan province had a smaller number of girls' secondary schools than the central guberniia, fewer local women qualified for admission as regular auditors. Moreover, as was the case during the "thaw," the women of this university town showed no sustained interest in higher education. Consequently, the Kazan Courses had to rely on *volnye slushatel'nitsy* from outside the capital for much of their income. Initially, this caused no problem: the admission of 63 external auditors boosted enrolment to 96 in 1876; and for the next two years, unqualified women continued to outnumber regular auditors.[34] In the fall of 1879, however, only 8 *volnye slushatel'nitsy* attended, thus reducing total enrolment to 45. For the next six years, enrolment never exceeded 47, and even dropped to a low of 24 in 1883. Had local professors not taught for little or no remuneration, the Kazan Courses would have collapsed long before Delianov closed admissions to them in 1886.

Undoubtedly, the apathy of local women helped cripple the Kazan Courses. At the same time, however, Tolstoi's policies bear much of the responsibility for the sharp decline in enrolment. The minister continued to reject petitions to add a third year to the course program,[35] thus forcing those who sought more extensive education to attend higher courses elsewhere. Even more important, Tolstoi imposed stringent regulations on all women's higher courses in 1879.[36] The new requirements for external auditors drastically reduced admissions to the Kazan Courses: only women residing with local families in Kazan or who had secured special permission from the district curator could now be admitted as *volnye slushatel'nitsy*. In addition, all prospective auditors required a certificate of political reliability from the local police. A woman under twenty-one years also needed the written consent of her parents, guardian, or husband. Besides the prohibition on smoking and rowdiness that had been in effect since their opening, women were now forbidden to gather on the premises of the courses except when their classes met. But it was not the behaviour of auditors that prompted the minister to tighten control over women's courses. Instead, Russian radicalism had once again cast a dark shadow over women's pursuit of higher education.

During the late 1870s, the resurgence of student activism and intensification of the radical movement gave new vigour to old suspicions about the revolutionary potential of higher education. By 1877, the police had arrested 1611 persons suspected of anti-government activities.[37] Of the 525 deemed the most serious offenders and held over for trial, student youth constituted the largest majority. The 80 women indicted also included 7 auditors of the midwifery courses in the Medical-Surgical Academy, as well as the Fritschi who were prosecuted in the Trial of Fifty in 1877. Pre-trial confinement, however, significantly reduced the number of defendants in the second mass trial, which ended in January 1878: illness, mental breakdown, and suicide in cramped detention cells left only 193 facing judgment. The court sentenced 103 to various terms of prison and exile, but most of those convicted were released because they had already served equivalent time awaiting trial. The remaining 90 were acquitted. Contrary to the expectations of the police, mass arrests and imprisonment failed to intimidate contemporary radicals. Such measures only drove the more desperate to embrace terrorism.

The Trial of 193 was barely over when Vera Zasulich, a twenty-eight-year-old radical who had already served a two-year prison term and equal time in exile, shot and wounded Trepov, the governor of St Petersburg.[38] Zasulich's action had nothing to do with Trepov's earlier attempt to shut down the St Petersburg Public Lectures. She shot the governor because he had ordered the flogging of a political prisoner. Her crime, however, went unpunished. Portrayed by her defence attorney as a "selfless slave" who "raised the bloody hand" against cruelty and injustice, Zasulich was acquitted by jury trial in the spring of 1878.[39] The government immediately ordered her re-arrest, but Zasulich escaped abroad. In the aftermath of Zasulich's trial, more state officials became the targets of violent revolutionists. In August, terrorists killed the head of the Third Department, V.N. Mezentsov. His successor, A.R. Drentel'n (1878–80), and the emperor himself, escaped assassination attempts the following spring. The governor of Kharkov was not so fortunate: he was fatally wounded in March. Compounding the crisis situation created by terrorism was the new wave of student disorders, which began in Kharkov in late 1878 and rapidly spread to other university towns.[40]

Auditors of the higher courses, except for a rare few, stayed away from student demonstrations and terrorist organizations. But the nation's security forces believed otherwise. Shortly before Timashev was dismissed in November 1878 for failing to curb domestic unrest, he warned Tolstoi that an anti-government movement in Kiev attracted many young women who threatened to transform the higher courses into a forum for radical propaganda. Drentel'n also reported irregularities in the management and organization of the Bestuzhevskie Courses, and claimed that they harboured a large number of Jews "known for their political untrustworthiness."[41] Given the crisis atmosphere in top government circles, these allegations put Tolstoi in the unusual position of defending the women's courses. In February 1879, this reluctant ally of higher courses countered Drentel'n's charges, insisting that "nothing extraordinary" had transpired in the Bestuzhevskie Courses since their opening, and only sixty Jews attended.[42] Recalling the Zurich investigation, the minister also advised that higher courses deterred Russian women from attending foreign universities where they learned dangerous ideas and habits. Tolstoi skilfully argued for the continued operation of existing women's courses but by no means dispelled suspicions about them. Indeed, the minister himself viewed the higher courses primarily as a safety valve, a mechanism to control women's educational pursuits. Contemporary turmoil in university towns had also convinced Tolstoi that the courses were now more susceptible than ever to infection by youthful radicalism. Thus, he introduced more stringent regulations that restricted enrolment to women known to state educational authorities and approved by the local police.

At the time, most leading statesmen were groping for the causes and cures of domestic unrest. In the spring of 1879, the emperor had appointed a special conference of ministers to investigate internal problems, particularly the spread of subversive ideas among Russian youth.[43] Chaired by P.A. Valuev, the minister of state domains, the conference included Tolstoi, Drentel'n, L.S. Makov, the new minister of internal affairs (1878–80), as well as Finance Minister S.A. Greig and Count S.N. Urusov, the head of

the Second Department entrusted with the codification of Russian law. Measures to tighten control over the universities dominated the proceedings. But
complaints against *kursistki* by security personnel guaranteed that restrictions
would also be placed on women's higher courses. Besides approving Tolstoi's new regulations for the existing courses, the conference declared
additional courses "undesirable" and inadmissible unless approved by the
chief of gendarmes, minister of internal affairs, and governor general.[44] This
ensured that no other courses would be opened while Drentel'n remained
in office. Convinced that higher courses, especially those which attracted
Jews, were radical hotbeds, the head of the Third Department could not be
reconciled to existing courses, much less agree to the creation of new ones.
In 1879, Drentel'n, along with Makov, rejected a petition to establish higher
courses in Odessa.[45] And in early 1880, with hopes of shutting down the
Kiev Courses, the chief of gendarmes forwarded to Tolstoi an anonymous
and unsubstantiated report of political terrorists among local auditors. Subsequent investigation by the Kiev curator revealed that no such activists
attended the courses: only two former auditors had been arrested as political
suspects and were expelled from the city by administrative order.[46]

Not only higher courses for women came under fire in the Valuev Conference. Any further increase in girls' gymnasia was also deemed "undesirable."[47] Instead, the conference favoured Delianov's plan to establish
girls' elementary schools and vocational courses that required neither higher
nor even secondary education. This reform would undoubtedly make education more accessible to the lower social orders. At the same time, however,
it was also designed to halt women's progression through the education
system. Thus, almost three years before Delianov became minister of education, he could anticipate significant high-level support for his forthcoming
assault on the women's higher courses.

Indeed, the deliberations of the Valuev Conference did not bode well for
the future of women's education. The new regulations imposed on higher
courses in 1879, nevertheless, failed to hamper the development of courses
in St Petersburg, Moscow, and Kiev. Only in Kazan did strict entrance
requirements for *volnye slushatel'nitsy* precipitate a dramatic decline in
admissions.

In Kiev, consistently high enrolments promoted the expansion of the two-
year arts and science courses into a full four-year program of university
study. From their opening in October 1878 to the closure of admissions in
1886, over 300 women attended the courses annually. Most had completed
the gymnasium and enrolled as regular auditors. A few entered as *volnye
slushatel'nitsy*, but their number declined from 37 in 1878 to 11 during the
academic year 1881–2.[48] Almost half the auditors came from the gentry or
official circles (see table 6). Women from clerical families constituted 23
percent, whereas the daughters of merchants and craftsmen represented

TABLE 6

Social status and religious affiliation of auditors of the women's higher courses in Kiev, 1878–82

| Social Status | | | Religious Affiliation | | |
|---|---|---|---|---|---|
| | Number | Percent | | Number | Percent |
| Gentry | 95 | 13.42 | Orthodox | 536 | 75.71 |
| Officials, | | | Jewish | 112 | 15.82 |
| military | | | Roman Catholic | 52 | 7.34 |
| officers | 241 | 34.04 | Lutheran | 8 | 1.13 |
| Clergy | 163 | 23.02 | | | |
| Honoured | | | | | |
| citizens | 15 | 2.12 | | | |
| Merchants | 94 | 13.28 | | | |
| Craftsman | 64 | 9.04 | | | |
| Peasants | 8 | 1.13 | | | |
| Cossacks, | | | | | |
| soldiers | 2 | 0.28 | | | |
| Foreigners | 6 | 0.85 | | | |
| Unknown | 20 | 2.82 | | | |
| Total | 708 | 100.00 | | 708 | 100.00 |

Source: TSGIAL, f. 733, o. 191, d. 322, l. 222.

another 21 percent. The 50-ruble tuition fee, as well as inadequate academic preparation, discouraged enrolment from the nation's underprivileged rural estates. During the first four years, only a total of 10 auditors (1.4 percent) came from the ranks of peasants, soldiers, and Cossacks. At the same time, the enrolment of 112 Jews (15.8 percent) can be explained, for the most part, by the location of the courses within the Pale of Settlement. This large contingent of Jews had, undoubtedly, increased the urgency of Drentel'n's demands for investigation of the Kiev Courses. Orthodox kursistki, who constituted two-thirds of the local auditors, nevertheless, were not above suspicion.

Like most women attending higher courses, Kiev kursistki also suffered financial hardship. These provincial courses, however, rallied much more popular support than those in Kazan. Members of the Trustees Committee made small annual donations, in addition to organizing concerts and bazaars which, during the first four years, yielded more than 4400 rubles.[49] As a result, slightly more than one-quarter of all contemporary auditors received grants of 25 rubles each. Several provincial zemstvos also assisted needy women: the zemstvo boards of Chernigov, Bessarabia, and Saratov, for example, provided stipends for a few auditors born in their respective guberniias.[50] Although the contributions of zemstvos and private patrons were too small to eliminate completely the economic distress of their recipients, they encouraged, if not enabled, a significant number of women to study in the Kiev Courses. Because admission fees represented over 90 percent of the total income,[51] it was this continued high enrolment that facilitated the expansion of the courses.

By 1881, the Kiev Courses constituted an unofficial women's university, albeit without degree-granting powers.[52] The historical-philological faculty offered twenty-five different courses, of which the following were obligatory: Russian historical grammar; the history of the Russian language; the history of Greek, Roman, medieval, and modern literature; ancient, medieval, and modern history; statistics; psychology; pedagogy; and either the French or German language. The physical-mathematical department required the completion of ten of its twenty-four courses: algebra, algebraic analysis, geometry, analytical geometry, trigonometry, differential and integral calculus, physics, chemistry, astronomy, and French or German.

Transformation of the Kiev Courses into a de facto women's university occurred after both Tolstoi and Drentel'n had been removed from office in 1880. Baron A.P. Nikolai, the short-term minister of education, had authorized the extensive four-year program.[53] Yet, while the new minister granted this major concession, he failed to respond to repeated appeals for teaching rights for the graduates. Inexperience explains, in part, his somewhat erratic response to petitions concerning the Kiev Courses. According to a contemporary statesman, Nikolai confessed that "questions of women's education were completely alien to him."[54] The turmoil of the time, however, must also be taken into consideration. During the period 1880–1, the surge in revolutionary activities that had precipitated the reshuffling of statesmen monopolized the attention of government officials, thereby relegating the higher courses to the periphery of their concerns. Given the crisis situation, it is not surprising that Nikolai simultaneously endorsed and ignored appeals concerning women's education.

Kiev offered the most extensive educational opportunities for women outside the capital. Had the government allowed higher courses in Odessa, however, there is little doubt that they, too, would have expanded. Professor A.S. Trachevskii, who petitioned for them, had organized special secondary courses to prepare local women for university study.[55] In 1879, their enrolment exceeded three hundred. At the same time, Odessa City Duma had allocated 10,000 rubles for the establishment of higher courses. In Kharkov, by contrast, it was not only state policy that darkened prospects for women's higher courses. Here, the activities of local women and professors represent one of the least successful, but most colourful, episodes in the struggle for women's higher education in Russia.

In 1870, Kharkov women staged the first public demonstration for women's rights in Russian history: they confronted Tolstoi before the steps of Kharkov University with a petition to reform girls' secondary schools and to admit women to the university.[56] Their tactics clearly distinguished these women from the sponsors of higher courses elsewhere. Their misunderstanding of the education system also served to undermine their efforts. As well as appealing for university admission, they called on the minister to "promote the reform of girls' secondary schools into *real* [schools] with a program adapted to the university course."[57] Thus Tolstoi had good cause to reject their petition: the gymnasium offered university preparation, whereas the *real* school qualified pupils for matriculation in advanced technical institutes. The unusual request for *real* schools suggests that local professors had not helped draft the petition. Whether Kharkov women solicited their aid is unknown. It appears, however, that the local academic community made no effort to establish women's courses during the 1870s. At least, in the fall of 1878, Tolstoi informed Timashev that he had received no appeals for higher courses in Kharkov.[58]

Archives of the Ministry of Education also indicate that Kharkov professors first petitioned for higher courses in early 1881.[59] Their timing was unfortunate: their petition was buried in the administrative upheaval that followed the March regicide.[60] Failure to secure official approval, however, did not deter four local professors. In September 1882, A. Kirpichnikov established literature courses for women in a vocational school.[61] He was soon joined by mathematician K. Andreev and physicist A. Shimkov. Enrolment in individual courses ranged from twelve to twenty-five.[62] Philologist A. Potebnia also opened classes for women in his own home. Rumours of the unauthorized courses soon reached Delianov, but the new minister of education had some difficulty tracking down Kharkov's wayward academics.

Initially, the local curator was unco-operative. When Delianov first requested information about the courses in December 1882, M.S. Maksimovskii replied that such investigations were matters for the secret police, and that he could not afford his own "secret service." An additional letter from Delianov two months later, however, secured the curator's assistance. But Kharkov professors remained defiant. When confronted by Maksimovskii, Kirpichnikov refused to admit the irregularity of his actions, and divulged no information about his colleagues. Andreev responded that he did not need permission for private meetings with acquaintances. When Potebnia was accused of teaching unauthorized courses to women, he winked at the apparent gravity of his offence: "I consider it awkward to refuse myself and my acquaintances scholarly discussions over a cup of tea." Shimkov responded with a defence of professorial autonomy: "As a teacher in two higher educational institutions, I consider myself entitled to give lessons in the subject of my speciality without asking for special permission."[63] Even after the ministry ordered the courses in the vocational school closed, Shimkov still flaunted his independence: he provided the curator with his home address where, he announced, he would continue to teach women.

Indeed, when Kharkov professors finally took up the cause of women's higher education, they were much more audacious than their colleagues in other university towns. They seemed to welcome the opportunity to defy educational administrators and declare the autonomy of scholars. Such autonomy, they knew quite well, would not survive the new regime of Alexander III. His conservative entourage was preparing a frontal assault on higher education. In 1884, the government would impose new strictures on both the academic and administrative affairs of the university. The destruction of women's higher courses began two years later.

The only higher courses to survive the reign of Alexander III were the Bestuzhevskie of St Petersburg.[64] From their founding in 1878, they enjoyed extensive local support. Osinin again provided gymnasium facilities where the courses were held in the evenings. Professors who had taught the Vladimirskie Courses now supervised seminars, laboratories, and examinations, and read lectures as well. They also modelled the three-year courses after the regular university curricula. During the first year, the historical-philological faculty offered a liberal arts program equivalent to Guerrier's Courses.[65] The syllabus of the physical-mathematical department included algebra, geometry, physics, chemistry, mechanics, botany, and zoology. In 1879, a special mathematics division was opened with courses in higher algebra, trigonometry, analytical geometry, differential and integral calculus, higher mechanics, and thermo-chemistry. Two years later, a fourth year of study was added. The Bestuzhevskie Courses, like the Kiev Courses, had become a women's university.

Over 700 enrolled annually during the first eight years.[66] It was not only high enrolments, however, that allowed the Bestuzhevskie Courses to prosper. Within weeks of their opening, Filosofova, Stasova, Trubnikova, and other local sponsors established a new philanthropic organization, the Society for Funding Women's Higher Courses. By 1886, membership approached 1000, and private donations exceeded 30,000 rubles. This society also received an initial grant of 2500 rubles from the Ministry of Education and, beginning in 1879, an annual subsidy of 3000 rubles. Tolstoi was generous, but only in comparison to his treatment of other higher courses. The minister's subsidy represented less than 3 percent of the total income of the courses: proceeds from concerts and bazaars brought in more than twice that amount. In 1882, the St Petersburg City Duma also awarded the courses an annual grant of 3000 rubles. Thanks to public and private patronage, the Bestuzhevskie Courses, unlike those in Moscow and the provinces, established considerable financial reserves. This would prove crucial to their continued operation after admissions were closed in 1886.

Women from privileged society also dominated enrolment in the Bestuzhevskie Courses (see table 7). Merchant and artisan families contributed the second largest group of auditors, which constituted more than 32 percent of admissions in 1883–5. Like Kiev *kursistki*, most had completed the gymnasium and enrolled as regular auditors. Representation from the clerical estate, however, was much lower, ranging between 3 and 12 percent of the total enrolment during the first eight years. The attendance of Jews also exceeded Tolstoi's earlier estimate to the Valuev Conference: they represented almost 17 percent of all auditors in 1885–6.[67] In terms of religious conformity and social status, nevertheless, *kursistki* bore a marked resemblance to local university students: more than two-thirds were Orthodox, and over half came from families of gentry and officials.[68]

Education in the higher courses was also equivalent to the four-year university program. Sechenov, who taught the same course at both the university and Bestuzhevskie Courses, found that men would do better on examinations one year, and women would perform best in the next year. He also reported that, during his forty years as a teacher, his best pupil was a woman.[69] Unlike their male counterparts, however, Bestuzhevskie graduates received neither status in the Table of Ranks nor employment commensurate with their academic preparation. Among those who found jobs, most occupied positions that required only secondary education.[70] Of the more than 1000 women who graduated during the period 1882–9, over 36 percent became teachers in private homes, elementary schools, and the lower classes of girls' secondary institutions. Completion of the gymnasium would have qualified them for these positions. Fewer than 6 percent entered the medical field: several enrolled in foreign universities or courses in the Medical-Surgical Academy and became physicians, but the majority trained as midwives, masseuses, and paramedics (*fel'dsheritsy*). University-level education was not prerequisite to admission to these vocations. Another 20 percent engaged in various types of literary, theatrical, laboratory, and office work. No employment information is available on the remaining 303 graduates, except that the majority married after completing the courses. Because there are no data on the number who failed in their efforts to secure positions, it is difficult to estimate the unemployment rate of Bestuzhevskie graduates. Nevertheless, increased competition among both gymnasium and university graduates for teaching posts[71] suggests that a significant number of St Petersburg *kursistki* could not find work. Women from higher courses in the less urbanized provinces undoubtedly encountered greater difficulty earning a living.

Tolstoi's refusal to award higher courses any degree-granting powers had

TABLE 7

Social status and educational background of auditors of the Bestuzhevskie Courses, 1878–86

| | 1878–9 | | 1879–80 | | 1880–1 | |
|---|---|---|---|---|---|---|
| Total Number | 793 | | 789 | | 840 | |
| Social status | | % | | % | | % |
| Daughters and wives of gentry, officials, military officers | 591 | 74.53 | 681 | 86.31 | 548 | 65.24 |
| Clergy | 63 | 7.94 | 26 | 3.29 | 85 | 10.12 |
| Merchants, artisans | 131 | 16.52 | 77 | 9.76 | 194 | 23.09 |
| Peasants | 8 | 1.01 | 4 | 0.51 | 13 | 1.55 |
| Foreigners | 0 | | 1 | 0.13 | 0 | |
| New Admissions | 793 | | 330 | | 295 | |
| Previous education | | | | | | |
| Gymnasium | 596 | 75.16 | 240 | 72.73 | 221 | 74.92 |
| Institute | 78 | 9.84 | 68 | 20.61 | 41 | 13.90 |
| Parish school | 19 | 2.39 | 6 | 1.82 | 16 | 5.42 |
| Domestic teachers | 88 | 11.10 | 11 | 3.33 | 2 | 0.68 |
| Former auditors of pedagogical or other higher courses | 12 | 1.51 | 5 | 1.51 | 15 | 5.08 |

a Records of the Ministry of Education, cited in note 26, give 717 as the total. It is possible that eleven women either entered or dropped the courses after one of the two sets of figures was drawn up.

b Indicates combined enrolment of merchants, artisans, peasants, and foreigners. Separate figures for these groups are not given for 1885–6.

Source: Adapted from table v, SPBVzhK, 1878–1903, 252.

even restricted *kursistki*'s employment as teachers in girls' schools, the most acceptable female occupation of the time. Unlike Fisher's graduates, they were barred from the senior classes of girls' gymnasia. Yet, no matter how arbitrary the minister's policies, it should also be noted that career preparation was not the main purpose of the higher courses. Scholarship was the single most important concern of professors who organized and taught them.[72] In the mid 1880s, when Delianov suggested transforming the Bestuzhevskie Courses into a pedagogical institute, both Beketov and Bestuzhev-Riumin insisted that the courses retain the "character of a higher educational institution of the university type with no utilitarian function."[73] In other words, the women's courses must be preserved as a bastion of *nauka*. This was particularly important after the new University Statute of 1884 had robbed professors of the autonomy they had enjoyed for two decades. Commitment to *nauka*, which itself was a defence of academic freedom, demanded that

| 1881–2 | | 1882–3 | | 1883–4 | | 1884–5 | | 1885–6 | |
|---|---|---|---|---|---|---|---|---|---|
| 990 | | 891 | | 905 | | 851 | | 728[a] | |
| | % | | % | | % | | % | | % |
| 617 | 62.32 | 523 | 58.7 | 493 | 54.48 | 498 | 58.52 | 415 | 57.0 |
| 118 | 11.92 | 98 | 11.0 | 105 | 11.6 | 56 | 6.58 | 73 | 10.03 |
| 238 | 24.04 | 253 | 28.4 | 290 | 32.04 | 279 | 32.78 | | |
| 17 | 1.72 | 17 | 1.9 | 17 | 1.88 | 14 | 1.65 | 240[b] | 32.97 |
| 0 | | 0 | | 0 | | 4 | 0.47 | | |
| 293 | | 397 | | 349 | | 250 | | 233 | |
| | | | | | | | | | |
| 240 | 81.91 | 341 | 85.89 | 287 | 82.23 | 215 | 86 | 198 | 84.98 |
| 30 | 10.24 | 29 | 7.31 | 46 | 13.18 | 18 | 7.2 | 9 | 3.86 |
| 15 | 5.12 | 10 | 2.52 | 9 | 2.58 | 11 | 4.4 | 11 | 4.72 |
| 6 | 2.05 | 7 | 1.76 | 4 | 1.15 | 5 | 2.0 | 10 | 4.29 |
| 2 | 0.68 | 10 | 2.52 | 3 | 0.86 | 1 | 0.4 | 5 | 2.15 |

scholarship, not the employment of *kursistki*, receive top priority. Consequently, the higher courses created a large contingent of well-educated women who were denied both economic and social advancement.

This frightened Georgievskii: he envisioned the emergence of an unemployed "female intellectual proletariat."[74] Among contemporary Russian officials, the very term "proletariat" evoked the spectre of social upheaval.[75] Although from a far different vantage point, Soviet scholars also view *kursistki*, particularly those of St Petersburg, in terms of the proletarian struggle. They applaud the Bestuzhevskie Courses as an advanced school in the "glorious revolutionary-democratic tradition."[76] But this commendation hardly applies to the courses during the reigns of Alexander II and Alexander III. Only after Witte's industrialization drive of the 1890s precipitated significant social dislocation and the burgeoning of the labour movement, did increasing numbers of Bestuzhevskie auditors join the revolutionary camp. Until then, few *kursistki* were political radicals. That, of course, was not the impression given by contemporary police. Their reports of suspect auditors were alarming, particularly during the early reign of Alexander III. In 1886, for example, they informed Delianov that over 200 women who attended the Bestuzhevskie Courses during the past five years had attracted police surveillance. Of that number, more than half allegedly belonged to various propaganda and revolutionary circles.[77] Given the few arrests and expulsions of auditors, however, these figures appear highly inflated. Beketov, who based his defence of *kursistki* on information from the St Petersburg governor, reported that only 39 local auditors were recognized as "more or less" suspect by the administration: 7 auditors were expelled from the courses in 1879; during the period 1882–5, 17 women were exiled from the northern capital, and another 15 required clearance from the "secret" police.[78] Among the last group, several had left the courses after police investigation, but 5 had remained to complete the program. Not one of these suspects, moreover, was charged with participating in any kind of serious anti-government activity. Further testimony to the political loyalty or indifference of auditors was their noticeable absence from university disorders and political demonstrations.

Such evidence made little impression on the police who had distrusted the studious woman since the "thaw." Professors like Sechenov and Beketov, though, had proved staunch allies of female auditors. This long-term alliance of academics and women boasted remarkable achievements: thousands of Russian women had access to university-level education during the late 1870s and early 1880s. The higher courses, nevertheless, accomplished little in terms of promoting women's careers in late nineteenth-century Russia. Tolstoi remained adamant in his opposition to expanding their employment opportunities. Fortunately, his rival Miliutin held different views. In spite of Tolstoi's most strenuous efforts, the war minister would train female physicians in the Medical-Surgical Academy.

CHAPTER FIVE

# Women Doctors and
# the War Ministry

One can affirmatively state that this country, in its present condition, needs female physicians still more than physicians in general, although even the number of the latter is disproportionately small in comparison to the contemporary need for them. The historical fortunes of Russia impose upon the Russian woman special and lofty responsibilities, in the fulfilment of which she has already demonstrated as much capacity for self-sacrifice as ability for honest and steadfast work.

I.S. TURGENEV (1882)[1]

The medical courses of the War Ministry occupy a unique place in the history of women's education during the reign of Alexander II. Unlike the higher courses, which provided no access to male professions, the ministry's advanced midwifery courses enabled women to become physicians. The first graduating class served as surgeons and medical assistants in the Russo-Turkish War of 1877–8, and shortly thereafter became general practitioners for the zemstvo. In 1880, the emperor granted medical *kursistki* the title of *zhenskii vrach* or woman doctor and the right to independent medical practice.

I

Contributing to women's advance in medicine was the traditionally low status of Russian physicians.[2] Although the post-graduate degree of Doctor of Medicine often commanded respect and a high administrative or teaching post in the medical establishment, such benefits did not accrue to the ordinary *vrach* or practitioner who completed the five-year program at the university or Medical-Surgical Academy. His diploma of *lekar'* garnered little pay or prestige. Indeed, until the close of the nineteenth century, the privileged classes shunned medical practice as the occupation of their social inferiors. As late as 1880, students of clerical origin exceeded 25 percent of enrolment in university medical faculties; the sons of tradesmen, artisans, peasants, and labourers totalled 19 percent. Another sure sign of the physician's humble status was the high enrolment of Jews: they constituted over 10 percent of all contemporary medical students. Discriminatory legislation encouraged the Jew's pursuit of a medical degree: Russian law confined most Jews to the Pale of Settlement, but allowed Jewish physicians to reside in other parts of the empire. The relatively large number of Jewish practitioners thus gave the Russian *vrach* the stigma of racial, as well as social, inferiority. It is no wonder, then, that women made their first inroads in medicine, rather than the more reputable legal or academic professions.

Breaking down the barriers to women's medical practice in this paternalistic empire, nevertheless, required not a small show of skill and fortitude on the part of Russian women. They would demonstrate both in the field hospitals and medical stations during the Russo-Turkish War. Yet even more important to the emergence of female physicians was the patronage of Miliutin: his favoured status in the entourage of Alexander II would give women's medical education a powerful advocate in top government circles, whereas the Medical-Surgical Academy would provide the teaching staff and clinical facilities for training women doctors. Miliutin, however, could claim no monopoly on the emperor's confidence. Nor did the jealous nature of autocratic rule under Alexander II allow him to control the entire medical establishment: university medical schools fell under the jurisdiction of the Ministry of Education; the Medical Council, under the purview of the Ministry of Internal Affairs. All legislation concerning medical education and practice, therefore, automatically involved Tolstoi and Timashev. Although they could not interfere in the internal affairs of the War Ministry and thus prevent the establishment of women's courses in the academy, the fragmented nature of the medical administration would allow them to block all efforts to give the courses legal status as a regular educational institution. As a result, the very survival of women's medical courses remained totally dependent upon Miliutin.

The individual who took the initiative in promoting women's medical education in the War Ministry was N.I. Kozlov, the chief war-medical inspector. His daughter, the future physician Praskoviia N. Tarnovskaia, encouraged her father's efforts on women's behalf.[3] In January 1870, Kozlov petitioned the Medical Council to approve a four-year midwifery program for women.[4] Courses specializing in obstetrics, pediatrics, and gynecology, he suggested, could be established separately from male students in the academy and other medical schools having the necessary facilities. Graduates would receive the title of *uchenaia akusherka* or advanced midwife, and the right to independent obstetrical and gynecological practice, as well as to treat children and syphilitic diseases in localities lacking physicians. Unlike the *povival'naia babka*, the traditional midwife who was not trained nor licensed to treat illness or perform obstetrical operations, the advanced midwife would provide qualified and extensive medical care.

The Medical Council welcomed Kozlov's proposal. Russia desperately needed trained medical personnel. During the 1870s, only the capitals could boast a relatively large number of doctors. For the rest of the empire, excluding Siberia and Turkestan where medical services were virtually non-existent, there was only one physician for every 7600 inhabitants.[5] By comparison, in the previous decade, France had one doctor for every 2000 residents. In Prussia and Austria, the ratio was 1:2800 and 1:4800 respectively. Admittedly, the advanced midwife could not perform all the functions of the regular physician, yet she would be specially trained to deal with two of Russia's most pressing health problems: infant mortality and syphilis. Fifty percent of all newborns died within their first year.[6] The spread of venereal disease also assumed staggering proportions.[7] In St Petersburg, for example, the incidence of syphilis more than doubled in less than a decade, increasing from 6353 in 1861 to 14,895 in 1868. In rural areas, venereal disease had become even more widespread. Official statistics record tens of thousands of syphilitics, but the actual number far exceeded reported cases in both town and country: on the one hand, the social stigma of the affliction prompted many to seek confidential medical attention; on the other, the short supply of doctors left the less fortunate undiagnosed and untreated. The nation's health care obviously demanded drastic improvement, and Kozlov's proposal promised at least a partial solution to the problem. Moreover, both Suslova and Kashevarova had recently become licensed physicians, thus proving women's ability to master medical science. Consequently, in April 1870, the Medical Council recommended the creation of advanced midwifery courses in the Medical-Surgical Academy and university medical faculties to the ministries of war, education, and internal affairs.[8]

Miliutin agreed without hesitation. Once again, his wife and daughter urged him to sponsor women's courses. Anna Filosofova also appealed to her husband, Miliutin's trusted assistant in the ministry. That is not to suggest, however, that familial ties or personal loyalties fully explain Miliutin's promotion of women's medical education. Much more fundamental was the war minister's liberal philosophy. His commitment to the courses was serious: he not only offered to train advanced midwives in the Academy, but attempted to inscribe the degree of *uchenaia akusherka* in law. Legal status would secure the rights of graduates, as well as protect the courses from bureaucratic onslaught. Thus, when Miliutin approved the Medical Council's recommendation, he also proposed that the degree of advanced midwife be established "in the legal order, on the basis of an agreement between the War Ministry and the Ministry of Internal Affairs."[9]

Timashev would make no such agreement. Unlike Miliutin, the minister of internal affairs feared that the expansion of women's professional activities would have damaging repercussions on the entire fabric of society. Nevertheless, he formally endorsed the Medical Council's proposal for advanced midwifery courses.[10] These seemingly contradictory gestures, however, did not emerge from any ambivalence on Timashev's part toward women's medical education. Instead, they illustrate his cautious policy of minimal concessions when pressured by an influential office or public opinion. As was the case with women's higher courses, he was willing to grant limited concessions, but only as temporary privileges, never as rights that would legally admit women to established professions. Respect for the Medical Council prompted Timashev's quasi-approval of the courses, but his suspicions of the social dangers of women's medical practice ensured that he would deny the courses any legal recognition.

Tolstoi proved even less accommodating. He could hardly be expected to endorse any plan to expand women's medical education, much less one promoted by Miliutin's ministry. Jurisdictional rivalries, as well as philosophical differences, fuelled the antagonism of these statesmen. This became particularly apparent during the early 1870s.[11] Miliutin, for example, not only opposed Tolstoi's plan to allow only students of the classical gymnasium to matriculate in a university, but after the proposal became law in 1871, he continued to admit candidates without a gymnasium certificate into the Medical-Surgical Academy. At the same time, Tolstoi made several attempts to wrest control of the academy from the war minister. He also waged a vigorous campaign against Miliutin's military reforms, which granted privileges, on the basis of education, to those entering military service. Tolstoi's efforts failed: Miliutin remained in charge of the academy, and educational privileges were written into the Universal Military Conscription Statute of 1874. Given the jurisdictional disputes and mutual hostility that strained the relations of these two ministers, Miliutin's approval of advanced midwifery courses was bound to harden Tolstoi's resistance to them.

But Tolstoi did not reject the courses outright. His efforts to sabotage them were much more subtle. He first resorted to delaying tactics. Although he rarely consulted the professorial community on educational issues, he now solicited its advice on the Medical Council's recommendation.[12] Only professors of Moscow and Dorpat had modified their views since the "thaw": they now joined their colleagues on other university councils and medical faculties in approving the expansion of women's medical education and practice.[13] They also agreed that women fulfil similar requirements and pass the same examinations as male medical students. Tolstoi ignored their response and refused to sanction women's courses in university medical schools. Instead, he requested further study of women's medical training in Russia and abroad.[14] The minister also tried to persuade the Medical Council that the country's health services could be improved without resorting to advanced midwifery courses for women: he suggested opening similar courses for men.

Tolstoi's manoeuvres failed to obstruct the creation of women's medical courses. Before he had even responded to the Medical Council, Miliutin had independently petitioned Alexander II to allow their establishment under the War Ministry. A private donation of 50,000 rubles from a wealthy patron, Lidiia A. Rodstvennaia, enabled Miliutin to assure the emperor that private funding, not the state treasury, would finance their organization.[15] On 6 May 1872, Alexander II authorized advanced midwifery courses in the Medical-Surgical Academy as a four-year experiment.[16] Later, he also approved Miliutin's plan to expand the program and subsidize the courses with an annual grant of 8200 rubles.[17] Such actions clearly demonstrate that the emperor championed Miliutin's command of the War Ministry, but they reveal little about his attitude toward women's medical training: he also accepted Tolstoi's ban on women in the universities and Timashev's refusal to accord the courses legal status. Indeed, the coexistence of these competing policies suggests that Alexander II had formulated no definite views on women's advanced education, although it is highly likely that the contemporary exodus of Russian women to Zurich's medical faculty helped convince him of the utility of opening midwifery courses in St Petersburg. At the same time, these courses were also in keeping with the Imperial Order of 14 January 1871, which sanctioned the expansion of women's midwifery training. Their establishment on an experimental basis and under the sole jurisdiction of the war minister, however, would facilitate their closure after Miliutin lost his ministerial post in 1881.

II

Advanced midwifery courses opened in the Medical-Surgical Academy in November 1872. Tuition fees and academic requirements similar to those of the Bestuzhevskie Courses controlled admissions, although prospective auditors also took entrance examinations in all subjects of the girls' gymnasium.[18] In the first year, 86 of the 130 applicants qualified for admission.[19] Their numbers increased gradually, bringing the total enrolment during the first eight years to 796.[20] Like the Bestuzhevskie auditors, most medical *kursistki* had completed the gymnasium. In the midwifery courses, however, the traditionally privileged classes did not dominate enrolment to the same extent as in the capital's higher courses: just 50 percent came from the families of gentry, officials, and military officers (see table 8). The middling ranks of urban society – merchants, honoured citizens, and professionals – represented 25 percent, whereas the lower orders who paid the poll tax constituted slightly more than 16 percent. Among the latter group, the overwhelming majority were of artisan status; daughters of clerics remained

TABLE 8

Social status, marital status, and religious affiliation of auditors of the women's medical courses, 1872–9

|  | Number enrolled | Percentage of total enrolment | |
|---|---|---|---|
| *Total* | 796 | 100 | |
| *Social status* | | | |
| Gentry, officials, military officers | 398 | 50 | |
| Merchants, honoured citizens | 138 | 17.34 | |
| Physicians, students | 41 | 5.15 | 25 |
| Free professions[a] | 20 | 2.51 | |
| Clergy | 59 | 7.41 | |
| Artisans[b] | 105 | 13.19 | |
| Petty officials[b] | 13 | 1.63 | 16.45 |
| Peasants, colonists, menials[b] | 9 | 1.13 | |
| Shopkeepers, tradesmen[b] | 4 | 0.50 | |
| Foreigners | 8 | 1.01 | |
| Unknown | 1 | 0.13 | |
| *Marital status* | | | |
| Single | 712 | 89.4 | |
| Married | 71 | 9.0 | |
| Widowed | 13 | 1.6 | |
| *Religious affiliation* | | | |
| Orthodox | 572 | 72.0 | |
| Jewish | 169 | 21.1 | |
| Roman Catholic | 38 | 4.8 | |
| Lutheran | 17 | 2.1 | |

[a] Includes engineers, professors, teachers, and medical personnel.

[b] Signifies poll-taxed estates.

*Source*: Table adapted from Gertsenshtein, "Zhenskie vrachebnye kursy," 556–7.

below 8 percent of the total enrolment. Only a small number of widows and married women attended: almost 90 percent were single women in their early twenties.[21] Jews also flocked to the courses, exceeding 20 percent of all admissions. Advanced medical education, they hoped, would free them from the Pale. Because the courses lacked legal recognition and the right to grant a physician's diploma, however, only exceptional circumstances would allow Jewish graduates to practise in other regions of the empire.

Originally, the courses offered a four-year medical program.[22] In the first year, auditors attended twenty-two hours of lectures in physics, chemistry, botany, zoology, anatomy, and histology every week, and spent most evenings in the laboratory. With each successive year of study, the number of subjects and hours of practical work increased. The fourth year course included lectures in gynecology, opthamology, dermatology, syphilis, and children's diseases, as well as clinical studies in obstetrics, surgery, gynecology, and internal medicine. In 1876, when the War Ministry transferred the courses to Nikolaevskii War Hospital, Kozlov expanded them into a five-year program equivalent to a university medical faculty. And to signify that the courses offered much more than midwifery training, they now received the more prestigious title of women's medical courses (*zhenskie vrachebnye kursy*).

Strict regulations governed the behaviour of auditors.[23] An inspectress supervised the corridors and classrooms to ensure that women had no contact with male students. Nor were they allowed to express censure or approval of their instructors. One alumna recalled that fear of expulsion prevented several women from thanking a particularly helpful professor. In addition, all auditors were required to present verification from the clergy to prove that they had fulfilled their religious obligations. Proper deportment was paramount, and the dress code enforced: hair nets and long skirts were mandatory. With the exception of the ban on smoking, which seems to have been a national pastime of contemporary youth, women complied with the internal regulations of the courses. In fact, they appeared so obedient and serious that male students mockingly called them "the perfect ones" (*parfetki*) and "crammers" (*zubrilki*).[24] Despite their good conduct, medical *kursistki* aroused considerable fear and distrust in conservative quarters. Katkov warned that the women's medical courses threatened to transform the academy into a local "Geneva."[25] At the same time, St Petersburg buzzed with bizarre rumours about the auditors: "they cut up corpses at night, walk around with bones in their hands, and carry intestines in their pockets."[26]

Memoirs of contemporary *kursistki* paint a far less colourful picture.[27] Most auditors studied at the academy or hospital for ten hours a day, then returned to cramped and crowded quarters where they pored over lecture notes until late into the night. Fatigue and poverty were constant companions: a sixteen-hour work day and a single meal rationed to last two days were not uncommon. Few received financial assistance, although Trubnikova organized a benefit society to aid needy auditors; and while several zemstvo boards also provided stipends to *kursistki* who agreed to serve the zemstvo after graduation, their number was too small to improve the lifestyle of most auditors.[28] As late as 1879, for example, only 6 percent of all medical *kursistki* enjoyed some form of financial aid. Economic hardship and the general severity of daily life exacted a heavy toll on several women: among those expected to graduate in 1877, seven had died of consumption and two had committed suicide.[29] Another, Varvara S. Nekrasova, died of typhus in the Russo-Turkish War.

Military conflict once again tested the courage and medical skills of Russian women. In 1877, twenty-five *kursistki* joined the Turkish campaign as medical personnel with the army and Red Cross.[30] The following year, when typhus broke out among troops on the Danube, another contingent of advanced midwives went to the Balkan front. A total of fifty-two *kursistki* served in the war effort: forty as physicians, and twelve as paramedics. Few women could have envisioned the carnage that awaited them in the south. And none had anticipated sexual abuse by Russian officers. Nekrasova, who was molested by one officer and publicly propositioned by others, chronicled the brutalization of military personnel at medical stations: "The men here have completely ceased to be human beings – they have turned into some kind of devils: they are ready to set up entire harems and become sultans in them."[31] How *kursistki* mustered the strength to resist the advances and assaults of army officers is itself amazing. Even without sexual harassment, the onerous and brutal conditions of wartime service were enough to exhaust their physical and spiritual reserves: where medical facilities were lacking, women crawled on hands and knees among patients, struggling to keep the diseased and wounded alive;[32] in hospitals, they performed amputations, removed bullets, and tended the sick for fifteen to eighteen hours at a stretch.[33] Indeed, to serve in the Turkish campaign required the physical stamina of Russia's legendary Amazons, as well as the moral courage of Pushkin's Tatiana. At the same time, Nekrasova's correspondence indicates that the more contemporary struggle for women's admission to the medical profession had also fortified her resolve: "In the name of advancing our movement forward, I could come to terms with worse conditions: I would not only walk in the mud, but wallow in it. My only fear is of falling ill."[34]

Nekrasova's fear became a reality, but so, too, did her hopes for women's advance in medicine. *Kursistki*'s performance in the Russo-Turkish War had proven their competence as physicians. Some even won medals of honour. Within two years of the war, several became general practitioners for the zemstvo. According to one contemporary medical expert, zemstvo boards often preferred to hire women, rather than male doctors, because they were conscientious, gentle, and, no less important, were paid a smaller salary than men.[35] The first female practitioners employed by the zemstvo earned between 450 and 800 rubles annually; their male counterparts, on the average, received between 800 and 900 rubles. Until the early twentieth century, the salaries of women doctors remained generally lower than men. Given the zemstvo's limited financial resources, it made good budgetary sense to employ women. Zemstvo boards, however, did not control the hiring of female physicians. The minister of internal affairs refused to delegate this power to the zemstvo. Deep distrust of the female physician, moreover, also prevented the introduction of any general policy on the employment of women as zemstvo doctors. Instead, provincial governors, in co-operation with the minister and the head of the Third Department, assessed each female applicant separately.[36] As a result, the success or failure of each candidate was determined not so much by the applicant's medical qualifications or the needs of the zemstvo, as by the views of these state officials concerning the political reliability of the *zhenskii vrach*. This meant that women's access to positions as zemstvo doctors varied according to the shifting political currents of top government circles, as well as from province to province. Such arbitrary hiring practices seriously curtailed women's employment by the zemstvo, but did not completely frustrate the career ambitions of all: a few became interns and assistants in their alma mater; many more served as physicians in urban and rural areas.[37]

It should also be noted that women were employed as physicians although they had no legal status as such. Even the widespread acclaim won by medical *kursistki* in the Turkish War had failed to reconcile Timashev to women's medical practice. In early 1878, he rejected the Medical Council's recommendation to grant the advanced midwife official recognition as a general practitioner without restricting her patients to women and children.[38] Timashev insisted that women's medical practice was a social issue beyond the competence of medical experts. Confident of Tolstoi's support, he proposed that the issue be resolved by a joint commission of the ministries of education, war, and internal affairs. The emperor agreed that women's medical education now demanded greater scrutiny by the government. Police investigation of radical movements during the late 1870s had revealed that many youthful offenders were students in the Medical-Surgical Academy;[39] and ten former auditors of Zurich's medical faculty had stood in the dock in the Trial of Fifty.[40] The nexus of medicine and radicalism had become so apparent that Alexander II ordered an official inquiry into the women's medical courses by state security officials, as well as medical and educational personnel. In November 1878, he appointed N.V. Isakov, the head of the War-Medical Administration, chairman of the special commission of middle-level administrators from the ministries of war, education and internal affairs, and the Third and Fourth departments.[41]

Ironically, when the Isakov Commission launched its investigation, the chief opponents of the medical courses rallied little support in Russian ruling circles. Revolutionary terrorism cost Timashev his ministerial post in November 1878; and Tolstoi's failure to curb burgeoning student activism left him with few allies in court. The Isakov Commission reflected the temporary eclipse of conservative statesmen: the majority adopted a conciliatory attitude toward women's medical education and practice. Riding the political tide of high government circles is usually expedient and almost natural for middle-level bureaucrats, particularly in autocratic regimes; but the Third Department's defence of medical *kursistki* was nothing less than an about-face. Under Shuvalov's command, the political police had consistently opposed women's admission to traditionally male professions. However, the recently promoted Drentel'n, who seemed preoccupied by the hunt for revolutionists in the Kiev and Bestuzhevskie Courses, failed to provide the department with such authoritative leadership. In the Isakov Commission, Third Department delegate A. Severtsov championed women's advance in medicine.

Severtsov played a crucial role in persuading commission members that medical *kursistki* posed no serious threat to the autocratic regime. He testified that the women's medical courses, in comparison to the other higher institutions of the northern capital, harboured few political dissidents: whereas 3 percent of St Petersburg University students and 4.28 percent of the students in the academy had been convicted of criminal and administrative offences, only 1.75 percent of medical *kursistki* had received similar convictions. During the past five years, only 46 of the 648 women enrolled in the courses had been indicted on charges of political crimes. Of that number, the courts had convicted 4 auditors of criminal offences, 7 of administrative infractions, and had banned 2 women from the capital. Severtsov not only minimized the political dangers of the courses, but also argued that women's employment as medical practitioners would prove a boon to social morality. Medical practice, he maintained, would provide careers to women who, lacking a regular source of income or relatives to support them, might otherwise turn to prostitution.[42]

Severtsov's report helped to convince commission members to overrule the proposal of Georgievskii, who now insisted that women's medical practice be limited to midwifery and the treatment of women's and children's diseases.[43] The latter had also charged that advanced medical training would rob women of "the sense of modesty and decency." In spite of Georgievskii's objections, the final report of the Isakov Commission recommended granting the graduates of the courses the title of female physician and the right to medical practice without restricting treatment to women and children. In September 1879, the War Ministry submitted the report to the Ministry of Education.[44] Following Tolstoi's review, it was to be forwarded to the Ministry of Internal Affairs for introduction to the Council of Ministers.

Revolutionary terrorism disrupted consideration of the Isakov Commission report. The bombing of the Winter Palace in February 1880 temporarily foreclosed official discussion of women's medical education; however, the consequent reshuffling of statesmen left liberals and moderates dominating Russia's top ministries. Within a week of the dynamiting of the imperial residence, Alexander II named Count M.T. Loris-Melikov, an associate of Miliutin's liberal circle and opponent of Tolstoi, chairman of the Supreme Executive Committee to co-ordinate all state agencies and, several months later, minister of internal affairs. In April 1880, Loris-Melikov secured

Tolstoi's resignation, and the more congenial A.A. Saburov became minister of education. By the summer of 1880, then, moderate and progressive officials controlled the ministries reviewing the recommendations of the Isakov Commission.

Undoubtedly, the more consistently liberal complexion of the tsar's chief advisers prompted Alexander II to take a more definite stand on the issue of women's medical practice. On 14 June 1880, the emperor awarded the graduates of the women's medical courses the title of *zhenskii vrach* and the right to independent medical practice.[45] He failed, however, to inscribe their new right and title in the legal code. Similarly, the medical courses that trained female physicians remained a provisional establishment totally dependent upon the sponsorship of Miliutin.

On 1 March 1881, the assassination of Alexander II forced Miliutin's resignation and left the courses defenceless against the conservative reaction initiating the reign of Alexander III. Within a few months of Miliutin's ouster, P.S. Vannovskii, the new war minister, announced the forthcoming expulsion of the courses from the War Ministry. On 5 August 1882, an Imperial Order closed admissions to the courses, stipulating that they would be abolished once current auditors had completed their medical training.[46]

The impending destruction of the country's only advanced medical school for women galvanized the professors of the courses into action. Determined to secure a new institutional base for the women's courses, they appealed to the St Petersburg City Duma, which agreed to assume jurisdiction over them so long as adequate funding and hospital facilities were found.[47] At the same time, professors enlisted the services of the progressive press to rally popular support: *Golos, Novoe vremiia,* and *Vrach* numbered among the many newspapers and journals that featured articles extolling women's medical practice. *Vrach* also published the growing list of benefactors of the courses, which included composer N.A. Rimskii-Korsakov and painter V.V. Vereshchagin. Particularly active in garnering the support of such cultural celebrities was A.P. Borodin who acquired greater fame as a composer than as a chemistry professor in the Medical-Surgical Academy and the women's courses. *Vrach,* moreover, did its best to ensure that any endorsement by the nation's most illustrious sons did not go unnoticed. Thus, after *Golos* printed I.S. Turgenev's letter praising women doctors, the medical journal reported on its publication so that the great writer's sympathies would become more well known.[48]

Once aware of the plight of the courses, individuals and organizations throughout the empire offered immediate financial assistance: Moscow merchants, Kiev attorneys, St Petersburg students, members of the Tver provincial zemstvo, and physicians from Irbit, Kaluga, and Voronezh made donations to the Duma. The size of individual contributions varied greatly, ranging from the 6-ruble gift of an anonymous donor in the Crimean town of Kerch to the large 10,000-ruble grant of General A.L. Shaniavskii, the husband of Lidiia Rodstvennaia who gave 50,000 rubles to the courses in the early 1870s. By late November 1882, the Duma had received 24,000 rubles in contributions, and another 51,000 rubles had been pledged to the courses over a ten-year period.[49] The press campaign supporting the courses had barely begun. If private funding could save the courses, and many believed it could, then the future of the women's medical courses was secure.

The government decided otherwise: it refused to allow the transfer of the courses to the Duma. The two most powerful statesmen in the court of Alexander III guaranteed that the training of female physicians would cease. Tolstoi, who became minister of internal affairs in 1882, had already opposed the courses for over a decade and, now that the new tsar had returned him to power, he was not about to surrender to public pressure. Concession and conciliation were even more alien to K.P. Pobedonostsev, the tutor of the former tsarevich and Procurator of the Holy Synod. He wanted no expansion of woman's activity beyond her traditional role of wife, mother, and elementary teacher. The new minister of education, Delianov, also had a long history of opposition to women's higher education. These statesmen, nevertheless, could not completely ignore public reaction to the closure of the medical courses.

To end speculation about the courses' future, a special meeting of ministers, chaired by Tolstoi, clarified the government's position on women's medical education. Its members – Pobedonostsev, Delianov, Vannovskii, and K.K. Grot of the Fourth Department – reached a quick accord. On 4 December 1882, they unanimously declared that the women's medical courses could not continue in their present form. Reiterating some of the same arguments used to justify the government's expulsion of women from Russian universities in the early 1860s, they maintained that "deceptive" agitation about the so-called "woman question" had promoted women's demand for advanced medical education, and that the training of female physicians disrupted family life. In addition to these old complaints, statesmen now had practical grounds for closing the women's medical courses: the state, which was the main employer of medical personnel, simply did not have enough jobs for the growing number of male physicians, much less women doctors. At the time, competition for medical posts with the government was fierce. Consequently, the ministers' meeting recommended restricting women to the lower ranks of the profession, particularly to the traditional female vocation of midwifery. It proposed the establishment of a four-year women's midwifery institute to confer the title of *uchenaia akusherka*, not *zhenskii vrach*.[50] The employment opportunities of these midwives would also be seriously curtailed. Although they could enter private practice, they were barred from all salaried positions except those in women's and children's hospitals, maternity homes, and girls' educational institutions. The government, moreover, did not plan to finance the new midwifery institute. Funding would have to come from the private sector.

Two months later, on 3 February 1883, Delianov established a special commission to prepare the regulations and training program for the proposed midwifery institute.[51] Two of its three members probably welcomed the new restraints on women's medical education and practice. The chairman, Prince M.S. Volkonskii, had a formidable reputation as a "person with totally reactionary views,"[52] and Georgievskii had long displayed his opposition to female physicians. The third member was E.N. Mamonov, the director of the Medical Department of the Ministry of Internal Affairs. His contributions to the development of the Russian medical profession were much more well known than his political philosophy. Before joining the Medical Department in 1876, he had founded the Moscow Society of Russian Physicians and edited the journal, *Moskovskaia Meditsinskaia Gazeta*. These three individuals had no difficulty drafting preliminary plans for the midwifery institute that strictly followed the guidelines set by the ministers' meeting of the previous year. Before the end of June, they submitted their project to the nation's medical experts: deans of university medical faculties, directors of hospitals, professors of the Medical-Surgical Academy, and members of the Medical Council were invited to evaluate their proposal.

The overwhelming majority of medical specialists rejected the plans of the Volkonskii Commission. High on their list of objections was the limited medical education to be offered in the midwifery institute. To emphasize the dangers of creating ill-prepared medical personnel, Professor N.V. Sklifasovskii, the dean of the medical faculty of Moscow University, warned that such an institute would lead to "charlatanism in medical practice." K.A. Raukhfaus, the director of a children's hospital and teacher in the women's medical courses, expressed similar fears: the struggle for survival would give the *uchenaia akusherka* only two options – "to be a medical proletarian or a medical charlatan." Other experts focused on the need for physicians in the countryside and the employment of women doctors by the zemstvos. N.I. Rozov, the former director of the Medical Department, insisted that rural Russia required general practitioners, not midwives, and pointed to the stipends provided by various zemstvos to secure the services of women doctors in their localities.[53] The Russian Medical Council found the project of the Volkonskii Commission so deficient that it proposed a fundamentally different type of institute: the *Journal of the Medical Council* of 8 June 1888 included plans for a women's medical institute with a five-year course of study equivalent to a university medical faculty.[54] Graduates were to receive a physician's diploma and the title of *zhenskii vrach*.

Opposition from the nation's leading medical authority, coupled with the fear of creating quacks and charlatans, prompted Delianov to change his position on the issue of women doctors. He shelved the original plans of the Volkonskii Commission and, in August, solicited Tolstoi's approval of the Medical Council's proposal. Tolstoi refused to endorse it. Delianov, however, did not yield to his influential colleague. Instead, he now championed the women's medical institute. Although Delianov remained antagonistic to the women's higher courses, his preference for vocational training made him far more amenable to advanced medical education for women. He was also keenly aware of the shortage of medical personnel in the countryside; and, to increase rural health services, his ministry was promoting paramedical training. The women's medical institute, which was assured extensive private patronage, would allow further expansion of rural health care at little expense to the government. Indeed, it is ironic that the individual who had so eagerly assisted Tolstoi in frustrating women's professional ambitions during the 1870s and early 1880s now struggled in vain to win his former mentor's support for a school to train female physicians. Tolstoi would not budge. Until his death in 1889, he continued to insist that the country had no need for women doctors.[55] The following year, Delianov introduced the project for the women's medical institute to the State Council. But Pobedonostsev was there to block its passage.[56] Thus the training of female physicians came to a halt in Imperial Russia when Vannovskii expelled the women's courses from the War Ministry. Women's medical education would make no further progress until the next autocrat, Nicholas II, approved the establishment of the St Petersburg Medical Institute for Women in 1895.

III

Despite the short life span of the women's medical courses, they had trained a contingent of women doctors far outnumbering that of any contemporary European state. The Russian Medical Register of 1884 listed 385 female physicians.[57] Within four years, after all women enrolled in the courses had graduated, their number increased to 698.[58] By contrast, the medical profession in France included only 95 women doctors in 1900, and England still lagged behind Russia with 258 female physicians.[59] Given the desperate need for doctors in rural Russia, one would assume that the graduates of the women's medical courses would contribute significantly to peasant health care. But such was not the case: only 148 served as zemstvo doctors and private practitioners in the countryside.[60] That is not to deny, of course, the individual achievements of several female physicians. During a six-year struggle to control the outbreak of smallpox in Moscow guberniia, for example, one woman doctor prepared more than 400,000 vaccinations;[61] those adventurous few who practised in the Muslim borderlands sometimes treated as many as 80 or 100 patients in a day.[62] In general, however, women doctors had far less impact on the nation's health care than their numbers or expertise warranted. And, as anomalous as it might appear, the overwhelming majority could not secure regular posts as physicians.

Less than one quarter of Russia's women doctors held salaried positions.[63] Because the state had failed to develop the administrative network to provide regular employment for the growing number of physicians, 540 women were forced into private practice, a highly insecure occupation in a country where few, particularly among the peasantry, could afford to pay for medical treatment. Consequently, over 90 percent of these private practitioners remained in the capitals or large provincial towns that offered greater opportunity for supplementary employment, as well as the amenities of urban life. Only fifty-six women risked private practice in the countryside. Similarly, most male doctors avoided the peasant village. They too suffered an employment crisis in the late nineteenth century. Indeed, state appointments for doctors had become so scarce that the Ministry of Internal Affairs freed its stipendaries in medical schools from their service obligations.[64] By 1888, 60 percent of Russia's 19,032 physicians struggled to earn a living by private practice.

Among that fortunate minority of women who received medical appointments, sixty-six remained in St Petersburg.[65] Most were hired by local hospitals or the City Duma. The remaining ninety-two worked for various zemstvos: some in the hospitals of district and provincial capitals; others in more remote areas where the average size of a physician's bailiwick was 3000 kilometres and the population exceeded 50,000.[66] In remote regions, medical practice obviously entailed greater physical discomfort, as well as cultural isolation. Employment in major centres of the zemstvo, however, could also have its drawbacks. Here, women doctors were sometimes hired as paramedics, rather than physicians. This always meant low pay and little prestige, but seldom any diminution of their medical responsibilities. That was the situation of both Julia A. Kviatkovskaia and Mariia P. Rashkovich who graduated from the courses in 1886 and subsequently accepted posts as paramedics in a zemstvo hospital in Moscow guberniia. Although they fulfilled all the obligations of physicians, their annual pay was only 300 rubles.[67] At that time, a male doctor on the zemstvo received an average salary of 1315 rubles; a female physician, 944 rubles.[68] As a result of the shrinking job market, however, such pay differentials were not women's primary concern: the chronic insecurity of private practice encouraged many to apply for salaried posts as lower-level medical personnel.[69]

By the late nineteenth century, increasing competition for medical appointments had generated considerable antagonism toward women doctors from the middling and lower ranks of the Russian medical profession. Male physicians frequently challenged the professional qualifications of the *zhenskii vrach*. Natalia P. Dragnevich, a woman doctor in the zemstvo hospital of Kirilov, complained that her male colleagues taunted her: "It would be nice to know by what right and on the basis of what documents you practise medicine."[70] Similarly, Kviatkovskaia's experiences convinced her that male doctors, as a whole, were the "main enemies" of female physicians.[71] Lower-level medical personnel also refused to acknowledge the *zhenskii vrach* as a physician. In 1882, for example, a pharmacy in Pskov guberniia refused to fill the prescriptions of women doctors employed by the district zemstvo because their names did not appear on the list of physicians published by the Medical Department of the Ministry of Internal Affairs.[72] Admittedly, Russian women doctors had no legal status: they were not included in the official medical register until 1883, and the law made no mention of the *zhenskii vrach* or *uchenaia akusherka*.[73] At the same time, however, it is more likely that women's intrusion into the glutted job market, rather than legal concerns, underlay such obstructionism. After all, the hiring of women as zemstvo physicians required the approval of state officials. Moreover, most members of the upper echelons of the medical establishment – professors of medicine, deans of medical schools, and directors of clinics and hospitals – endorsed the training and practice of women doctors.[74] Unlike the regular *vrach*, pharmacist, or paramedic, however, Russia's medical elite had no reason to fear the female physician as a threat to personal economic well-being.

Rivalry with male medical personnel increased the hardships of women doctors, particularly in rural areas where educated companionship was scarce. Here, physicians of both sexes complained of loneliness and cultural isolation.[75] Village teachers also lamented the solitude of the so-called "God-forsaken corners" of the empire: "You sit and your soul is seized by melancholy, the tormenting melancholy of solitude."[76] For the woman doctor who also suffered rejection by her male colleagues in the district, the sense of estrangement must have been profound. In the peasant village, however, the female physician did have one important advantage over her male counterpart: she was less suspect in the eyes of the local population. Unlike the male practitioner, she had never served as an agent of state power in the countryside. Before the reforms of the 1860s, the Russian doctor examined recruits for military service, a fate viewed as the death sentence by the peasantry; he performed autopsies, which rural folk viewed as acts of mutilation; and he sometimes supervised corporal punishment.[77] Female practitioners, in contrast, had never been associated with the punitive arm of the state. In fact, the peasantry had traditionally taken their health problems to women: the *povitukha*, the untrained village midwife, or the *znakharka*, the faith healer who specialized in herbal remedies, or the noblewoman on the landlord's estate. Consequently, the peasantry harboured no fear of female physicians, but regarded them as natural healers.[78]

Regrettably, women's acceptance as healers did not break peasant resistance to modern medicine, which, in the late nineteenth century, meant radical change in the diet and hygiene of rural Russia. Given the social and economic conditions of the peasant village, such reform entailed nothing less than a cultural revolution in the broadest sense. All the good intentions and advice of the physician had little impact on peasant hygiene when the village population used the same bath houses, or had a limited water-supply, or simply lacked sufficient clothing to change after bathing.[79] How could she convince a mother not to wrap her newborn in the father's soiled shirt when the peasant believed that this practice would make the father love the child and the child respect the father? And, although the *zhenskii vrach* had special training in obstetrics, her expertise was no match for the traditional methods of the *povitukha* who had long *stazh* (service) in the village. The *povitukha* was an age-old member of the local community, had tended the birth of much of its population, and, like the peasant mother, viewed parturition as a mystical event to be celebrated with appropriate ritual. In addition, the woman doctor, unlike the village midwife, had neither the time nor the inclination to perform domestic chores for the peasant household for two days following the delivery. A physician could not hope to cure a child suffering from dysentery when the only food in the peasant hut was *pushnoi khleb*, a mealy bread of grain and chaff that frequently caused digestive disorders. Under such conditions, one woman doctor lamented, the loneliness and isolation of rural practitioners were "nothing" compared to their sense of helplessness: "The worst was that I did not feel any sense of satisfaction in my work." All her attempts to bring modern medicine to the village, she despaired, "had no impact on the peasantry."[80]

Few would fault the female physician for failing to alleviate the health problems endemic to peasant life. Male doctors experienced no greater success. At the same time, however, there is reason to doubt that the graduates of the women's courses served as the most effective bearers of medical reform in rural Russia. Most came from the upper and middling classes who had little understanding of village life and little empathy for peasant custom. And, although women were accepted as healers, as outsiders they could hardly inspire the confidence needed to effect the dramatic change in peasant lifestyle that modern medicine required. As well, women doctors from the non-privileged classes, after studying medicine in the nation's capital for five years, could easily come to despise the squalor and poverty of the peasant village. Undoubtedly, it was more than the economic insecurity of private practice in the countryside that prompted physicians of both sexes to remain in urban areas.

Even the new government of Alexander III recognized that the social and economic conditions of rural Russia often "paralysed" the activities of physicians.[81] And Delianov attempted to improve peasant health care by training more paramedics (*fel'dshery*). Between 1882 and 1891, the number of *fel'dshery* more than doubled, increasing from 6182 to 14,303.[82] Given the cultural alienation experienced by most rural doctors, there was reason to believe that the *fel'dsher* might better serve peasant health needs than the physician. Paramedics, who were generally drawn from the lower social orders and whose education did not entail five years amidst the more secular, cosmopolitan culture of St Petersburg, might more easily bridge the gap between modern medicine and village tradition. Also important, the paramedic's salary was much lower than the physician's, and thus would allow the government and zemstvos to employ more medical personnel in rural areas. Regrettably, however, the medical expertise of many paramedics was too limited and their overall number too small. By the early 1890s, it was abundantly clear that the *fel'dsher*, like the physician, was no remedy for the poverty that bred poor nutrition and hygiene among the peasantry. The high death toll and widespread suffering in the famine of 1891–2 and the cholera epidemic of the following year dramatically exposed the government's failure to improve the health and welfare of rural Russia.

When famine and cholera struck the country, the burgeoning population had even less access to physicians than when the women's courses were first created. In 1890, there was one doctor for every 9600 inhabitants of European Russia.[83] For the entire empire, the ratio was worse: 1:10,800. And, despite Delianov's recent promotion of lower-level medical personnel, the ratio of paramedics was only slightly better: 1:9200 in European Russia, and 1:9900 for the empire. It should be noted, however, that in zemstvo provinces, doctors outnumbered *fel'dshery* by almost three to two.[84] Like the education system, then, the Russian medical establishment was not only inadequate, but ill-balanced. Indeed, one contemporary compared the Russian medical profession to an army "in which the number of officers is greater than the number of soldiers."[85] Most of these "officers," of course, remained in large urban centres. In the northern capital in particular, graduates of the women's medical courses swelled the ranks of physicians who could find no regular employment as doctors. Like the *kursistki* of the higher courses who vied with gymnasium graduates for highly competitive teaching posts, women doctors, as Georgievskii had warned, appeared well on their way to becoming an unemployed "female intellectual proletariat." Few Russian physicians, however, revealed any of the revolutionary potential of the legendary proletariat – at least until the twentieth century.[86] But the regime of Alexander III had placed no bets on women doctors. Nor did it put any trust in educated youth of either sex: the assault on the universities and higher courses would quickly follow the closure of women's medical courses.

### CHAPTER SIX

# The Bitter End:
# The Conservative Assault
# on Higher Education

But what will follow the thaw? If spring and a bountiful summer, good, but if that thaw is temporary and then frost once again fetters everything, it will be even more painful.

VERA S. AKSAKOVA (1855)[1]

After the regicide, Prince Meshcherskii, the editor of *Grazhdanin* and influential friend of the new tsar, advised Alexander III: "All political criminals are, by their very birth, the first charges of the education system; *there began their gangrene*."[2] Russia's new ruling party agreed that contemporary education bred political radicalism and indicted the universities and women's higher courses as the chief culprits. Pobedonostsev regarded students as "crowds of monsters and scoundrels," and scorned the liberal academic community as "the great herd of intellect" that threatened the very foundation of Russian autocracy.[3] Tolstoi had begun preparations to dismantle the liberal university reforms as early as 1875, when he named Delianov chairman of a special commission to draft a new university statute.[4] With his appointment as minister of education in 1882, the eminently practical Delianov redoubled his efforts to promote vocational and technical training at the expense of university education. For guidance, he turned to Katkov who, until his death in 1887, exercised increasing influence backstage of the new regime.[5] And Georgievskii, who served as Delianov's right hand in the ministry, could always be counted on to execute counter-reform in higher education.

Despite unanimity among the crown's chosen advisers concerning the dangers of existing educational institutions, the new government did not replace the liberal university statute with a restrictive charter until 1884, and it waited two more years before closing admissions to the women's higher courses. Conservative legislation governing the press and the zemstvo was also postponed. Public discontent ran so high during the early years of Alexander III's reign that statesmen feared that the wholesale introduction of the counter-reforms would spark a new wave of terrorist activity. Peasant disorders were on the increase in the countryside, and student demonstrations again rocked university towns. In particular, the government was apprehensive about provoking student unrest before the coronation celebrations of 1883, and thus delayed the offensive against higher education.[6]

But it was not only forces outside the government that prevented rapid implementation of the counter-reforms. The State Council also resisted drafting legislation that would undo the reforms of Alexander II.[7] Composed of former ministers, senators, and other dignitaries of the realm, the State Council was the uppermost level of the bureaucracy. Here, projected legislation was reviewed, debated, and given its final form before presentation to the emperor. Both the prestige of the State Council and its level of expertise had been greatly enhanced during the period of "Great Reforms": much of the reform legislation was prepared by departments of the State Council or by special commissions under its authority. Consequently, when Alexander III assumed the throne, many members of the State Council, which then numbered seventy-five, identified with the reforms of his predecessor and opposed their rescission.[8] When entrusted with the formulation of the ultraconservative legislation demanded by the court circle, the majority of state counsellors often prepared only moderate revisions of the "Great Reforms."

Alexander III was thus saddled with an unco-operative State Council and he could not rule without it. On the one hand, the emperor needed its expertise. Economic and social developments in nineteenth-century Russia made the governing of the empire far too complex for the tsar and his close associates. On the other hand, the State Council gave an aura of legitimacy to autocratic rule. To ignore or abolish the State Council, which helped to create the impression that the emperor ruled in co-operation with the nation's leading experts and according to regular legal procedures, would seriously damage the reputation of the autocrat both at home and abroad. And although there was nothing to prevent the tsar from replacing several recalcitrant state counsellors with new members who were more co-operative, he could not afford to dismiss all those who resisted the counter-reforms. To do so would be equivalent to declaring the unreliability of the highest level of the state bureaucracy.[9]

Obstructionism in the State Council, which prolonged the debate over projected legislation, delayed the introduction of the counter-reforms, but it could not prevent their eventual implementation. The emperor was not bound to accept the recommendations of the State Council. Moreover, when disagreement among state counsellors resulted in the formulation of two different legislative projects, one supported by the majority and another by the minority, it was the tsar's prerogative to decide which project became law. When the majority failed to produce the desired legislation, as it did on the question of university reform, Alexander III simply rejected its proposal. Instead, he approved the new university statute sponsored by Tolstoi's minority.[10] The late Alexander II had used the same method to override opposition in the State Council: his endorsement of Tolstoi's classical gymnasium statute of 1871 is a prime example. Under his successor, the dissenting majority of state counsellors also proved unable to prevent the imposition of stringent controls over Russian universities in the fall of 1884.

The new statute uncompromisingly subordinated the university to the Ministry of Education.[11] Rectors and deans were no longer elected by the local professoriate, but appointed by the minister. He also controlled the hiring, promotion, and dismissal of professors. University courts were abolished, and the powers of the district curator expanded. Most destructive to academic freedom was the creation of special state commissions to conduct university examinations. Professors now had to tailor their classes to prepare students for state examinations, and their lectures required advance approval by the Ministry of Education. In sum, the new statute of 1884 stripped Russian universities of their former autonomy.

A worse fate awaited the women's higher courses. Delianov planned to abolish them altogether, but that was not clear at the outset. Fear of exacerbating the discontent pervading academic circles after the government shackled the universities prompted the minister to resort to subterfuge. Rather than launch a frontal assault on the women's courses, he publicly declared what could be construed as their temporary closure. On 8 May 1886, *Pravitel'stvennyi vestnik* announced that no new auditors would be admitted to the courses pending the review of women's educational facilities by a special government commission. One of the many functions of this commission, which was also chaired by M.S. Volkonskii, was to prepare new regulations for the higher courses. If such regulations were not established before the last auditors admitted to the courses graduated, then the courses would close by default.

Delianov had established this commission in 1884, after the tsar drew his attention to the critique of women's education that Baroness E.F. von Raden had presented to the empress.[12] Von Raden had not only complained about the higher courses, asserting that women's contemporary struggle for higher education had "all the characteristics of a morbid passion"; she had also criticized girls' primary and secondary schools.[13] As a result, Delianov instructed the commission to investigate the entire organization of women's education in the empire.[14] The task was enormous: it involved the study of the numerous regulations of the Ministry of Education and Fourth Department, the records of previous commissions on women's education, as well as the reports Volkonskii solicited from individual teachers, professors, school directors, district curators, and provincial governors.

Only in March 1888 did the Volkonskii Commission finish its work: ten different projects on various aspects of women's education, including new regulations for the higher courses and a proposal for advanced language courses, were submitted to Delianov.[15] By this time, only the two-year courses in Kazan had ceased operations. The minister, however, was determined that the other women's courses would soon follow suit. He failed to act on the commission's recommendations. Consequently, the courses in Moscow and Kiev shut down in rapid succession: Guerrier's Courses closed in 1888; those in Kiev and on the Lubianka perished the following year. Delianov also took steps to guard against their future rehabilitation. When he finally submitted the proposals of the Volkonskii Commission to the State Council in 1893, the projects for the higher courses and advanced language courses were excluded.[16] The ancient capital and provincial university towns would remain without women's higher courses until Nicholas II approved their re-establishment in the early twentieth century.

Only the personal intervention of Alexander III saved the Bestuzhevskie Courses from annihilation. In January 1889, after Delianov had repeatedly refused to allow the enrolment of new auditors, Elena I. Likhacheva, the president of the courses' funding society, appealed directly to the tsar. Undoubtedly, the society's extensive financial resources and numerous patrons of high social rank helped garner the emperor's support. At the same time, however, Likhacheva's petition was formulated in such a way so as to convince the tsar that the continued operation of the courses would help preserve traditional moral and social values. The educated woman, for example, was here described as "the true custodian of religion, morality and order in the family and society." More persuasive was Likhacheva's reiteration of Tolstoi's earlier justification of higher courses: they deterred Russian women from studying at foreign universities, which spawned "ideas and morals incompatible with our way of life."[17] In fact, the closure of admissions to the women's medical and higher courses had already precipitated another exodus of Russian women abroad. During the academic year 1888–9, over 100 Russian women were enrolled in Swiss universities.[18] Within a month of Likhacheva's appeal, the emperor requested Delianov to consider her petition to reopen admissions to the Bestuzhevskie Courses.

Delianov had no choice but to revise his position concerning the higher courses in the capital. The tsar's new-found sympathy for the Bestuzhevskie Courses, however, did not stop the minister from expressing his reluctance about their reopening. He specifically declared that he considered women's medical courses "much more expedient and useful" than higher courses.[19] In terms of deterring women from studying abroad, the minister was right: of the 103 women enrolled in Swiss universities in that year, 81 studied medicine.[20] In deference to the emperor, Delianov agreed to allow the higher courses of St Petersburg to resume operations but only under new regulations that would tighten his ministry's control over them.

Thus, when the Bestuzhevskie Courses reopened in September 1889, they were subject to the same type of strict controls the government had recently imposed on the universities.[21] The minister now appointed all managerial and administrative personnel, including the director and trustees committee. His approval was also necessary for the hiring of academic and supervisory staff. In addition, the district curator exercised close supervision over the courses and regulated their expenditures. Despite increased governmental control, the Bestuzhevskie Courses, nevertheless, remained classified as a private educational institution and, as such, granted no degrees to expand the employment opportunities of *kursistki*. But then, it was not the issue of women's employment that had won the emperor's support for the continued operation of the courses. Indeed, their new director, V.P. Kulin, made this perfectly clear in his speech celebrating their reopening. He admonished the new auditors to engage in serious intellectual work "but not with the aim of preparing yourself for any kind of professional activity, no, – you are preparing for life, mainly family life."[22]

Such preparation, the new admission requirements guaranteed, would remain beyond the grasp of the lower social orders. Financial barriers blocked their access to the courses. Each auditor, even if she planned to enrol on a part-time basis, was now required to prove that she had sufficient funds for the entire four-year course. And no matter how few subjects she studied, the part-time auditor now paid the same annual 50-ruble fee as full-time *kursistki*. To discourage poor but industrious women from attempting "to work their way" through the higher courses, the new regulations also stipulated that part-time auditors could not exceed 2 percent of the total enrolment. Discrimination against Jews was more explicit: non-Christians could constitute only 3 percent of the total number of auditors. This regulation was in keeping with the government's recent efforts to curb the educational opportunities of Jews and their migration to turbulent university towns. In 1887, the government had placed limits on the number of Jews admitted to the universities and gymnasia. A quota of 3 percent of the total enrolment was established for St Petersburg and Moscow, whereas other educational districts outside the Pale restricted the admission of Jews to 5 percent of the student body. The new regulations of the Bestuzhevskie Courses also limited the total number of auditors to 150 in the first year, and set the maximum enrolment figure at 400 when the full four-year program was in operation.[23] By 1894, however, so many applicants qualified for admission that Delianov lifted the enrolment ceiling. The number of admissions increased dramatically and, six years later, enrolment approached 1000.[24]

When the first class of auditors entered the courses in 1889, it was clear that the new admission requirements had achieved the government's desired results: the overwhelming majority came from Orthodox families of the upper social estates. Among the 144 women attending the courses, 90 percent were Orthodox and 77 percent were daughters of nobles and officials.[25]

Representatives of other religious faiths included 6 Roman Catholics, 5 Jews, and 3 Lutherans. Members of the lowest social orders were also underrepresented: the combined total of auditors of peasant, artisan, and clerical status was only 14 (9.7 percent). Women of the merchant class were somewhat more numerous and constituted 13 percent of the total enrolment. They would remain the second largest socio-economic group in the Bestuzhevskie Courses for well over a decade. However, they continued to lag far behind women of privileged society who exceeded, on the average, two-thirds of the total annual enrolment until the early twentieth century.[26] The government of Alexander III had thus succeeded in making the higher courses inaccessible to most women of the lower social orders. Indeed, opportunities for advanced education, even among well-to-do women, would be severely curtailed until after the next tsar assumed the throne in late 1894.

During his first decade in power, Nicholas II expanded both the educational facilities and employment opportunities of women. He not only approved the establishment of the St Petersburg Medical Institute for Women but, in 1904, granted its graduates the title of *lekar'* and the same rights as male physicians except status in the Table of Ranks.[27] Three years earlier, he had also enhanced the prestige and career options of women who completed the Bestuzhevskie Courses by allowing them to teach the upper classes of girls' gymnasia.[28] In 1900, moreover, the emperor sanctioned the reopening of Guerrier's Courses in Moscow.[29] Like the Bestuzhevskie Courses, they remained under the strict control of the Ministry of Education until 1905. In that tumultuous year, revolution precipitated massive education reform and induced the government to grant autonomy to the higher courses, as well as to the universities.

The first Russian Revolution ushered in a decade of unprecedented development of higher educational facilities for women. Besides the existing courses in St Petersburg and Moscow, women's higher courses opened in nine other towns of the empire: Kiev, Kazan, and Odessa (1906); Kharkov (1907); Tiflis and Dorpat (1908); Novocherkassk and Warsaw (1909); and Tomsk (1910).[30] Most courses consisted of two departments: historical-philological and physical-mathematical. Those in Kiev and Odessa, however, boasted medical faculties as well. Separate medical schools for women were also created in Moscow (1909) and Kharkov (1910). In addition, Russian women now had access to legal training: the higher courses in Kiev, Odessa, and Warsaw opened judicial faculties; and the Bestuzhevskie Courses added a department of law in 1906. Theological courses for women were also established in Moscow and Kazan (1909). As had been the case during the "thaw" following the Crimean War, Russian women were quick to exploit the new educational opportunities that came on the heels of the revolution. By the academic year 1911–12, enrolment in the various courses reached 22,000 and another 1400 women attended the St Petersburg Medical Institute.[31] Four years later, the total number of women in advanced educational facilities increased to 44,000: they now constituted approximately one-third of the entire student population in all higher educational institutions of the empire.[32]

By this time, both the prestige and employment opportunities of *kursistki* had increased dramatically. The major breakthrough came in late 1911 when the state recognized the academic program of the higher courses as equivalent to the curriculum of a regular university faculty. The law of 19 December 1911 granted the graduates of the higher courses the right to teach all classes of secondary schools, including the upper levels of boys' gymnasia, and the same salaries and pensions awarded male teachers in equivalent positions.[33] Even more important, on the basis of this law, they were now admitted to state examinations at the university. After more than fifty years of struggle, Russian women could qualify for the same degrees as male students. They had finally secured admission to professional careers that had long been the sole preserve of men. But Russian women never did gain access to the old regime's Table of Ranks.

The October Revolution would destroy the old hierarchy as well as sexual segregation in education. Women's higher courses, as separate educational institutions, ceased to exist in 1919, when the new Bolshevik authorities ordered their merger with local universities.

\* \* \*

The history of the women's movement in nineteenth-century Russia documents the dedication, talent, and courage of thousands of women who struggled for higher education. Some sought personal liberation from the fetters of ignorance; others hoped to find gainful employment; and most believed that knowledge would enable them to contribute to the welfare of their society. By mastering university study or establishing careers in teaching or medicine, these women helped undermine society's traditional views of the female sex. Whereas the medical degree awarded Nadezhda Suslova in 1867 may have only challenged time-honoured notions of woman's infirmity and inferiority, some two decades later, the inclusion of 698 female physicians in the Russian Medical Register should have been enough to put these fallacies to rest. And, although higher education failed to give all *kursistki* the opportunity to earn a living or to alleviate the illiteracy and disease that shackled much of the population, the less tangible gains of women who sought their "liberator" in knowledge cannot be dismissed. From professors of the higher courses in particular, they learned that *nauka* was an end in itself.

Until the early twentieth century, the very pursuit of knowledge was the main compensation for the material hardship and public censure suffered by most *kursistki*. The Revolution of 1905 changed this and much more: it not only brought dramatic improvement in women's educational and employment opportunities but also steered the women's movement into the political arena. Now Russian women began to struggle for female suffrage and equality of the sexes before the law. Educated women, of course, spearheaded the new campaign, and the three main feminist organizations drew their leadership largely from the graduates of the medical or higher courses. Anna N. Shabanova, who completed the medical courses of the War Ministry in the late 1870s, became the driving force behind the political activism of the Mutual Philanthropic Society. Another graduate, Doctor Mariia I. Pokrovskaia, founded the Women's Progressive Party. Two leading organizers of the All-Russian Union for Women's Equality – Anna S. Miliukova and Zinaida S. Mirovich – had attended Guerrier's Courses in Moscow. While these women now pursued political rights, they employed roughly the same tactics used in the earlier struggle for higher education. They still relied heavily on peaceful petitioning and a supportive press, although women, not men, were now the loudest champions of the women's cause. They also continued to seek allies in the liberal community. Such tactics, however, did not win them political rights. Why they failed requires an investigation of the problems confronting liberal reform movements in that turbulent last decade of Imperial Russia, and these have been explored by other scholars.

Women's struggle for higher education in nineteenth-century Russia was also a peaceful, legalistic movement that sought reform within the existing system. As such, its achievements and failures cannot be fully understood unless studied in the context of the political culture of the reform era. When viewed from this perspective, the history of the women's movement also sheds light on autocratic politics, as well as social developments, during the second half of the nineteenth century. First, it illustrates that the opinion of certain elements of educated society had become a factor in Russian political life. This public opinion confronted the autocracy on issues of educational reform and convinced state officials to temper their reactions to demands for increased educational opportunities for women. Second, the simultaneous development of competing policies on women's education under Alexander II clearly demonstrates the lack of co-ordination within the government administration. It also indicates that favoured statesmen enjoyed a relative degree of autonomy in matters on which the tsar held no definite views. This is particularly evident in the ministerial controversy over women's medical education. Third, the initial success and ultimate fate of the women's courses testify to both the personal nature of autocratic rule and the fragility of such legalistic reform movements in Imperial Russia. Just as Alexander II's ambiguous attitude toward advanced education for women allowed the creation of medical and higher courses, so, too, did it determine their precarious existence and thus facilitate their demise. As private, provisional establishments, most women's courses were easily swept away by the conservative reaction that followed the regicide.

Finally, the history of the women's movement provides a glaring example of the autocracy's mismanagement of the human resources at its disposal. During the reform era, the desire to serve society within the existing political structure fostered women's pursuit of university study. But government inefficiency, buttressed by long traditions of sexual discrimination and recurring fears of educated youth, denied many educated women the opportunity to contribute to the nation's social services. Failure to develop an adequate administrative network to support health care in the countryside also forced female physicians into the ranks of the urban unemployed while rural areas desperately needed medical personnel. Similarly, although most of the population was illiterate, the top-heavy education system could not satisfy the demands of graduates of girl's gymnasia and higher courses for teaching posts. The government's refusal to utilize the skill and service offered by *kursistki* illustrates one of the most tragic flaws of Russian autocracy: its inability to distinguish friend from foe. Such myopic vision would have grave consequences: it exacerbated the social tensions and polarities of Imperial Russia and, by the early twentieth century, alienated virtually all elements of society from the autocratic regime.

# Notes

ARCHIVAL REFERENCES

LGIA        Leningradskii gosudarstvennyi istoricheskii arkhiv
TSGIAL      Tsentral'nyi gosudarstvennyi istoricheskii arkhiv SSSR (Leningrad)
d.          *delo* (item)
f.          *fond* (record group)
l.          *list* (page)
ll.         *listy* (pages)
ob.         *oborotnaia storona* (reverse side of page)
o.          *opis'* (inventory)

OTHER SOURCES

*Istoricheskaia zapiska*   *Istoricheskaia zapiska k dokladu Vysochaishe uchrezhden-*
*Isakova*                  *noi komissii po voprosu o zhenskikh vrachebnykh kur-*
                           *sakh, meditsinskom obrazovanii i pravakh meditsinskoi*
                           *praktiki zhenshchin.* N.p., n.d. Materials of Isakov
                           Commission. St Petersburg, 1878–9.
*Istoricheskii obzor*      *Istoricheskii obzor pravitel'stvennykh rasporiazhenii po*
VVOZH                      *voprosu o vysshem vrachebnom obrazovanii zhenshchin.*
                           St Petersburg, 1883.
MNP                        Ministerstvo Narodnago Prosveshcheniia
*Sbornik postanovlenii*    *Sbornik postanovlenii po Ministerstvu Narodnago*
                           *Prosveshcheniia.* 17 vols. St Petersburg, 1864–1904.
*Sbornik rasporiazhenii*   *Sbornik rasporiazhenii po Ministerstvu Narodnago Pros-*
                           *veshcheniia.* 17 vols. St Petersburg, 1866–1905.
SPBVZhK, *1878–1903*       *S-Peterburgskie Vysshie Zhenskie Kursy za 25 let, 1878–*
                           *1903. Ocherki i materialy.* Ed. Komitet Obshchestva

dlia dostavleniia sredstv vysshim zhenskim kursam v
S-Peterburge. St Petersburg, 1903.

| | |
|---|---|
| *Trudy ZhO* | *Trudy Vysochaishe uchrezhdennoi komissii po voprosu o zhenskom obrazovanii.* St Petersburg, 1879. |
| *Zamechaniia* | *Zamechaniia na proekt obshchago ustava Imperatorskikh Rossiiskikh universitetov.* 2 parts. St Petersburg, 1862. |
| ZhMNP | *Zhurnal Ministerstva Narodnago Prosveshcheniia* |

### INTRODUCTION

1 *Volos dolog, da um korotok.* As quoted in V. Dal', *Poslovitsy russkogo naroda. Sbornik* (Moscow, 1957), 350. This collection was originally published in 1862.

2 As quoted in V. Binshtok, "Iz istorii zhenskago obrazovaniia v Rossii," part 1, *Obrazovanie*, 5 (October 1896): 51.

3 For the following figures, see E.D. Dneprov, "Zhenskoe obrazovanie v doreformennoi Rossii," in E.P. Fedosova, *Bestuzhevskie kursy – pervyi zhenskii universitet v Rossii (1878–1918 gg.),* ed. E.D. Dnepov (Moscow, 1980), 7, 14.

4 When first established by Catherine II in 1764, the institute's program was twelve years. It was shortened to nine years during Paul's reign, and reduced to six years by the mid-nineteenth century. Useful accounts of the institute include: J.L. Black, *Citizens for the Fatherland. Education, Educators, and Pedagogical Ideals in Eighteenth Century Russia* (Boulder, Colorado, 1979), 152–71, passim; S.S. Shashkov, *Istoriia russkoi zhenshchiny,* 2nd ed. (St Petersburg, 1879), 224–7; and V. Ia. Stoiunin, "Obrazovanie russkoi zhenshchiny (Po povodu dvadtsatipiatiletiia russkikh zhenskikh gimnazii)," *Istoricheskii vestnik,* 12 (April 1883): 125–35, passim.

5 *Zhenskoe pravo. Svod uzakonenii i postanovlenii otnosiashchikhsia do zhenskago pola* (St Petersburg, 1873), 110.

6 *Zhenshchina v prave. S prilozheniem vsekh postanovlenii deistvuiushchago zakonogatel'stva, otnosiashchikhsia do lits zhenskago pola,* ed. Ia. A. Kantorovich [ps. Orovich] (St Petersburg, 1895), 248–9.

7 Vera N. Figner, *Memoirs of a Revolutionist,* trans. Camilla Chapin Daniels and R.G. Davidson, ed. Alexander Kaun (New York, 1968), 27–9. For similar recollections by other *institutki,* see M. Dol---eva [Dolgomosteva], "Institutki," *Epokha* (October 1864): 1–40; and A. Lazareva, "Vospominaniia vospitannitsy Patrioticheskago instituta doreformennago vremeni," *Russkaia starina,* 8 (August 1914): 229–48.

8 Elizaveta N. Vodovozova, *Na zare zhizni i drugie vospominaniia,* 2 vols, ed. V.P. Koz'min (Moscow and Leningrad, 1934), 1: 457.

9 Nikolai Gogol, *Dead Souls,* trans. and intro. David Magarshack (New York, 1961), 36. When Gogol first published the novel in Moscow in 1842, the

censors compelled him to expand the title to *The Adventures of Chichikov, or Dead Souls* (*Pokhozhdeniia Chichikova, ili Mertvye dushi*).

10 N.I. Pirogov, "Voprosy zhizni," in *N.I. Pirogov. Izbrannye pedagogicheskie sochineniia*, ed. V.Z. Smirnov (Moscow, 1952), 81–2. "Questions of Life" was originally published in July 1856.

11 As quoted in *The Woman Question in Europe. A Series of Original Essays*, ed. Theodore Stanton (New York, 1884), 422, editorial note.

12 Figner, *Memoirs*, 29–30.

13 In Moscow alone, the courses of V.I. Guerrier (Ger'e) admitted 1232 women between 1872 and 1886. See L.A. Bobrova, "Vysshie zhenskie kursy professora Ger'e v Moskve, 1872–1888 gg.," in *Trudy Moskovskogo gosudarstvennogo istoriko-arkhivnogo instituta*, vol. 16, ed. S.O. Schmidt (Moscow, 1961), 266.

14 For Russia, see TSGIAL, f. 846 (Georgievskii), o. 1, d. 119, l. 89. For England and Europe, see Millicent Garrett Fawcett, "Women in Medicine," in *Woman Question in Europe*, 63–89; and Melina Lipinska, *Les femmes et le progrès des sciences médicales* (Paris, 1930), 165–76, 194–205.

15 For correspondence and contacts with foreign feminists, see O.K. Bulanova-Trubnikova, *Tri pokoleniia* (Moscow and Leningrad, 1928), 97–103; V. Cherkesova, "Mariia Vasil'evna Trubnikova," *Zhenskoe delo*, 1 (December 1899): 24, 30–3; E. Likhacheva, *Materialy dlia istorii zhenskago obrazovaniia v Rossii, 1856–1880* (St Petersburg, 1901), 507–10; and Vladimir V. Stasov, *Nadezhda Vasil'evna Stasova. Vospominanii i Ocherki* (St Petersburg, 1899), 189–234.

16 For example, *Sankt-Peterburgskie vysshie zhenskie (Bestuzhevskie) kursy (1878–1918 gg.)*. Sbornik statei, 2nd ed., ed. S.N. Valk et al. (Leningrad, 1973), 3, describes the Bestuzhevskie Courses as "a sensitive barometer which responded to all social-revolutionary events in Russia."

17 Richard Stites has produced the most comprehensive study of the Russian women's movement: *The Women's Liberation Movement in Russia. Feminism, Nihilism, and Bolshevism, 1860–1930* (Princeton, NJ, 1978). The broad scope of this work, however, has allowed Stites to devote little space to women's education. Barbara Alpern Engel, *Mothers and Daughters. Women of the Intelligentsia in Nineteenth-Century Russia* (Cambridge, England, 1983), focuses on the evolution of women's consciousness and the social forces that promoted women's increasing participation in the radical movement. Women's struggle for political rights in the early twentieth century dominates the following studies: Linda Harriet Edmondson, *Feminism in Russia, 1900–1917* (Stanford, 1984); and Rochelle Lois Goldberg, "The Russian Women's Movement: 1859–1917" (PH D dissertation, University of Rochester, 1976). Ruth A. Dudgeon, "Women and Higher Education in Russia, 1855–1905" (PH D dissertation, George Washington University, 1975), and "The Forgotten Minority: Women Students in Imperial Russia, 1872–1917," *Russian History*, 9

(1982): 1–26, carefully charts the development of women's higher educational facilities and provides a detailed analysis of enrolment statistics in the early twentieth century.

18 N.A. Nekrasov, "Frost, the Red Nose" (1862–3), as quoted in Dorothy Atkinson, "Society and the Sexes in the Russian Past," in *Women in Russia*, ed. Dorothy Atkinson, Alexander Dallin, and Gail Warshofsky Lapidus (Stanford, 1977), 27, n. 76.

### CHAPTER ONE

1 S.M. Solov'ev, *Zapiski Sergeia Mikhailovicha Solov'eva. Moi zapiski dlia detei moikh, i esli mozhno, i dlia drugikh* (St Petersburg, n.d.), 172. F.I. Tiutchev coined the term "thaw" for the period immediately following the death of Nicholas I. See V.S. Aksakova, *Dnevnik Very Sergeevny Aksakovoi, 1854–1855*, ed. and intro. N.V. Golitsyn and P.E. Shchegolev (St Petersburg, 1913), and Peter Thiergen, *Wilhelm Heinrich Riehl in Russland (1856–1886). Studien zur russischen Publizistik und Geistesgeschichte der zweiten Hälfte des 19. Jahrhunderts* (Giessen, 1978), 28.

2 As quoted in K.A. Timiriazev, "Probuzhdenie estestvoznaniia v tret'ei chetverti veka," in *Istoriia Rossii v XIX veke*, vol. 7 (St Petersburg, 1909), 2. *Nauka*, although often translated as science, encompasses all branches of learning, including the humanities. A comparable term is the German *wissenschaft*.

Recent studies that influenced my interpretation of educational reform under Alexander II are: Patrick L. Alston, *Education and the State in Tsarist Russia* (Stanford, 1969); R.G. Eimontova, "Universitetskaia reforma 1863 g.," *Istoricheskie zapiski*, 70 (1961): 163–96, and "Universitetskii vopros i russkaia obshchestvennost' v 50-60-kh godakh XIX v., *Istoriia SSSR*, 6 (1971): 144–58; Allen Sinel, *The Classroom and the Chancellery: State Educational Reform in Russia under Count Dmitry Tolstoi* (Cambridge, MA, 1973); and Alexander Vucinich, *Science in Russian Culture, 1861–1917* (Stanford, 1970). Likhacheva, *Materialy*, remains the most comprehensive and reliable study of women's education in nineteenth-century Russia.

Useful studies on the nature and workings of autocratic government include: Daniel Field, *The End of Serfdom: Nobility and Bureaucracy in Russia, 1855–1861* (Cambridge, MA, 1976); Marc Raeff, *Plans for Political Reform in Imperial Russia, 1730–1905* (Englewood Cliffs, NJ, 1966); Alfred J. Rieber, ed., *The Politics of Autocracy. Letters of Alexander II to Prince A.I. Bariatinskii, 1857–1864* (Paris and The Hague, 1966); Alfred J. Rieber, "Alexander II: A Revisionist View," *Journal of Modern History*, 43, no. 2 (March 1971): 42–58; S. Frederick Starr, *Decentralization and Self-Government in Russia, 1830–1870* (Princeton, NJ, 1972); George L. Yaney, *The Systematization of Russian Government: Social Evolution in the Domestic Administration of*

*Imperial Russia, 1711–1905* (Urbana, Chicago, and London, 1973); and P.A. Zaionchkovskii, *Rossiiskoe samoderzhavie v kontse* XIX *stoletiia* (Moscow, 1970).

3  Alston, *Education and the State*, 43–4; Sinel, *The Classroom and the Chancellery*, 24; and Vucinich, *Science in Russian Culture*, 35–7.

4  Although educational reform is not discussed by Terence Emmons, *The Russian Landed Gentry and the Peasant Emancipation of 1861* (Cambridge, England, 1968), or by Charles A. Ruud, "Censorship and the Peasant Question: The Contingencies of Reform Under Alexander II (1855–1859)," *California Slavic Studies*, 5 (Berkeley, Los Angeles, and London, 1970): 137–67, both historians agree that the exigencies of peasant reform prompted Alexander II to make conciliatory gestures to various interests outside the government and to invite their participation, however temporary, in the reform effort.

5  Charles A. Ruud, *Fighting Words: Imperial Censorship and the Russian Press, 1804–1906* (Toronto, 1982), 99.

6  Pirogov, "Voprosy zhizni," 81–2.

7  For Pirogov's views on the wartime activities of Russian nurses, see N.I. Pirogov, "Pis'mo k baronesse Raden," in Pirogov, *Izbrannye pedagogicheskie sochineniia*, 548–69. A useful secondary account is: John Shelton Curtiss, "Russian Sisters of Mercy in the Crimea, 1854–1855," *Slavic Review*, 25, no. 1 (March 1966): 84–100.

8  During his curatorship of Kiev educational district (1858–61), Pirogov significantly reduced the use of corporal punishment in the schools of the Ukraine. See Alston, *Education and the State*, 69.

9  Pirogov, "Voprosy zhizni," 83.

10  For further discussion of Ushinskii's activities during his inspectorship at Smolny, see D.D. Semenov, "Moe pervoe znakomstvo c K.D. Ushinskim," in D.D. Semenov, *Izbrannye pedagogicheskie sochineniia*, ed. N.A. Konstantinov (Moscow, 1953), 63–87; and Vodovozova, *Na zare zhizni*, 1: 534–623.

11  As quoted in *Sbornik pamiati Anny Pavlovny Filosofovoi*, 2 vols (Petrograd, 1915), vol. 1: A.V. Tyrkova, *Anna Pavlovna Filosofova i eia vremia*, 170.

12  K.D. Ushinskii, "Otchet komandirovannogo dlia osmotra zagranichnykh zhenskikh uchebnykh zavedenii kollezhskogo sovetnika K. Ushinskogo," in K.D. Ushinskii, *Izbrannye proizvedniia, prilozhenie k zhurnaly "Sovetskaia pedagogika,"* ed. V. Ia. Struminskii (Moscow and Leningrad, 1946), 179–80.

13  The following discussion is based primarily on M.L. Mikhailov, "Parizhskiia pis'ma. M.L. Mikhailova. Pis'mo v," in *Sochineniia D.I. Pisareva. Polnoe sobranie v shesti tomakh*, ed. F. Pavlenko (St Petersburg, 1894), 1: 111-16 (originally published in *Sovremennik* in 1859); and Richard Stites, "M.L. Mikhailov and the Emergence of the Woman Question in Russia," *Canadian Slavic Studies*, 3, no. 2 (Summer 1969): 178–99.

"Ukazatel' literatury zhenskago voprosa na russkom iazyke," *Severnyi vestnik*, 7 (July 1887): 1–32 (separate pagination); 8 (August 1887): 33–55, lists a total of 1785 articles and books on the woman question. For a more detailed discussion of the crystallization of social consciousness on the woman question, see Stites, *The Women's Liberation Movement in Russia*, 29–63, passim.

14 D.I. Pisarev, "Zhenskie tipy v romanakh i povestiakh Pisemskago, Turgeneva i Goncharova," in *Sochineniia D.I. Pisareva*, 1: 488 (originally published in *Russkoe slovo* in December 1861).

15 *Chto delat'?* was originally published in *Sovremennik* in March, April, and May 1863. My discussion of the novel is based on the following translation: *What Is To Be Done? Tales About New People*, trans. Benjamin R. Tucker with rev. by Ludmilla B. Turkevich, and intro. E.H. Carr (New York, 1961).

16 An informative, although somewhat laudatory, account of Chernyskevskii's life and work is Franco Venturi, *Roots of Revolution. A History of the Populist and Socialist Movements in Nineteenth Century Russia*, trans. Francis Haskell (New York, 1966), 129–86.

17 See T.A. Bogdanovich, *Liubov' liudei shestidesiatykh godov* (Leningrad, 1929), 58–63, 421–3.

18 An excerpt from the conservative newspaper, *Vest'*, no. 46 (1864), as quoted in Charles A. Moser, *Antinihilism in the Russian Novel of the 1860's* (London, The Hague, and Paris, 1964), 44.

19 "Dnevnik V.F. Odoevskogo 1859–1869 gg.," in *Literaturnoe nasledstvo*, 22–4 (1935), 211. Entry of 28 April 1866.

20 V.P. Meshcherskii, "'K delu!' Otvet russkoi zhenshchine," *Grazhdanin*, no. 31, 4 December 1872, 451.

21 Peter Gay, *The Bourgeois Experience: Victoria to Freud*, vol. 1: *Education of the Senses* (New York and Oxford, 1984), 193.

22 Excerpt from the *Richmond and Louisville Medical Journal* (January 1878), as quoted in the correspondence section of *The New England Journal of Medicine*, 295, no. 5 (29 July 1976): 296. Nancy and Julian Frieden brought this item to my attention.

23 *Ottsy i deti*, in I.S. Turgenev, *Polnoe sobranie sochinenii i pisem v dvadtsati vos'mi tomakh*, vol. 8 (Moscow and Leningrad, 1964), 258–64 (originally published in *Russkii vestnik* in March 1862). *Prestuplenie i nakazanie*, in F.M. Dostoevskii, *Sobranie sochinenii v desiati tomakh*, vol. 5 (Moscow, 1957), 382 (originally published in eight instalments in *Russkii vestnik* between January and December 1866).

24 K.A. Timiriazev, an influential scientist of the reform era, explained that the term "sixties" referred to the intellectual atmosphere of the decade following the death of Nicholas I: "The sixties, as is generally known, began in the mid-fifties ... That boundary was 18 February 1855. At that moment, it occurred to every thinking Russian that he stood at the crossroads, at the watershed of two historical epochs." See "Probuzhdenie estestvoznaniia v tret'ei chetverti veka," 1.

25  V.D. Sipovskii, "Polozhenie u nas voprosa o vysshem zhenskom obrazovanii," *Zhenskoe obrazovanie*, 1 (August 1876): 258–60.
26  E.A. Shtakenshneider [Stackenschneider], *Dnevnik i zapiski (1854–1866)*, ed. I.N. Rozanov (Moscow and Leningrad, 1934), 292.
27  E.F. Iunge, *Vospominaniia (1843–1860 gg.)* (Moscow, 1933), 479.
28  Ibid., 214–15.
29  MNP, *Sbornik postanovlenii*, vol. 3, no. 219, cols 214–16.
30  MNP, "Po povodu novago universitetskskago ustava (Iz *Zhurnala Ministerstva Narodnago Prosveshcheniia*, avgust, 1863 goda)" in MNP, *Universitetskii ustav 1863 goda* (St Petersburg, 1863), 89.
31  See the memoirs of a contemporary student: L.F. Panteleev, *Iz vospominanii proshlago* (St Petersburg, 1905), 133.
32  Eimontova, "Universitetskii vopros," 147.
33  Panteleev, *Iz vospominanii proshlago*, 135; Likhacheva, *Materialy*, 468; and SPBVZhK, *1878–1903*, 9–10.
34  Iunge, *Vospominaniia*, 216.
35  M. Mikhailov, "Zhenshchiny v universitete," *Sovremennik*, 86 (1861): 505–6.
36  Shchepkina, *Iz istorii zhenskoi lichnosti*, 288.
37  S.M. Dionesov, "Russkie tsiurikhskie studentki (Iz istorii vrachebnogo obrazovaniia russkikh zhenshchin)," *Sovetskoe zdravookhranenie*, 30 (May 1971): 68; and *Istoricheskii obzor* VVOZh, 8–9.
38  M.K. Korbut, *Kazanskii gosudarstvennyi universitet imeni V.I. Ul'ianova-Lenina za 125 let (1804/5–1929/30)*, 2 vols (Kazan, 1930), makes no reference to women in Kazan University during this period.
39  Shchepkina, *Iz istorii zhenskoi lichnosti*, 288.
40  Mikhail Lemke, "Molodost' Ottsa Mitrofana," *Byloe*, 1, no. 13 (January 1907): 202.
41  Suslova's father, a former serf of Count Sheremet'ev in Nizhninovgorod guberniia, proved unusually enterprising. By the time she was twelve, her father had acquired sufficient wealth to leave the countryside and resettle his family in the city, first in Moscow and subsequently in St Petersburg. Unlike most peasants who scoffed at educating girls, Suslova's parents encouraged her academic pursuits, including the study of French, German, English, and Latin. See M.S. Belkin, "Russkie zhenshchiny-vrachi – pionery vysshego zhenskogo meditsinskogo obrazovaniia," *Sovetskii vrachebnyi sbornik*, 14 (1949): 30.
42  I.M. Sechenov, *Autobiographical Notes*, ed. Donald B. Lindsley, trans. Kristan Hanes (Washington, DC, 1965), 103–4, 123.
43  As quoted in Vucinich, *Science in Russian Culture*, 35.
44  William L. Mathes, "The Origins of Confrontation Politics in Russian Universities: Student Activism: 1855–1861," *Canadian Slavic Studies*, 2, no. 1 (Spring 1968): 28–45, provides a detailed analysis of student activism, particularly in St Petersburg and Moscow. For the discussion of higher educa-

tional institutions as incubators of Russian radicalism, see Alain Besançon, *Éducation et société en Russie dans le second tiers du XIXᵉ siècle* (Paris and The Hague, 1974); and Daniel R. Brower, *Training the Nihilists. Education and Radicalism in Tsarist Russia* (Ithaca and London, 1975).

45 Eimontova, "Universitetskaia reforma," 166.

46 Mathes, "The Origins of Confrontation Politics," 38. *Istoriia Moskovskogo universiteta v dvukh tomakh, 1755–1955*, ed. M.N. Tikhomirov et al. (Moscow, 1955), 1: 243, n. 2 reports that two-thirds of Moscow University students were exempt from fee payments in 1859; Alston, *Education and the State*, 48, cites the same percentage of fee exemptions at St Petersburg University; and Eimontova, "Universitetskaia reforma," 167, n. 11, reports that approximately one-third of the St Petersburg students and one-half of the student body of St Vladimir University paid no fees during the period, 1859–61.

47 Mathes, "The Origins of Confrontation Politics," 39–42.

48 A.V. Nikitenko, *Dnevnik v trekh tomakh*, ed. N.L. Brodskii et al. (Moscow, 1955), 2: 213.

49 A.M. Skabichevskii, *Literaturnye vospominaniia*, ed. and intro. B. Koz'min (Moscow, 1928), 338, n. 38.

50 Mathes, "The Origins of Confrontation Politics," 41; V.D. Spasovich, "Vospominaniia o K.D. Kaveline," in *Sobranie sochinenii K.D. Kavelina*, vol. 2, ed. N. Glagolev (St Petersburg, 1900), xxii. For Kavelin's criticism of Putiatin's methods and his recommendations for restoring order to St Petersburg University, see K.D. Kavelin, "Zapiska o bezporiadkakh v s-peterburgskom universitete, osen'iu 1861 goda," in *Sobranie sochinenii K.D. Kaveline*, 2, cols 1191–1206.

51 For further discussion of the professoriate's views on *nauka* and the role of the university, see I.N. Borozdin, "Universitety v epokhu 60-kh godov," in *Istoriia Rossii v XIX veke*, vol. 4 (St Petersburg, 1907), 185–212; G.A. Dzhanshiev, *Epokha velikikh reform: istoricheskiia spravki*, 2nd ed. (St Petersburg, 1907), 266–71; and Eimontova, "Universitetskii vopros," 144–58. Two recent Western studies have contributed significantly to research on the academic intelligentsia. James C. McClelland, *Autocrats and Academics: Education, Culture, and Society in Tsarist Russia* (Chicago and London, 1979), emphasizes that the professoriate's demand for autonomous *nauka* contributed to the neglect of vocational education, thereby perpetuating social disparity and economic underdevelopment in tsarist Russia. Samuel David Kassow, "The Russian University in Crisis: 1899–1911" (PH D dissertation, Princeton University, 1976), focuses on the tumultuous period beyond the scope of my study. His dissertation provides a detailed and sympathetic analysis of liberal professors who were caught between the radicalism of students and intellectuals, on the one hand, and the repressive policies of the autocratic regime, on the other.

52 McClelland, *Autocrats and Academics*, 61.

53 Eimontova, "Universitetskaia reforma," 167–8.

54 MNP, *Zamechaniia*, part 2, 520–7.

55 The exception is the judicial faculty of St Vladimir's University, which approved only the admission of female auditors. To grant a woman a degree in law, the faculty pointed out, would be "superfluous" because Russian women were denied almost all rights conferred by such degrees. See ibid., part 2, 525.

56 Ibid., part 2, 520–1.

57 Ibid., part 2, 522.

58 *Universitetskii ustav 1863 goda*, 16–17, 28.

59 MNP, *Sbornik rasporiazhenii*, vol. 3, no. 577 (20 July 1863), cols 560–6. According to the report of the State Council, the prohibition of women did not demand special mention in the statute, but appertained to the administrative regulations to be issued by the Ministry of Education. See "Mnenie gosudarstvennago soveta" in TSGIAL, f. 733, o. 147, d. 195, ll. 28–9.

Eimontova, "Universitetskaia reforma," 175–9, convincingly argues that the implementation of these restrictions through a ministerial circular was a tactical manoeuvre designed to create the impression that these restrictions emanated not from the central authorities, but from the university councils.

60 "Pravila i Instruktsii, sostavleniia sovetami universitetov: S-Peterburgskago, Kazanskago, Khar'kovskago i sv. Vladimira i utverzhdeniia popechiteliami, na osnovanii universitetskago ustava 1863 goda," *zhMNP*, 120 (October–December 1863): 3, 14, 36, 59.

61 The following examples of the tardiness of Western universities to admit women are found in Gay, *The Bourgeois Experience*, 1: 182–3.

62 The following discussion of the provisions of the University Statute is based on *Universitetskii ustav 1863 goda*, 12, 14–18.

63 Alston, *Education and the State*, 55.

64 The analysis of zemstvo tactics by N.M. Pirumova, *Zemskoe liberal'noe dvizhenie. Sotsial'nye korni i evoliutsiia do nachala xx veka* (Moscow, 1977), 175–82, reveals that the address was the "favourite legal form" by which the zemstvo tried to influence the government, and that the majority of appeals concerned "small" questions and local issues. The reluctance of zemstvo deputies to adopt an openly oppositionalist stance vis-à-vis the government is emphasized in the following: Roberta Thompson Manning, *The Crisis of the Old Order in Russia: Gentry and Government* (Princeton, NJ, 1982), and "The Zemstvo and Politics, 1864–1914," in *The Zemstvo in Russia. An Experiment in Local Self-Government*, ed. Terence Emmons and Wayne S. Vucinich (Cambridge, MA, 1982), 133–75; and Starr, *Decentralization and Self-Government*.

Recent research contradicts the earlier thesis of George Fischer, *Russian Liberalism: From Gentry to Intelligentsia* (Cambridge, MA, 1958), which

argued that the "third element," the various specialists employed by the zemstvo, played an increasingly dominant oppositional role in zemstvo activities
during the late nineteenth century. Pirumova, *Zemskoe liberal'noe dvizhenie*,
provides a detailed analysis of the composition and leadership of the zemstvo
that demonstrates that gentry landowners dominated zemstvo liberalism
throughout the nineteenth century; Manning, *The Crisis of the Old Order*,
forcefully argues that the gentry leadership of the zemstvo attempted to use the
new institutions to recoup the influence of provincial landowners that had
been on the decline since the early nineteenth century; Nancy Mandelker Frieden, *Russian Physicians in an Era of Reform and Revolution, 1856–1905*
(Princeton, NJ, 1981), shows that zemstvo physicians, a significant component
of the "third element," were on the whole preoccupied with professional rather
than political goals; Robert E. Johnson, "Liberal Professionals and Professional Liberals: The Zemstvo Statisticians and Their Work," in *The Zemstvo
in Russia*, 343–63, draws a similar conclusion concerning zemstvo statisticians.
65 Starr, *Decentralization and Self-Government*, 301.
66 "Mnenie P.A. Dubovitskago otnositel'no vvedeniia v Rossii zvaniia samos-
toiatel'nykh vrachei zhenshchin" in TSGIAL, f. 1294, o. 6, d. 48, l. 5; l. 7.
67 *Iubileinyi sbornik imperatorskii voenno-meditsinskoi akademii*, ed. A. Ia.
Danilevskii and A.A. Likhachev (St Petersburg, 1902), 30.
68 Likhacheva, *Materialy*, 479.
69 For Kashevarova's medical training and practice, see Belkin, "Russkie
zhenshchiny-vrachi," 34–45; and V.P. Leikina-Svirskaia, *Intelligentsia v Rossii
vo vtoroi polovine XIX veke* (Moscow, 1971), 138–9. Further details concerning her personal life are found in Jeanette E. Tuve, *The First Russian Women
Physicians*, ORP Russian Biography Series, vol. 6 (Newtonville, MA, 1984),
46–56.
70 Sechenov, *Autobiographical Notes*, 117.
71 Geroid Tanquary Robinson, *Rural Russia Under the Old Regime: A History of
the Landlord-Peasant World and a Prologue to the Peasant Revolution of
1917* (Berkeley and Los Angeles, 1969), 129–37. Originally published in New
York in 1932, Robinson's book remains one of the best Western studies on
the economic crisis of the gentry during the post-emancipation period.
Manning, *The Crisis of the Old Order*, 1–24, provides a detailed analysis of
the increasing impoverishment of the landowning gentry throughout the
nineteenth and early twentieth century.
72 Ekaterina Nekrasova, "Zhenskie vrachebnye kursy v Peterburge. Iz vospominanii i perepiski pervykh studentok," *Vestnik evropy*, 17 (December 1882):
808.
73 In an appeal for a women's university, the contemporary press emphasized
that social propriety as well as the fragile physiognomy of gentry women
rendered them unfit for manual labour. See "Zhenskii universitet," *Otechestvennye zapiski*, 171 (December 1868): 369.

74 For the issues, other than women's medical education, that divided Miliutin and Tolstoi, see Alston, *Education and the State*, 92–5; D.A. Miliutin, *Dnevnik D.A. Miliutina*, 4 vols, ed. P.A. Zaionchkovskii (Moscow, 1947-50), 1: 55, 98, 107–9, 144–5, 171, 197–203; James Cobb Mills, Jr, "Dmitrii Tolstoi as Minister of Education in Russia, 1866–1880" (PH D dissertation, Indiana University, 1967), 64, 176; and Sinel, *The Classroom and the Chancellery*, 79-84, 147–9.

75 Raeff, *Plans for Political Reform*, 15–16; and Rieber, *The Politics of Autocracy*, 39–40, 55, 65, 94–6. Yaney, *The Systematization of Russian Government*, 299, suggests that Alexander II deliberately appointed ministers of opposing views to constrain one another. This interpretation is emphasized in the more recent study by Daniel T. Orlovsky, *The Limits of Reform: The Ministry of Internal Affairs in Imperial Russia, 1802–1881* (Cambridge, MA, 1981), 12.

76 Sinel, *The Classroom and the Chancellery*, 148–50.

CHAPTER TWO

1 Ekaterina Nekrasova, "Pervye zhenskie kursy v Moskve, izvestnye pod imenem Lubianskikh," *Otechestvennye zapiski*, 251 (July 1880): 5–6.

2 Suslova was the first accorded this privilege. By 1869, only eight Russian women, including Bokova, attended Zurich University. See the appendix in J.M. Meijer, *Knowledge and Revolution. The Russian Colony at Zurich (1870–1873). A Contribution to the Study of Russian Populism* (Assen, Netherlands, 1955), 208–12.

3 The term "flying universities" is quoted by Fedosova, *Bestuzhevskie kursy*, 35; and G.A. Tishkin, "Zhenskii vopros i pravitel'stvennaia politika 60-70-kh godov XIX v.," in *Voprosy istorii Rossii XIX-nachala XX veka* (Leningrad, 1983), 165.

4 Nekrasova, "Pervye zhenskie kursy," 3–4.

5 Useful studies of girls' secondary schools under the jurisdiction of the Ministry of Education and the Fourth Department during this period are: Dneprov, *Zhenskoe obrazovanie*, 13–24; Likhacheva, *Materialy*, 1–250, passim; S.V. Rozhdestvenskii, *Istoricheskii obzor deiatel'nosti Ministerstva Narodnago Prosveshcheniia, 1802–1902* (St Petersburg, 1902), 371–5, 456–9, 566–70; Stoiunin, "Obrazovanie russkoi zhenshchiny," 135–53; and S.S. Tatishchev, *Imperator Aleksandr II: ego zhizn' i tsarstvovanie*, 2 vols (St Petersburg, 1903), 2: 235, 239, 284–8.

6 Likhacheva, *Materialy*, 212.

7 Sophie Kropotkin, "The Higher Education of Women in Russia," *The Living Age*, 26 February 1898, 604.

8 Ministerial regulations governing the new schools stipulated their establishment in those towns that could maintain them by local funding and private contribu-

tions. See "O polozhenie o zhenskikh uchilishchakh vedomstva Ministerstva Narodnago Prosveshcheniia," *Sbornik postanovlenii*, vol. 3, no. 148 (30 May 1858), col. 314.

9   For the academic program and regulations, see ibid., cols 310–18; "O novom polozhenie o zhenskikh uchebnykh zavedeniiakh vedomstva Ministerstva Narodnago Prosveshcheniia," *Sbornik postanovlenii*, vol. 3, no. 268 (10 May 1860), cols 574–80; and "Tsirkuliarnoe predlozhenie po dely ob ustroistve zhenskikh uchilishch," *Sbornik rasporiazhenii*, vol. 3, no. 639 (March 1864), cols 687–9.

10  Rozhdestvenskii, *Istoricheskii obzor*, 567.

11  P.A. Zaionchkovskii, *Krizis samoderzhaviia na rubezhe 1870–1880-kh godov* (Moscow, 1964), 216.

12  Phrases used by Isaiah Berlin in reference to the views of author Leo Tolstoi. See Isaiah Berlin, *Russian Thinkers*, ed. Henry Hardy and Aileen Kelly (New York, 1979), 238.

13  Sinel, *The Classroom and the Chancellery*, 258.

14  Stoiunin, "Obrazovanie russkoi zhenshchiny," 149.

15  The remaining 17 percent came from various unspecified sources. See Dneprov, "Zhenskoe obrazovanie," 19.

16  Likhacheva, *Materialy*, 33–41.

17  Dneprov, "Zhenskoe obrazovanie," 22, 23.

18  Likhacheva, *Materialy*, 7–14.

19  "O polozhenie o zhenskikh uchilishchakh vedomstva Ministerstva Narodnago Prosveshcheniia," col. 315.

20  As quoted in Mills, "Dmitrii Tolstoi," 64.

21  "Po povodu zhenskago adresa podannago g. Ministru Narodnago Prosveshcheniia v Khar'kove," *zhMNP*, 149 (October 1870): 273.

22  For Katkov's influence on educational policy, see Martin Katz, *Mikhail N. Katkov: A Political Biography, 1818–1887* (The Hague, 1966), 37, 143–55, 168–9; Miliutin, *Dnevnik*, 1: 108; Mills, "Dmitrii Tolstoi," 61–2, 70–1; and Zaionchkovskii, *Rossiskoe samoderzhavie*, 66–74, 310–11. For discussion of the relationship between Tolstoi and the Moscow editor by an ardent admirer of Katkov, see E.M. Feoktistov, *Vospominaniia E.M. Feoktistova za kulisami politiki i literatury, 1848–1896*, ed. Iu. G. Oksman (Leningrad, 1929), 173–81.

23  For Katkov's views on women's education, see the numerous articles from *Moskovskie vedomosti* collected in M.N. Katkov, *O zhenskom obrazovanii. Stat'i sviazannyia s voznikoveniam i postepennym rostom Zhenskoi Klassicheskoi Gimnazii* (Moscow, 1897). For the quotation, see 61.

24  As quoted in Zaionchkovskii, *Rossiskoe samoderzhavie*, 311.

25  For a lively secondary account of Shuvalov's personality and politics, see Forrestt A. Miller, *Dmitrii Miliutin and the Reform Era in Russia* (Charlotte, NC, 1968), 172–7.

26 Ibid., 180, dismisses Timashev as "one of Shuvalov's creatures." No more flattering is the biographical sketch of Timashev by Orlovsky, *The Limits of Reform*, 84–93.

27 Stasov, *Nadezhda Vasil'evna Stasova*, 161–9.

28 Likhacheva, *Materialy*, 495–7.

29 The following discussion of Stasova's personal life is based on the biography by her brother: Stasov, *Nadezhda Vasil'evna Stasova*, 25–64. This book also provides much detail concerning the triumvirate's philanthropic activities and efforts to organize advanced educational facilities for women.

30 Goldberg, "The Russian Women's Movement," 38; Bulanova-Trubnikova, *Tri pokoleniia*, 97.

31 *Sbornik pamiati Anny Pavlovny Filosofovoi*, 1: 123–4.

32 Stasov, *Nadezhda Vasil'evna Stasova*, 120–3.

33 A.F. Koni, "Pamiati A.P. Filosofovoi," in *Sbornik pamiati Anny Pavlovny Filosofovoi*. Vol. 2: *Stat'i i materialy*, 4–5; vol. 1: 181.

34 Bulanova-Trubnikova, *Tri pokoleniia*, 155.

35 These conciliatory tactics and limited goals, it should be noted, did not appeal to the radical minority of contemporary women. Stites, *The Women's Liberation Movement in Russia*, clearly demonstrates that from the 1860s up to the Bolshevik Revolution of 1917, there were two separate women's movements: moderate feminism, which gave rise to the women's suffrage movement after 1905, and the socialist movement, which included such diverse individuals as the terrorist Sofiia Perovskaia and Bolshevik feminist Aleksandra Kollontai. Goldberg, "The Russian Women's Movement," which focuses on the struggle for women's political rights in the years 1905–17, also distinguishes between the socialist and non-socialist contingents of women's rights activists. Engel, *Mothers and Daughters*, 60–1, emphasizes that moderate feminist leaders deliberately excluded radical women in order to avoid antagonizing the authorities.

36 St Petersburg Women to K.F. Kessler (11 May 1868) in LGIA, f. 14, o. 1, d. 6623, ll. 17–32; ibid., l. 17.

37 Ibid. (13 May 1868), ll. 10–11.

38 Smolensk Women to K.F. Kessler (23 June 1868), ibid., ll. 4–9.

39 "V Sovete S-Peterburgskago universiteta: Komissii, naznachennoe Sovetom, dlia razsmotreniia zaiavleniia ot lits zhenskago pola kasatel'no uchrezhdeniia dlia nikh Kursov" (31 May 1868) in LGIA, f. 14, o. 1, d. 6623, ll. 2–3, 33–4; K.F. Kessler to M.V. Trubnikova (draft) (June 1868), ibid., l. 36; Stasov, *Nadezhda Vasil'evna Stasova*, 177–8, and 182–3 for a first-hand account of this meeting.

40 Stasov, *Nadezhda Vasil'evna Stasova*, 182, 183.

41 Nikitenko, *Dnevnik*, 3: 136.

42 D.A. Tolstoi to A.P. Filosofova (21 December 1868) in TSGIAL, f. 733, o. 191, d. 124, ll. 7–9.

43  Stasov, *Nadezhda Vasil'evna Stasova*, 237–9; and *SPBVZhK*, *1878–1903*, 38.

44  Alston, *Education and the State*, 83.

45  Miliutin, *Dnevnik*, 1: 37.

46  *SPBVZhK*, *1878–1903*, 39–40.

47  Cynthia H. Whittaker, "The Women's Movement during the Reign of Alexander II: A Case Study in Russian Liberalism," *Journal of Modern History*, 48, no. 2 (June 1976): 53.

48  P.A. Shuvalov to D.A. Tolstoi (16 June 1869) in TSGIAL, f. 733, o. 191, d. 124, ll. 44–8.

49  Sinel, *The Classroom and the Chancellery*, 87.

50  N.V. Mezentsov to D.A. Tolstoi (10 October 1869) in TSGIAL, f. 733, o. 191, d. 124, ll. 54–5; D.A. Tolstoi to P.A. Shuvalov (2 June 1869), ibid., ll. 42–3.

51  P.I. Liven to D.A. Tolstoi (26 May 1869), ibid., ll. 37–9. This letter names I.I. Mechnikov as the prospective teacher of zoology. Mechnikov's recent application for a position in St Petersburg's Medical-Surgical Academy, however, was rejected. Consequently, the zoologist taught at Odessa University during the period 1870–82. *SPBVZhK*, *1878–1903*, 41, reports that Wagner taught zoology in the public lectures.

52  Likhacheva, *Materialy*, 520, 593–4; M.L. Peskovskii, "Ocherk istorii vysshago zhenskago obrazovaniia v Rossii za 20 let," part I, *Nabliudatel'*, I (April 1882): 88–9; and *SPBVZhK*, *1878–1903*, 41–3.

53  Likhacheva, *Materialy*, 594; and *SPBVZhK*, *1878–1903*, 45.

54  "Memorandum of the Minister of Education" (3 November 1870) in TSGIAL, f. 733, o. 191, d. 124, l. 78.

55  Likhacheva, *Materialy*, 527.

56  "Zapiska o publichnikh zhenskikh kursakh chitaemikh Professorami S-Peterburgskago Universiteta" (12 March 1871) in TSGIAL, f. 733, o. 191, d. 124, ll. 87–90; ibid., l. 89, for all quotations.

57  D.A. Tolstoi to A.E. Timashev (7 April 1871), ibid., l. 91.

58  *Istoricheskaia zapiska Isakova*, 1–2.

59  "Otnositel'no dopuschcheniia zhenshchin na sluzhbu v obshchestvennyia i pravitel'stvennyia uchrezhdeniia," *Sbornik postanovlenii*, vol. 5, no. 5 (14 January 1871), cols 14–16. Published in *Pravitel'stvennyi vestnik*, 19 February 1871, 1.

60  For the top-level government debate surrounding the new gymnasium legislation, see Sinel, *The Classroom and the Chancellery*, 141–50.

61  "Memoranda of the Ministry of Education" (8 April 1872, 5 May 1873, 8 March 1875) in TSGIAL, f. 733, o. 191, d. 124, ll. 155, 222, 327.

62  Likhacheva, *Materialy*, 593.

63  See ibid., 514–15; and *SPBVZhK*, *1878–1903*, 36–7.

64  P.I. Liven to D.A. Tolstoi (4 February 1869) in TSGIAL, f. 733, o. 191, d. 124, ll. 37–9; D.A. Tolstoi to P.I. Liven (8 March 1869), ibid., ll. 6–6ob.

65 For a first-hand account of the activities of Alarchinskie women in the Chaikovskii Circle, see Aleksandra Kornilova-Moroz, "Perovskaia i osnovanie kruzhka Chaikovtsev," *Katorga i ssylka*, 22 (1926): 7–30.

66 For discussion of the family life, experiences, and personalities of women who joined the radical movement, see Engel, *Mothers and Daughters*, and her article, "From Separatism to Socialism: Women in the Russian Revolutionary Movement of the 1870s," in *Socialist Women. European Socialist Feminism in the Nineteenth and Early Twentieth Centuries*, ed. Marilyn J. Boxer and Jean H. Quataert (New York, 1978), 51–74.

67 Both Nekasova, "Pervye zhenskie kursy v Moskve," 4, and Likhacheva, *Materialy*, 515, report that a member of Moscow University Council informed local women that their petition would remain unanswered. Peskovskii, "Ocherk istorii vysshago zhenskago obrazovaniia," part 1, 81, states that the council either ignored or rejected the appeal.

68 A.N. Sheremetevskaia, "Stranitsa iz istorii vysshago zhenskago obrazovaniia," *Istoricheskii vestnik*, 65 (July 1896): 172.

69 K. Shokhol, "K voprosu o razvitii vysshago zhenskago obrazvaniia v Rossii," *ZhMNP* (New Series), 40 (August 1912): 170.

70 The inventory concerning women's courses in Moscow and St Petersburg during the period from 27 November 1868 to 2 May 1877 makes no reference to this appeal. See TSGIAL, f. 733, o. 191, d. 124.

71 For Korolev's petition, see A.P. Shirinskii-Shikhmatov to D.A. Tolstoi (14 April 1869), ibid., ll. 24–30; D.A. Tolstoi to the Main Administration of Moscow Educational Region (31 May 1869), ibid., l. 41; P.A. Shuvalov to D.A. Tolstoi (16 June 1869), ibid., ll. 47–8.

72 The following discussion, excluding detailed enrolment information, is based primarily on the accounts of two former auditors: Nekrasova, "Pervye zhenskie kursy v Moskve," 10–30; and Sheremetevskaia, "Stranitsa iz istorii," 173–84.

73 The sources consulted do not provide a complete list of all instructors throughout the existence of the courses. The most detailed information is found in "O sushchestvuiushchikh v Moskve zhenskikh kursakh" (1885) in TSGIAL, f. 733, o. 191, d. 674, ll. 38ob.–9. According to this report by the Moscow curator, only seven members of the teaching staff during the period 1878–85 came from the local university. Several docents are included in this number. The remaining thirteen instructors held positions in male vocational institutes and various secondary schools. The report also lists the family names of twenty-four others who occasionally taught the courses prior to 1878.

74 TSGIAL, f. 733, o. 191, d. 674, l. 39ob., records the following enrolment figures for the fall terms: 1870 – 181; 1871 – 158; 1872 – 138; 1873 – 120; 1874 – 118; 1875 – 116; 1876 – 120; 1877 – 95; 1878 – 86; 1879 – 111; 1880 – 126; 1881 – 107; 1882 – 120; 1883 – 110; 1884 – 117; 1885 – 150.

75 Moscow curator to minister of education (30 September 1882) in TSGIAL,
f. 733, o. 191, d. 322, l. 2080b.

76 Alston, *Education and the State*, 280, n. 48. After publication of the edicts of
July 1887, the number of persons of Jewish origin was limited to 3 percent
of the student body in both the gymnasia and universities of the capitals.

77 A large number of Jews also enrolled in the women's medical courses that
opened in St Petersburg in 1872. See chapter 5.

78 For Moscow province in the years 1881–2, 1882–3, and 1884–5, see I.P.
Bogolepov, *Gramotnost' sredi detei shkol'nago vozrasta v Moskovskom i
Mozhaiskom uezdakh Moskovskoi gubernii* (Moscow, 1894), 3. For the empire
in 1885, see A.G. Rashin, "Gramotnost' i narodnoe obrazovanie v Rossii v
XIX i nachale XX v.," *Istoricheskie zapiski*, 37 (1951): 62, table 36.

79 As quoted in Ben Eklof, "Peasant Sloth Reconsidered: Strategies of Education
and Learning in Rural Russia before the Revolution," *Journal of Social
History*, 14, no. 3 (Spring 1981): 373. The study conducted by Moscow
zemstvo reveals that most peasants considered girls' education an unnecessary
and useless expense. See Bogolepov, *Gramotnost' sredi detei shkol'nago
vozrasta*," 63–70.

80 Based on the budgetary figures for the academic years 1871–2 and 1884–5
found in Sheremetevskaia, "Stranitsa iz istorii," 180–1.

81 Nekrasova, "Pervye zhenskie kursy v Moskve," 27, points out that participation
in the meetings of the general assembly declined during the 1870s, thereby
allowing control to pass into the hands of a small number of women.

82 Based largely on Guerrier's archives in the Lenin Library, Bobrova, "Vysshie
zhenskie kursy professora Ger'e," 253–65, is indispensable to the following
discussion.

83 V. Ger'e, "Universitetskii vopros. Po povodu mnenie pr. Liubimova o
peresmotre Universitetskago Ustava, v *Rus. Vest.* 1873, fevral'," *Vestnik
evropy*, 8, no. 4 (April 1873): 818–36.

84 Sophie Satina, *The Education of Women in Pre-Revolutionary Russia*, trans.
Alexandra F. Poustchine (New York, 1966), 128.

85 Shokhol, "K voprosu o razvitii vysshago zhenskago obrazovaniia" (August
1912): 176–80.

86 "Ob ustroistve v Moskve publichnykh vysshikh zhenskikh Kursov," *Sbornik
rasporiazhenii*, vol. 5, no. 165 (6 May 1872), col. 427; ibid., col. 424.

87 Bobrova, "Vysshie zhenskie kursy professora Ger'e," 258.

88 Ibid., 256–7.

89 The following figures are given in ibid., 259–60.

90 Moscow curator to minister of education (30 September 1882) in TSGIAL, f.
733, o. 191, d. 322, l. 208.

91 Shokhol, "K voprosu o razvitii vysshago zhenskago obrazovaniia" (August
1912): 182.

121    Notes to pages 49–54

92  V. Ger'e, "Teorii i praktika zhenskago obrazovaniia," *Vestnik evropy*, 12, no.
    4 (April 1877): 645–700.
93  "Po povodu zhenskago adresa v Khar'kove," 269–74; Shokhol, "K voprosu o
    razvitii vysshago zhenskago obrazovaniia" (August 1912): 182–4; Korbut,
    *Kazanskii gosudarstvennyi universitet*, 2: 47–9.

CHAPTER THREE

 1  Vera Figner, *Zapechatlennyi trud. Vospominaniia v dvukh tomakh* (Moscow,
    1964), 1: 114.
 2  Konrad H. Jarausch, *Students, Society, and Politics in Imperial Germany. The
    Rise of Academic Illiberalism* (Princeton, NJ, 1982), 109–10.
 3  Patrick Kay Bidelman, "The Feminist Movement in France: The Formative
    Years, 1858–1889" (PH D dissertation, Michigan State University, 1975), 27.
 4  Likhacheva, *Materialy*, 490–2.
 5  The arrival and departure dates of individual Russian men and women studying
    in Zurich during the period 1864–74 are found in the appendix in Meijer,
    *Knowledge and Revolution*, 208–17.
 6  Enrolment figures for the summer of 1872, as given in Victor Bemert [Böh-
    mert], *Universitetskoe obrazovanie zhenshchin* (St Petersburg, 1973), 8–9.
 7  Meijer, *Knowledge and Revolution*, 47, 56.
 8  According to the report of the government commission investigating Russian
    women in Zurich, seven women came from the Caucasus, three from Siberia,
    and two from the Cossack hosts. See "O merakh k prekrashcheniiu priliva
    russkikh zhenshchin v Tsiurikhskii universitet i politechnikum" in TSGIAL, f.
    733, o. 191, d. 268, l. 25. The following is based on this report, ll. 25–6.
 9  P.N. Ariian, *Pervyi zhenskii kalendar' na 1899 god* (St Petersburg, 1899),
    139.
10  For further discussion of scientism in the 1860s, see Vucinich, *Science in
    Russian Culture*, 3–34, passim.
11  Meijer, *Knowledge and Revolution*, 56, 57.
12  Peter Kropotkin, *Memoirs of a Revolutionist* (Cambridge, MA, 1930), 269.
13  Meijer, *Knowledge and Revolution*, 56–7.
14  Kropotkin, *Memoirs*, 269.
15  Meijer, *Knowledge and Revolution*, 85–139, provides a detailed discussion of
    both revolutionary camps.
16  "O merakh k prekrashcheniiu priliva russkikh zhenshchin" in TSGIAL, f. 733,
    o. 191, d. 268, ll. 25–60b.
17  Sofiia Kovalevskaia, *Sonya Kovalevsky. Her Recollections of Childhood*,
    trans. Isabel F. Hapwood with a "Biography" by Anna Carlotta Leffler, trans.
    A.M. Clive Bayley (New York, 1895), 99.
18  Kantorovich, *Zhenshchina v prave*, 248–9.

19 Meijer, *Knowledge and Revolution*, 69; and, *Deiateli Revoliutsionnogo
   dvizheniia v Rossii: Bio-bibliograficheskii slovar'*. Vol. 2: *Semidesiatye gody*,
   ed. A.A. Shilovoi and M.G. Karnaukhova (Moscow, 1929), 508.
20 Her elder sister Anna had hoped that paleontologist V.O. Kovalevskii would
   become her own "fictitious" husband. Instead, he agreed to marry the eighteen-
   year-old Sofiia in 1868. The following year, Kovalevskaia began her studies
   in Germany, first in Heidelberg and later in Berlin where Karl Weierstrass
   privately supervised her work. In 1874, the German professor assisted Kovalevskaia in persuading the Dean of Göttingen's Faculty of Philosophy to
   award her a doctorate in absentia. That August, she was granted the degree of
   doctor of philosophy in mathematics, summa cum laude. Kovalevskaia's
   academic credentials, however, failed to impress Russian educational authorities who would only allow her to teach arithmetic in the lower classes of
   girls' gynmasia. In 1883, she accepted the post of private docent at Stockholm
   University. See P. Ia. Polubarinova-Kochina, *Zhizn'i deiatel'nost' S.V.
   Kovalevskoi (k 100-letiiu do dnia rozhdeniia)* (Moscow and Leningrad, 1950),
   10–23, passim.
21 N.A. Charushin, *O dalekom proshlom. Ch. I i II. Kruzhok Chaikovtsev.
   Iz vospominanii o revoliutsionnom dvizhenii 1870-kh gg.* (Moscow, 1926),
   104–6.
22 Also see Brower, *Training the Nihilists*, 25–7.
23 Ekaterina Breshko-Breshkovskaia, *The Little Grandmother of the Russian
   Revolution. Reminiscences and Letters of Catherine Breshkovsky*, ed. Alice
   Stone Blackwell (London, 1918), 28.
24 Kovalevskaia, *Sonya Kovalevsky*, 168.
25 The Fritschi Circle included the Figner sisters: Vera and Lidiia; the Liubatovich
   sisters: Vera and Olga; three Subbotina sisters: Mariia, Nadezhda, and
   Evgeniia; Betia Kaminskaia; Varvara Aleksandrova; Dora Aptekman; and
   Anna Toporkova. See Vera Figner, "Studencheskie gody," *Golos minuvshego*,
   10, no. 2 (March–April 1922): 168.
26 Meijer, *Knowledge and Revolution*, 52, uses this Kantian term in reference to
   the puritanical relations between the sexes at Zurich.
27 Vera Figner's account of the incident is quoted in ibid., 176, n. 17.
28 As quoted in Vera Broido, *Apostles into Terrorists. Women and the Revolutionary Movement in the Russia of Alexander II* (New York, 1977), 137.
29 Vera Figner, *Pol'noe sobranie sochinenii v shesti tomakh*, vol. 5 (Moscow,
   1929), 184.
30 As pointed out by Stites, *The Women's Liberation Movement in Russia*, 137,
   n. 26. See *Deiateli revoliutsionnogo dvizheniia v Rossii: Biobibliograficheskii
   slovar'*, 2. Also see the following discussion of Shuvalov's memorandum
   to Tolstoi.
31 Figner, "Studencheskie gody," 10, no. 2, 181. Italics are in the original.

32  Figner, "Studencheskie gody," *Golos minuvshego*, 11, no. 1 (January–February 1923): 39; ibid., no. 2 (March–April 1923): 139.
33  Ibid., 10, no. 2, 178.
34  As recommended by the special commission. See "O merakh k prekrashcheniiu priliva russkikh zhenshchin," 1. 26.
35  Over fifty books, articles, and items on women's education, and another ten on women and medicine, were published in Russia during the years 1870–3. See "Ukazatel' literatury zhenskago voprosa na russkom iazyke," *Severnyi vestnik*, 8 (August 1887): 36–51, passim.
36  The number of Russian women enrolled in Zurich University dropped from 102 in summer 1873 to 12 in summer 1874. See Ariian, *Pervyi zhenskii kalendar'*, 139.
37  Dionesov, "Russkie tsiurikhskie studentki," 69.
38  Ariian, *Pervyi zhenskii kalendar'*, 139; Figner, *Pol'noe sobranie sochinenii*, 5: 79; and Meijer, *Knowledge and Revolution*, 145–6.
39  Stephanie Wolicka to D.A. Tolstoi (3/15 December 1873) in TSGIAL, f. 733, o. 191, d 268, l. 45; Third Department to D.A. Tolstoi (13 December 1873), ibid., ll. 47–9; D.A. Tolstoi to heads of educational districts (22 December 1873), ibid., ll. 53–5, labelled "Confidential."
40  Figner, *Pol'noe sobranie sochinenii*, 5: 162–5.
41  Orlovsky, *The Limits of Reform*, 166–8.
42  A.L. Potapov (1874–6), N.V. Mezentsov (1876–8), and A.R. Drentel'n (1878–80).

CHAPTER FOUR

1  *Zhurnaly Vysochaishe uchrezhdennoi komissii po voprosu ob izyskanii glavneishikh osnovanii dlia luchshei postanovki zhenskago obrazovaniia v Imperii: Zasedanie 12 (14 January 1886)* in TSGIAL, f. 733, o. 191, d. 695, l. 55.
2  Useful accounts of the Delianov Commission, including quotations from its proceedings, are: *Istoricheskii obzor vvozh*, 27–42; Likhacheva, *Materialy*, 584–94; "O vydache posobiia uchrezhdennym v S-Peterburge vysshim zhenskim kursam," *Sbornik postanovlenii*, vol. 7, no. 355 (20 February 1879), cols 943–7; and *SPBVZhK, 1878–1903*, 63–71.
3  The Fourth Department delegation consisted of M.B. Chistiakov, president of the Academic Committee; I.T. Osinin, head of St Petersburg Girls' Gymnasia; V.I. Liadov, inspector of Aleksandrovskii School; and I.F. Rashevskii, inspector of Vasiliostrovskii Girls' Gymnasium. Representatives from the Ministry of Education held similar administrative positions: Georgievskii, president of the Academic Committee; V. Kh. Lemonius, director of St Petersburg's Third Gymnasium; I.M. Belliarminov, president of the Historical-

Philological Institute; and N.I. Sabinov, inspector of St Petersburg Educational District.

4 Fourth Department to Ministry of Education (14 July 1873) in TSGIAL, f. 733, o. 191, d. 268, ll. 13-15.

5 Likhacheva, *Materialy*, 585.

6 Quoted in *SPBVzhK, 1878–1903*, 64.

7 For the most detailed description of the report, see *Istoricheskii obzor vvozh*, 31–4.

8 "O vvedenii prepodavaniia Latinskago i Grecheskago iazykov i Pedagogiki v kurs zhenskikh gimnazii, kak neobliazatel'nikh predmetov dlia zhelaiushchikh," *Sbornik postanovlenii*, vol. 6, no. 91 (13 August 1874), cols 489–90.

9 Likhacheva, *Materialy*, 572–7.

10 As minister of education (1882–97), Delianov would promote considerable expansion of boys' technical and trade schools. Paul W. Johnson, "Taming Student Radicalism: The Educational Policy of I.D. Delianov," *Russian Review*, 33, no. 3 (July 1974): 259–68, reveals that Delianov's policies aimed at promoting modernization while, at the same time, curbing student radicalism.

11 McClelland, *Autocrats and Academics*, 9, emphasizes that the Russian education system "was built from the top down."

12 Literate men constituted 29.3 percent of the population; literate women, 13.1 percent. See Rashin, "Gramotnost' i narodnoe obrazovanie v Rossii," 47.

13 At the time, only 13.4 percent of the population lived in urban areas. Here, male literacy was more than double that in the countryside: 54 percent versus 25.2 percent. Literacy among urban women was more than thrice that of female peasants: 35.6 percent versus 9.8 percent. See ibid., 37, 39.

14 The following figures are found in the survey on the graduates of girls' gymnasia and unemployed women teachers that was conducted by the Ministry of Education in 1885: TSGIAL, f. 733, o. 191, d. 652, ll. 1–194. Regrettably, many provincial governors who responded to the ministerial poll provided only fragmentary information.

15 Moscow curator to Ministry of Education (2 December 1888) in TSGIAL, ibid., d. 666, l. 23–230b.

16 Likhacheva, *Materialy*, 590.

17 For excerpts from his letter (2 February 1876) protesting the report, see ibid., 590–1; and "O vydache posobiia," cols 944–6.

18 Based on the tables of income and expenditures found in *SPBVzhK, 1878–1903*, 244–7.

19 "O predostavlenii chastnoi zhenskoi klassicheskoi Gimnazii, soderzhimoi v Moskve g-zheiu Fisher, prav i preimushchestve zhenskikh gimnazii Ministerstva Narodnago Prosveshcheniia," *Sbornik postanovlenii*, vol. 6, no. 509 (19 November 1876), cols 1699–1701.

20 MNP, *Sbornik deistvuiushchikh postanovlenii i rasporiazhenii po zhenskim gimnaziiam i progimnaziiam Ministerstva Narodnago Prosveshcheniia*, ed. Mikhail Rodevich (St Petersburg, 1884), 140–2.

21 In response to the ministerial survey of 1885, the Moscow governor reported that there was no accurate information concerning the employment of Fisher's graduates, but added: "Many, having sufficient means, do not need positions." See TSGIAL, f. 733, o. 191, d. 652, l. 125ob.

22 Kiev curator to minister of education (13 September 1883), ibid., d. 322, l. 222ob.

23 The following figures are found in *Obshchestvo dlia dostavleniia sredstv vysshim zhenskim kursam (Osnovano 4-go Oktiabria 1878 g.). Otchet za 1885–1886g.* (St Petersburg, 1887), 100–2.

24 One of the St Petersburg women was enrolled in the medical courses of the northern capital. See M.L. Peskovskii, "Ocherk istorii vysshago zhenskago obrazovaniia v Rossii za 20 let," part 3, *Nabliudatel'*, 1 (June 1882): 117–18.

25 As quoted in *Sankt-Peterburgskie vysshie zhenskie (Bestuzhevskie) kursy*, 2nd ed., 10. Tsebrikova's account is confirmed by the memoirs of a former auditor: E. K---aia, "Iz nedavnikh vospominanii kursistki," *Zhenskoe obrazovanie*, 11 (November 1886): 635–40.

26 "O vozobnovlenii priema slushatel'nits na vysshie zhenskie kursy v S-Peterburge," *Sbornik postanovlenii*, vol. 11, no. 170 (25 June 1889), col. 708.

27 *SPBVZhK, 1878–1903*, 79.

28 This quotation and excerpts from the letters exchanged by the minister of education and the Kiev curator who investigated the charges are found in ibid., 79–80. For the full text of the curator's letter, see Kiev curator to minister of education (19 January 1879) in TSGIAL, f. 733, o. 191, d. 301, ll. 148–50.

29 "Zapiska dlia pamiati: Po Vysochaishemu poveleniiu" (12 March 1879) in TSGIAL, f. 733, o. 191, d. 301, ll. 169–70.

30 Of the total enrolment of 1288, more than 60 percent (793) attended the Bestuzhevskie Courses; Guerrier's Courses admitted 107; the Lubianskie Courses, 86; the Kiev Courses, 324; the Kazan Courses, 85. See *SPBVZhK, 1878–1903*, 252; Bobrova, "Vysshie zhenskie kursy professora Ger'e," 254; TSGIAL, f. 733, o. 191, d. 674, l. 390ob., and d. 322, l. 212ob., and d. 813, l. 39–390ob.

31 Secondary accounts of the Kazan Courses are few and brief: Korbut, *Kazanskii gosudarstvennyi universitet*, 2: 47–9; Likhacheva, *Materialy*, 597–8; and Shokhol, "K voprosu o razvitii vysshago zhenskago obrazovaniia" (August 1912): 182–5.

32 "Ob ustroistve v Kazani publichnykh vysshikh zhenskikh kursov," *Sbornik rasporiazhenii*, vol. 6, no. 67 (8 May 1876), cols 981–2.

33 "Chastnyia pravila dlia slushatel'nits i vol'nykh slushatel'nits publichnykh vysshikh zhenskikh kursov v g. Kazani (1878)" in TSGIAL, f. 733, o. 191, d. 322, l. 66ob.; ibid., ll. 64–5.

34 All enrolment figures are based on the confidential letter of the Kazan curator: P.N. Maslennikov to M.S. Volkonskii (12 March 1886) in TSGIAL, ibid., d. 813, ll. 39–41.

35 Kazan curator to minister of education (18 November 1883), ibid., d. 322, l. 188.

36 The following is based on "Pravila dlia slushatel'nits i vol'noslushatel'nits vysshikh zhenskikh kursov v g. Kazani (1879)," ibid., ll. 62–3. Also see "Pravila dlia slushatel'nits S-Peterburgskikh Vysshikh Zhenskikh Kursov," in *Obshchestvo dlia dostavleniia sredstv ... Otchet za 1884–1886 g.*, 137–8.

37 N.I. Sidorov, "Statisticheskie svedeniia o propagandistakh 70-kh godov v obrabotke III otdeleniia: Zapiska M.M. Merkulova o propagandistakh 70-kh godov," *Katorga i ssylka*, 38 (1928): 29–56, passim.

38 Zasulich's memoirs vividly describe the preparation and execution of this terrorist act. For the English translation, see "Vera Zasulich," in *Five Sisters: Women against the Tsar*, ed. and trans. Barbara Alpern Engel and Clifford N. Rosenthal (New York, 1977), 78–85.

39 For the trial, see Samuel Kucherov, *Courts, Lawyers and Trials under the Last Three Tsars* (New York, 1953), 214–25. For the quotation, see the excerpt from the memoirs of A.F. Koni, the president of the court at Zasulich's trial, in ibid., 220.

40 Tatishchev, *Imperator Aleksandr II*, 2: 602.

41 A.E. Timashev to D.A. Tolstoi (18 October 1878) in TSGIAL, f. 733, o. 191, d. 301, l. 89; A.R. Drentel'n to D.A. Tolstoi (28 December 1878), ibid., l. 134.

42 V.M. Friche, "Vysshaia shkola v kontse veka," in *Istoriia Rossii v XIX veke*, vol. 9 (St Petersburg, 1911), 161–2.

43 See Tatishchev, *Imperator Aleksandr II*, 2: 605–14. A succinct account of the conference's discussion of women's education is found in Zaionchkovskii, *Krizis samoderzhaviia*, 179.

44 Zaionchkovskii, *Krizis samoderzhaviia*, 179.

45 Shokhol, "K voprosu o razvitii vysshago zhenskago obrazovaniia" (March 1913): 25.

46 A.R. Drentel'n to D.A. Tolstoi (20 February 1880) in TSGIAL, f. 733, o. 191, d. 301, ll. 200–1; P.A. Antonovich to D.A. Tolstoi (19 March 1880), ibid., ll. 204–9.

47 Zaionchkovskii, *Krizis samoderzhaviia*, 179.

48 For admissions in 1878, see Kiev curator to minister of education (10 October 1878) in TSGIAL, f. 733, o. 191, d. 301, l. 87. The lowest enrolment was 308 during the academic year 1885–6. See Kiev curator to St Petersburg Department of Education (6 May 1886), ibid., d. 813, l. 87. For the academic year 1881–2, see ibid., d. 322, l. 210ob.

49 Ibid., l. 220ob.

50 *Istoricheskaia zapiska i otchet o Kievskikh vysshikh zhenskikh kursakh za pervoe chetyrekhletie (1878–1882)* (Kiev, 1884), 23.

51 Ibid., 21, records the total income as 63,394 rubles, 51 kopeks, including fee payments that totalled 59,230 rubles.

52 Ibid., 13–15.
53 Minister of education to Kiev curator (17 May 1881) in TSGIAL, f. 733, o. 191, d. 301, l. 252. Nikolai served as minister of education from 24 March 1881 to 16 March 1882. A.A. Saburov held this position during the year immediately following Tolstoi's dismissal.
54 K.P. Pobedonostsev, *Pis'ma Pobedonostseva k Aleksandru III*, 2 vols, ed. M.N. Pokrovskii (Moscow, 1925–6), 1: 375.
55 Shokhol, "K voprosu o razvitii vysshago zhenskago obrazovaniia" (March 1913): 20–5.
56 According to the account in the ministry's journal "Po povodu zhenskago adresa v Khar'kove," 269–74.
57 An excerpt from the petition quoted in *Golos* and reprinted in ibid., 269.
58 D.A. Tolstoi to A.E. Timashev (11 November 1878) in TSGIAL, f. 733, o. 191, d. 301, l. 194.
59 Twenty-four professors and teachers proposed a three-year program for women. See M.S. Maksimovskii to A.S. Saburov (22 January 1881), ibid., d. 369, ll. 2–16ob.
60 Eleven days before the assassination of Alexander II, Saburov forwarded the petition to the Ministry of Internal Affairs. See ibid., l. 17–17ob.
61 Report of A. Kirpichnikov to Kharkov curator (22 February 1883), ibid., l. 34–34ob.
62 Ibid. Shimkov reported that between sixteen and twenty auditors attended his classes; the Kharkov governor stated that twelve women, mainly local teachers, were enrolled in the courses. See ibid., ll. 36, 42ob.
63 I.D. Delianov to M.S. Maksimovskii (17 December 1882), ibid., ll. 21–2; M.S. Maksimovskii to I.D. Delianov (31 December 1882), ibid., ll. 24–24ob.; I.D. Delianov to M.S. Maksimovskii (13 February 1883), ibid., ll. 25–6; M.S. Maksimovskii to I.D. Delianov (6 April 1883), ibid., ll. 27–30; report of K. Andreev to Kharkov curator (25 February 1883), ibid., l. 39–39ob.; report of A. Potebnia to Kharkov curator (25 February 1883), ibid., l. 32; report of A. Shimkov to Kharkov curator (25 February 1883), ibid., l. 36.
64 Particularly useful studies which provide the basis for the following discussion are *SPBVZhK, 1878–1903* and *Obshchestvo dlia dostavleniia sredstv ... Otchet za 1885–1886 g.*
65 *SPBVZhK, 1878–1903*, 74.
66 For the following figures, see ibid., 244–7.
67 "O vozobnovlenii priema slushatel'nits," col. 708.
68 *Obshchestvo dlia dostavleniia sredstv ... Otchet za 1885–1886 g.*, 102.
69 I.M. Sechenov, "O Bestuzhevskikh Kursakh," in *Sankt-Peterburgskie vysshie zhenskie (Bestuzhevskie) kursy*, 2nd ed., 7.
70 The following is based on the table following p. 242 in *Pamiatnaia knizhka okonchivshikh kurs na S-Peterburgskikh vysshikh zhenskikh kursakh 1882–1889 gg., 1893–1903 gg.*, 4th ed. (St Petersburg, 1903).

71 See part I of chapter 4.

72 That is not to suggest that professors were blind to women's need for employment. As has been shown in chapter 2, part IV, Guerrier defended the higher courses on the grounds that they would not only raise the level of girls' education by training more qualified teachers, but also provide increased employment opportunities for the growing number of unmarried women in Russia.

73 SPBVZhK, 1878–1903, 159.

74 Georgievskii frequently referred to graduates of higher courses and women's medical courses as "*umstvennyi proletariat – zhenskago*" and "*uchebnyi zhenskii proletariat.*" See "O zhenskom meditsinskom obrazovanii 1871–1886 gg." in TSGIAL, f. 846, o. I, d. 119, ll. 49, 51.

75 For fears of the proletariat in the 1840s and 1850s, see Reginald E. Zelnik, *Labour and Society in Tsarist Russia. The Factory Workers of St Petersburg, 1855–1870* (Stanford, 1971), 25–8.

76 *Sankt-Peterburgskie vysshie zhenskie (Bestuzhevskie) kursy*, 2nd ed., 3.

77 D.A. Tolstoi to I.D. Delianov (17 March 1886) in TSGIAL, f. 733, o. 191, d. 813, ll. 25–8. The Corps of Gendarmes operated under the Department of Police of the Ministry of Internal Affairs after the Third Department was abolished in 1880. Tolstoi headed this ministry from 1882 to his death in 1889.

78 A.N. Beketov to M.S. Volkonskii (30 March 1886), ibid., l. 99–99ob.

CHAPTER FIVE

1 Letter of I.S. Turgenev, *Golos*, 10 December 1882, 2.

2 A useful history of medicine and health care in Imperial Russia is P.E. Zabludovskii, *Istoriia Otechestvennoi Meditsiny* (Moscow, 1960). N.M. Frieden has contributed significantly to the study of the Russian medical profession. The following analysis of religious affiliation and social origins of medical students is based on Frieden, *Russian Physicians*, 202–3, tables 9.1 and 9.2. V.I. Grebenshchikov, "Opyt razrabotki resultatov registratsii vrachei Rossii," in *Spravochnaia kniga dlia vrachei*, vol. 1, ed. Meditskinskii departament (St Petersburg, 1890), 110–11, reports that Jews constituted 13.43 percent of all physicians in Russia according to the official registration of 1890, but suggests that the percentage might actually be higher. In filing their registration cards, many Jewish physicians put down their nationality as Russian, Polish, or German. Although those who recorded their religion as Yiddish were automatically transferred to the Jewish category, it is probable, given the discrimination against Jews, that several failed to indicate their Jewish heritage.

3 Anna Filosofova claimed that Praskoviia exercised so much influence over her father that she deserves the credit for the creation of the courses. See *Sbornik pamiati Anny Pavlovny Filosofovoi*, 1: 222–3, n. 1.

4 For Kozlov's proposal, see *Istoricheskii obzor vvozh*, 5–16; and *Istoricheskaia zapiska Isakova*, 5–9.

5 Comparative figures for European countries are also found in N.I. Kozlov, *Zapiska po voprosu o vysshem, v osobennosti meditsinskom, obrazovanii zhenshchin* (St Petersburg, 1879), 18.

6 *Zapiska po zhenskomu voprosu (Okonchanie)* (St Petersburg, 1879), 34.

7 The following discussion of syphilis is based on Shashkov, *Istoriia russkoi zhenshiny*, 306–7.

8 *Istoricheskaia zapiska Isakova*, 7–8.

9 As quoted in ibid., 8.

10 Approved by the minister of internal affairs on 23 April 1870. See "Otnoshenie Voennago Ministra k Ministru Vnutrennikh Del" (12 June 1872), in *Trudy ZhO*, part 1, 8–9.

11 For Miliutin's account of the disputes, particularly Tolstoi's opposition to his administration of the Medical-Surgical Academy, see *Dnevnik*, 1: 78–9, 98, 112–15, 197–203, 207. A lively discussion of the controversy over the military reforms is found in Miller, *Dmitrii Miliutin*, 182–240, passim.

12 "Iz otzyva Ministra Narodnago Prosveshcheniia" (11 May 1872), in *Trudy ZhO*, part 1, 8.

13 For the replies of the university councils, see "Izvestiia o deiatel'nosti i sostoianii nashikh uchebnykh zavedenii," *zhMNP*, 157 (October 1871): 164–77. The reports of the medical faculties are found in TSGIAL, f. 846, o. 1, d. 119, ll. 1–3.

14 *Istoricheskaia zapiska Isakova*, 8.

15 "Doklad po Glavnomu voenno-meditsinskomu Upravleniiu o kapitale na uchrezhdenie kursov" (2 March 1872), in *Trudy ZhO*, part 1, 3–5.

16 "Otnoshenie Voennago Ministra k Ministru Vnutrennikh Del," 10.

17 *Istoricheskii obzor vvozh*, 124–5.

18 "Vremennoe Polozhenie ob osobom zhenskom kurse pri Imperatorskoi Mediko-khirurgicheskoi Akademii dlia obrazovaniia uchenikh akusherok," in *Trudy ZhO*, part 1, 12–15.

19 Nekrasova, "Zhenskie vrachebnye kursy," 818.

20 The following statistical analysis is based on G.M. Gertsenshtein, "Zhenskie vrachebnye kursy. Statisticheskie materialy k istorii ikh," *Vrach*, 1, no. 34 (August 1880): 554–7.

21 Twenty was the minimum age requirement until 1876. Women of eighteen and nineteen years represented approximately 15 percent of the total enrolment during the period 1876–9. See ibid., 554–5.

22 For the curriculum, see *Trudy ZhO*, part 1, 47–9.

23 Nekrasova, "Zhenskie vrachebnye kursy," 821–30.

24 Anna Shabanova, "Zhenskoe vrachebnoe obrazovanie v Rossii (K 35-letiiu pervykh zhenshchin-vrachei v Rossii)," *Istoricheskii vestnik*, 131 (March 1913): 955.

25 Katz, *Katkov*, 158.
26 Shabanova, "Zhenskoe vrachebnoe obrazovanie," 956.
27 For the reminiscences of two of the first graduates, see ibid., 952–61; and Nekrasova, "Zhenskie vrachebnye kursy," 807–45.
28 Gertsenshtein, "Zhenskie vrachebnye kursy," 558; and Kozlov, *Zapiska*, 12.
29 Nekrasova, "Zhenskie vrachebnye kursy," 841–2.
30 For the figures, see A.A. Shibkov, *Pervye zhenshchiny-mediki Rossii* (Leningrad, 1961), 81–2. Essential to the following discussion are the memoirs and correspondence of *kursistki*: Natalia P. Dragnevich, "Iz vospominanii zhenshchiny-vracha (K 25-letiiu deiatel'nosti zhenshchin-vrachei)," *Russkoe bogatstvo*, no. 1 (January 1903): 61–9; Varvara S. Nekrasova, "Studentka na voine. Pis'ma s voiny 1877 goda," *Russkaia mysl'*, nos 6–7 (June–July 1898): 35–55, 100–22; and "Pis'ma studentkoi Nekrasovoi, v koikh deistvuiushchiia litsa: general Krenke, ionyi ofitser," *Otechestvennye zapiski*, vol. 238, no. 5 (May 1878): 124–8.
31 "Pis'ma studentkoi Nekrasovoi," 127.
32 Nekrasova, "Studentka na voine," 47.
33 Dragnevich, "Iz vospominanii zhenshchiny-vracha," 63–4.
34 Nekrasova, "Studentka na voine," 116.
35 E.E. Eikhvald to M.S. Volkonskii (20 June 1883) in TSGIAL, f. 733, o. 191, d. 617, l. 101. For salaries, see Leikina-Svirskaia, *Intelligentsiia v Rossii vo vtoroi polovine XIX veka*, 141–2; and Grebenshchikov, "Opyt razrabotki resultatov registratsii vrachei Rossii," 119–20.
36 *Istoricheskaia zapiska Isakova*, 16.
37 P.P. Sushchinskii, *Zhenshchina-vrach v Rossii. Ocherk desiatiletiia zhenskikh vrachebnykh kursov, 1872–1882 g.* (St Petersburg, 1883), 17.
38 Kozlov had proposed this expansion of women's rights to medical practice: "Zapiska, vnesennaia v Meditsinskii Sovet Ministerstva Vnutrennikh Del Tainym Sovetnikom Kozlovym" (1 February 1878), in *Trudy ZhO*, part 1, 54–5. For the response of the Medical Council, see "Vypiska iz Doklada v Meditsinskii Sovet Komissii po peresmotru Pravil ispytaniia na meditsinskaia, farmatsevicheskaia i veterinarnyia stepeni i raz'iasneniiu prav lits zhenskago pola na vrachebnuiu praktiku" (24 June 1878), in ibid., 57. For Timashev's objections, see minister of internal affairs to minster of education (15 July 1878) in TSGIAL, f. 733, o. 191, d. 310, l. 2.
39 Sidorov, "Statisticheskie svedeniia o propagandistakh 70-kh godov, 32.
40 Figner, *Pol'noe sobranie sochinenii*, 5: 184.
41 For the membership of the Isakov Commission, see *Istoricheskii obzor vvozh*, 69.
42 "Mnenie chlena ot III-go otdeleniia Sobstvennoi Ego Imperatorskago Velichestva kantseliarii," in *Trudy ZhO*, part 2, 81–6.
43 A.I. Georgievskii, "Po povodu mneniia chlenov komissii t. s. Kozlova i d. s. s. Severtsova," in *Trudy ZhO*, part 2, 143–6. For the quotation, see 145.
44 *Istoricheskii obzor vvozh*, 101, 107.

45 *Pravitel'stvennyi vestnik*, 29 June 1880, 1.

46 *Istoricheskii obzor vvozh*, 118, 122–3.

47 For the reaction of the professors and the press to the closure of the courses, see Sushchinskii, *Zhenshchina-vrach v Rossii*, 24–8. Another useful study, which also includes the government's response to the upsurge of public support, is Z.N. Okun'kova-Gol'dinger, "Materialy k istorii zhenskago meditsinskago obrazovaniia v Rossii," in *Delo. Sbornik literaturno-nauchnyi izdannyi Moskovskom otdeleniem obshchestva dlia usileniia sredstv* SPB *zhenskago meditsinskago instituta* (Moscow, 1899), 16–30.

48 "Khronika i melkiia izvestiia," *Vrach*, 3, no. 47 (November 1882): 804; ibid., no. 50 (December 1882): 851.

49 *Izvestiia S-Peterburgskoi gorodskoi dumy*, no. 42 (December 1882): 2985.

50 For the record of the meeting, see *Zhurnal osobago soveshchaniia po "voprosu o zhenskom vrachebnom obrazovanii"* (4 December 1883) in TSGIAL, f. 733, o. 191, d. 616, ll. 4–11; ibid., l. 8–80b., l. 7–70b., ll. 9–100b.

51 The voluminous records of the Volkonskii Commission, including correspondence concerning the projected women's institute, are located in TSGIAL, ibid., dd. 510, 511, 616, 617, 618.

52 Zaionchkovskii, *Rossiiskoe samoderzhavie*, 311.

53 For the evaluations by individual medical experts, see TSGIAL, f. 733, o. 191, d. 617, ll. 1–136; those quoted or mentioned specifically are found in ibid., l. 47, l. 1090b., ll. 640b.–5.

54 See *Zhurnal Meditsinskago Soveta* (8 June 1888) in TSGIAL, ibid., d. 511, ll. 88–101.

55 I.D. Delianov to D.A. Tolstoi (13 August 1888) in TSGIAL, ibid., ll. 76–7; I.D. Delianov to D.A. Tolstoi (30 March 1889), ibid., ll. 104–13; D.A. Tolstoi to I.D. Delianov (19 April 1889), ibid., ll. 130-6.

56 Shabanova, "Zhenskoe vrachebnoe obrazovanie v Rossii," 960.

57 *Otchet meditsinskago departamenta za 1884 god* (St Petersburg, 1887), 141.

58 D.A. Tolstoi to I.D. Delianov (25 November 1888) in TSGIAL, f. 733, o. 191, d. 511, l. 860b.

59 Mary Roth Walsh, *"Doctors Wanted: No Women Need Apply." Sexual Barriers in the Medical Profession, 1835–1975* (New Haven and London, 1977), 181.

60 TSGIAL, f. 733, o. 191, d. 511, l. 87.

61 D.N. Zhbankova, "O zhenshchinakh-vrachakh," *Vrach*, 10, 31 (August 1889): 686.

62 E. Shchepkina, "Pamiati dvukh zhenshchin-vrachei," *Obrazovanie*, 5 (May–June 1896): 101.

63 Only 158 held regular posts. See TSGIAL, f. 733, o. 191, d. 511, ll. 860b.–7.

64 Ibid., l. 87 and ll. 850b.–6.

65 Ibid., ll. 860b.–7.

66 These figures refer to the physician's bailiwick in zemstvo districts in 1880.

See Samuel C. Ramer, "The Zemstvo and Public Health," in *The Zemstvo in Russia*, 292, table 8.1.

67 *Vospominaniia vrachei Iulii A. Kviatkovskoi i Marii P. Rashkovich* (Paris, 1937), 176–7.

68 Grebenshchikov, "Opyt razrabotki resultatov registratsii vrachei Rossii," 119.

69 TSGIAL, f. 733, o. 191, d. 511, l. 86ob.

70 Dragnevich, "Iz vospominanii zhenshchiny-vracha," 73.

71 *Vospominaniia Kviatkovskoi*, 82.

72 "Khronika i melkiia izvestiia," *Vrach*, 3, no. 46 (November 1882): 787.

73 Shabanova, "Zhenskoe vrachebnoe obrazovanie," 957; and "Doklad Vysochaishe uchrezhdennago Komiteta dlia sostavleniia proekta Polozheniia o Zhenskom Meditsinskom institute" in TSGIAL, f. 733, o. 191, d. 511, l. 67ob.

74 See earlier references to Tolstoi's poll of university medical faculties and the views of medical experts consulted by the Volkonskii Commission on the women's midwifery institute.

75 D. I---va [Dora Aptekman], "Iz zapisok zemskago vracha," *Russkaia mysl'*, no. 12 (December 1884): 77–8; and Sergei I. Mitskevich, *Zapiska vracha-obshchestvennika (1888–1918)*, 2nd ed. (Moscow, 1969), 78.

76 As quoted in Jeffrey Brooks, "The Zemstvo and the Education of the People," in *The Zemstvo in Russia*, 261–2.

77 For the police functions of doctors, see Mitskevich, *Zapiska*, 58–9.

78 D. I---va, "Iz zapisok zemskago vracha," 58–9.

79 Recent Western scholarship has explored rural Russia's resistance to modern medicine. See, for example, Nancy Mandelker Frieden, "Child Care: Medical Reform in a Traditionalist Culture"; and Samuel C. Ramer, "Childbirth and Culture: Midwifery in the Nineteenth-Century Russian Countryside," in *The Family in Imperial Russia. New Lines of Historical Research*, ed. David L. Ransel (Urbana, Chicago, and London, 1978): 218–59.

80 D. I---va, "Iz zapisok zemskago vracha," 66, 78.

81 "Vypiska iz zhurnala Uchenago Komiteta Ministerstva Narodnago Prosveshcheniia" (31 March 1886) in TSGIAL, f. 733, o. 191, d. 863, l. 7.

82 A.N. Strannoliubskii, "O zhenskom professional'nom obrazovanii," part 1, *Obrazovanie*, 5 (February 1896): 45.

83 Ibid., 44.

84 At that time, the doctor-*fel'dsher* ratio was 1:0.65. Three years earlier, in both St Petersburg and Moscow, the number of physicians was more than double that of paramedics. See ibid.

85 Ibid., 46.

86 An outstanding exception is Sergei I. Mitskevich who joined the political struggle of Russian Marxists in 1893.

CHAPTER SIX

1 *Dnevnik Very Sergeevny Aksakovoi*, 102.
2 From Meshcherskii's diary addressed to Alexander III, as quoted in N.V. Zeifman, "Srednee obrazovanie v sisteme kontrreform 1880–kh godov" (PH D dissertation, Moscow University, 1973), 3, n. 2. A decade earlier, Meshcherskii's press had attempted to poison the public's attitude toward women's higher education. See, for example, "Eshche o zhenskom voprose. Otvet baronesse Korf," *Grazhdanin*, 11 September 1872, 33–5; "Nash zhenskii vopros," ibid., 28 February 1872, 299–301, and 6 March 1872, 331–3; and "K delu! Otvet russkoi zhenshchine," ibid., 4 December 1872, 449–53.
3 Robert F. Byrnes, *Pobedonostsev: His Life and Thought* (Bloomington and London, 1968), 243; and Konstantin P. Pobedonostsev, *Reflections of a Russian Statesman*, trans. Robert Crozier Long (Ann Arbor, MI, 1968), 75.
4 Zaionchkovskii, *Rossiiskoe samoderzhavie*, 317–18.
5 When Miliutin heard of Delianov's appointment, he noted in his diary: "It is as if Katkov had been appointed; it is the restoration of Count Tolstoi's ministry which was hated by all Russia." See Miliutin, *Dnevnik*, 4: 130.
6 Zaionchkovskii, *Rossiiskoe samoderzhavie*, 318–19.
7 A particularly useful study that focuses on the State Council's resistance to counter-reform in the zemstvo administration and judicial system is Heidi W. Whelan, *Alexander III & the State Council. Bureaucracy & Counter-Reform in Late Imperial Russia* (New Brunswick, NJ, 1982). For the State Council's opposition to the projected university statute, see G.I. Shchetinina, *Universitety v Rossii i ustav 1884 goda* (Moscow, 1976), 127–45.
8 Whelan, *Alexander III & the State Council*, 55, 95.
9 Ibid., 30, 36.
10 Shchetinina, *Universitety v Rossii*, 143.
11 The following discussion of the provisions of the statute is based on ibid., 150–8; and Vucinich, *Science in Russian Culture*, 183–90.
12 Ministry of Education to Fourth Department (26 May 1884) in TSGIAL, f. 733, o. 191, d. 651, l. 7.
13 "Zapiska Baronessy von Raden" in TSGIAL, ibid., ll. 3–5. For the quotation, see l. 3.
14 "Doklad Vysochaishe uchrezdennoi komissii po voprosu ob izyskanii glavneishikh osnovanii dlia luchshei postanovki zhenskago obrazovaniia v Imperii" in TSGIAL, ibid., d. 695, ll. 1–4. The commission first met on 20 February 1885; its last and fifty-fifth session was held on 7 March 1888. Records of the meetings are located in ibid., ll. 5–180.
15 For the projects, see ibid., ll. 185–243.
16 *SPBVZhK, 1878–1903*, 161.
17 E.I. Likhacheva to Alexander III (21 January 1889) in TSGIAL, f. 733, o. 191, d. 813, ll. 151–3ob.

18  Ariian, *Pervyi zhenskii kalendar'*, 140.

19  "Vozvrashcheno ot Gosudaria Imperatora 23 fevralia 1889g. s obshchimi rezoliutsiiami na poslednei stranitz. Graf Delianov" in TSGIAL, f. 733, o. 191, d. 814, l. 5.

20  Ariian, *Pervyi zhenskii kalendar'*, 140.

21  For the new regulations, see "O vozobnovlenii priema slushatel'nits na vysshie zhenskie kursy v S-Peterburge," *Sbornik postanovlenii*, vol. 11, no. 170 (25 June 1889), cols 691–738.

22  As quoted in I.P. Novikov (St Petersburg curator) to I.D. Delianov (13 October 1889) in TSGIAL, f. 733, o. 191, d. 814, l. 293.

23  "O vozobnovlenii priema slushatel'nits," cols 696 and 733.

24  *SPBVZhK, 1878–1903*, 253, table V.

25  For the following figures, see TSGIAL, f. 733, o. 191, d. 814, ll. 290–2.

26  *SPBVZhK, 1878–1903*, p. 253, table V.

27  D.S. Margolin, *Vademekum po vysshemu zhenskomu obrazovaniiu. Polnyi sbornik pravil priema i programm vsekh vysshikh zhenskikh obshcheobrazovatel'nykh, spetsial'nykh i professional'nykh, pravitel'stvennykh, obshchestvennykh i chastnykh uchebnykh zavedenii v Rossii* (Kiev, 1915), 11.

28  Fedosova, *Bestuzhevskie kursy*, 68.

29  Margolin, *Vademekum po vyshemu zhenskomu obrazovaniiu*, 11.

30  Ibid., 13.

31  N. Ivanov, "Zhenskoe obrazovanie," in *Novyi entsiklopedicheskii slovar'*, ed. F.A. Brockhaus and I.A. Efron, vol. 17 (St Petersburg, 1915), cols 808, 810.

32  Dudgeon, "The Forgotten Minority," 8.

33  Ivanov, "Zhenskoe obrazovanie," col. 812.

# Selected Bibliography

ARCHIVAL COLLECTIONS

*Leningradskii gosudarstvennyi istoricheskii arkhiv*

*fond* 14     Petrogradskii universitet
*fond* 113    Petrogradskii vysshie zhenskie kursy (Bestuzhevskie)

*Tsentral'nyi gosudarstvennyi istoricheskii arkhiv* SSSR *(Leningrad)*

*fond* 733    Departament Narodnago Prosveshcheniia
*fond* 846    A.I. Georgievskii
*fond* 1294   Meditsinskii sovet Ministerstva Vnutrennikh Del

OFFICIAL DOCUMENTS, GOVERNMENT
PUBLICATIONS, AND COMMISSION
REPORTS

*Istoricheskaia zapiska k dokladu Vysochaishe uchrezhdennoi komissii po voprosu o zhenskikh vrachebnykh kursakh, meditsinskom obrazovanii i pravakh meditsinskoi praktiki zhenshchin.* N.p. n.d. Materials of Isakov Commission. St Petersburg, 1878–9.
*Istoricheskii obzor pravitel'stvennykh rasporiazhenii po voprosu o vysshem vrachebnom obrazovanii zhenshchin.* St Petersburg, 1883.
Ministerstvo Narodnago Prosveshcheniia. *Alfavitnyi sbornik postanovlenii i rasporiazhenii po S-Peterburgskomu uchebnomu okrugu za 1876–1882. Izvlecheniia iz izdannykh okrugom tsirkuliarov.* Edited by S. Komarov. St Petersburg, 1884.
– *Sbornik deistvuiushchikh postanovlenii i rasporiazhenii po zhenskim gimnaziiam i progimnaziiam Ministerstva Narodnago Prosveshcheniia.* Edited by Mikhail Rodevich. St Petersburg, 1884.

– *Sbornik postanovlenii po Ministerstvu Narodnago Prosveshcheniia*. 17 vols. St Petersburg, 1864–1904.
– *Sbornik rasporiazhenii po Ministerstvu Narodnago Prosveshcheniia*. 17 vols. St Petersburg, 1866–1905.
– *Universitetskii ustav 1863 goda*. St Petersburg, 1863.
– *Zamechaniia na proekt obshchago ustava Imperatorskikh Rossiiskikh universitetov*. St Petersburg, 1862.
– *Zhurnal Ministerstva Narodnago Prosveshcheniia*. St Petersburg, 1834–1917.
– *Zhurnaly zasedanii uchebnago komiteta glavnago pravleniia uchilishch po proektu obshchago ustava Imperatorskikh Rossiiskikh universitetov*. St Petersburg, 1862.
Ministerstvo Vnutrennikh Del. *Otchet meditsinskago departamenta za 1884 god*. St Petersburg, 1887.
*Pravitel'stvennyi vestnik*. St Petersburg, 1869–1917.
*Trudy Vysochaishe uchrezhdennoi komissii po voprosu o zhenskom obrazovanii*. St Petersburg, 1879.
*Zhenskoe pravo. Svod uzakonenii i postanovlenii otnosiashchikhsia do zhenskago pola*. St Petersburg, 1873.

MEMOIRS, DIARIES, LETTERS, AND
MISCELLANEOUS PRIMARY SOURCES

Aksakova, V.S. *Dnevnik Very Sergeevny Aksakovoi, 1854–1855*. Edited and introduced by N.V. Golitsyn and P.E. Shchegolev. St Petersburg, 1913.
Breshko-Breshkovskaia, Ekaterina. *The Little Grandmother of the Russian Revolution. Reminiscences and Letters of Catherine Breshkovsky*. Edited by Alice Stone Blackwell. London, 1918.
Chernyshevskii, N.G. *What Is To Be Done? Tales about New People*. Translated by Benjamin R. Tucker with revisions by Ludmilla B. Turkevich. Introduced by E.H. Carr. New York, 1961.
Dobroliubov, N.A. *N.A. Dobroliubov. Sobranie sochinenii*. 9 vols. Edited by B.I. Bursov et al. Vol. 4. Moscow and Leningrad, 1962.
Dragnevich, Natalia P. "Iz vospominanii zhenshchiny-vracha (K 25-letiiu deiatel'nosti zhenshchin-vrachei)." *Russkoe bogatstvo*, no. 1 (January 1903): 61–74.
Feoktistov, E.M. *Vospominaniia E.M. Feoktistova: za kulisami politiki i literatury, 1848-1896*. Edited by Iu. G. Oksman. Leningrad, 1929.
Figner, Vera N. *Memoirs of a Revolutionist*. Translated by Camilla Chapin Daniels and G.R. Davidson. Edited by Alexander Kaun. New York, 1968.
– *Pol'noe sobranie sochinenii v shesti tomakh*. Vol. 5. Moscow, 1929.
– "Studencheskie gody." Parts 1–3. *Golos minuvshego*, 10 (March–April 1922): 165–81; 11 (January–February, March–April 1923): 27–45, 125–45.
– *Zapechatlennyi trud. Vospominaniia v dvukh tomakh*. Moscow, 1964.
Georgievskii, A.I. *Kratkii istoricheskii ocherk pravitel'stvennykh mer i prednachertanii protiv studencheskikh bezporiadkov*. St Petersburg, 1890.

Ger'e (Guerrier), V. "Teorii i praktika zhenskago obrazovaniia." *Vestnik evropy*, 12, no. 4 (April 1877): 645–700.

– "Universitetskii vopros. Po povodu mnenie pr. Liubimova o peresmotre Universitetskago Ustava, v *Rus. Vest.* 1873, febral'." *Vestnik evropy*, 8, no. 4 (April 1873): 818–36.

Giliarov-Platonov, N.P. *Universitetskii vopros. ("Sovremenniia izvestiia," 1868–1884 gg.).* Edited by K.P. Pobedonostsev. St Petersburg, 1903.

*Istoricheskaia zapiska i otchet o Kievskikh vysshikh zhenskikh kursakh za pervoe chetyrekhletie (1878–1882)*. Kiev, 1884.

Iunge, E.F. *Vospominaniia (1843–1860 gg.)*. Moscow, 1933.

I---va, D. [Dora Aptekman]. "Iz zapisok zemskago vracha." *Russkaia mysl'*, no. 12 (December 1884): 48–82.

Katkov, M.N. *O zhenskom obrazovanii. Stat'i sviazannyia s voznikoveniam i postepennym rostom Zhenskoi Klassicheskoi Gimnazii*. Moscow, 1897.

Kavelin, K.D. *Sobranie sochinenii K.D. Kavelina*. Vol. 2. Edited by N. Glagolov. St Petersburg, 1900.

Kovalevskaia, Sofiia. *Sonya Kovalevsky. Her Recollections of Childhood*. Translated by Isabel F. Hapwood. With a "Biography" by Anna Carlotta Leffler. Translated by A.M. Clive Bayley. New York, 1895.

Kozlov, N.I. *Zapiska po voprosu o vysshem, v osobennosti meditsinskom, obrazovanii zhenshchin*. St Petersburg, 1879.

K---aia, E. "Iz nedavnikh vospominanii kursistki." *Zhenskoe obrazovanie*, 11 (November 1886): 635–41.

Meshcherskii, V.P. *Moi vospominaniia*. 2 vols. St Petersburg, 1897–8.

Mikhailov, M. "Zhenshchiny v universitete." *Sovremennik*, 86 (1861): 499–507.

Miliutin, D.A. *Dnevnik D.A. Miliutina*. 4 vols. Edited by P.A. Zaionchkovskii. Moscow, 1947–50.

Mitskevich, Sergei I. *Zapiska vracha-obshchestvennika (1880–1918)*. 2nd ed. Moscow, 1969.

Nekrasova, Ekaterina. "Zhenskie vrachebnye kursy v Peterburge. Iz vospominanii i perepiski pervykh studentok." *Vestnik evropy*, 17 (December 1882): 807–45.

– "Pervye zhenskie kursy v Moskve, izvestnye pod imenem Lubianskikh." *Otechestvennye zapiski*, 251 (July 1880): 1–39.

Nekrasova, Varvara S. "Studentka na voine. Pis'ma s voiny 1877 goda." Parts 1, 2. *Russkaia mysl'*, nos 6, 7 (June, July 1898): 35–55, 100–22.

Nikitenko, A.V. *Dnevnik v trekh tomakh*. Edited by N.L. Brodskii et al. Moscow, 1955.

*Obshchestvo dlia dostavleniia sredstv vysshim zhenskim kursam (Osnovano 4-go oktiabria 1878 g.). Otchet za 1885–1886 g.* St Petersburg, 1887.

Odoevskii, V.F. "Dnevnik V.F. Odoevskogo 1859–1869 gg." *Literaturnoe nasledstvo*, 22–4 (1935): 79–308.

*Pamiatnaia knizhka okonchivshikh kurs na S-Peterburgskikh vysshikh zhenskikh kur-*

*sakh: 1882–1889 gg., 1893–1903 gg.* 4th ed. Edited by N.A. Vetvenitskaia. St Petersburg, 1903.

Panteleev, L.F. *Iz vospominanii proshlago.* St Petersburg, 1905.

Pirogov, N.I. *N.I. Pirogov. Izbrannye pedagogicheskie sochineniia.* Edited by V.Z. Smirnov. Moscow, 1952.

Pisarev, D.I. *Sochineniia D.I. Pisareva. Polnoe sobranie v shesti tomakh.* Edited by F. Pavlenko. Vol. 1. St Petersburg, 1894.

Pobedonostsev, K.P. *K.P. Pobedonostsev i ego korrespondenty. Pis'ma i zapiski.* 2 vols. Edited by M.N. Pokrovskii. Petrograd, 1923.

– *Pis'ma K.P. Pobedonostseva k Aleksandru III.* 2 vols. Edited by M.N. Pokrovskii. Moscow, 1925–6.

– *Reflections of a Russian Statesman.* Translated by Robert Crozier Long. Ann Arbor, MI, 1968.

*Sbornik pamiati Anny Pavlovny Filosofovoi.* Vol. 1: A. Tyrkova, *Anna Pavlovna Filosofova i eia vremia.* Vol. 2: *Stat'i i materialy.* Petrograd, 1915.

Sechenov, I.M. *Autobiographical Notes.* Edited by Donald B. Lindsley. Translated by Kristan Hanes. Washington, DC, 1965.

Semenov, D.D. *Izbrannye pedagogicheskie sochineniia.* Edited by N.A. Konstantinov. Moscow, 1953.

Shabanova, Anna. "Zhenskoe vrachebnoe obrazovanie v Rossii (K 35-letiiu pervykh zhenshchin-vrachei v Rossii)." *Istoricheskii vestnik*, 131 (March 1913): 952–61.

Shchepkina, E. "Pamiati dvukh zhenshchin-vrachei." *Obrazovanie*, 5 (May–June 1896): 92–105.

Shtakenshneider [Stakenschneider], E.A. *Dnevnik i zapiski (1854–1886).* Edited by I.N. Rozanov. Moscow and Leningrad, 1934.

Skabichevskii, A.M. *Literaturnye vospominaniia.* Edited and introduced by V.P. Koz'min. Moscow and Leningrad, 1928.

Solov'ev, S.M. *Zapiski Sergeia Mikhailovicha Solov'eva. Moi zapiski dlia detei moikh, i esli mozhno, i dlia drugikh.* St Petersburg, n.d.

Trachevskii, A.S. *Vysshie zhenskie kursy v Odesse professora Trachevskago.* Odessa, 1879.

Ushinskii, K.D. *K.D. Ushinskii. Izbrannye proizvedeniia, prilozhenie k zhurnaly "Sovetskaia pedagogika."* Edited by V. Ia. Struminskii. Moscow and Leningrad, 1946.

– *K.D. Ushinsky. Selected Works.* Edited by A.I. Piskunov. Moscow, 1975.

Vodovozova, Elizaveta N. *Na zare zhizni i drugie vospominaniia.* 2 vols. Edited by V.P. Koz'min. Moscow and Leningrad, 1934.

*Vospominaniia vrachei Iulii A. Kviatkovskoi i Marii P. Rashkovich.* Paris, 1937.

## SECONDARY WORKS

Abramov, Ia. *Zhenskie vrachebnye kursy.* St Petersburg, 1886.

Alston, Patrick L. *Education and the State in Tsarist Russia.* Stanford, 1969.

Ariian, L.N. *Pervyi zhenskii kalendar' na 1899 god.* St Petersburg, 1899.

Ashevskii, S. "Russkoe studenchestvo v epokhu shestidesiatnykh godov (1855–1863)." Parts 1, 2. *Sovremennyi mir*, 2 (June, August 1907): 12–26, 19–36.

Atkinson, Dorothy, Alexander Dallin, and Gail Warshofsky Lapidus, eds. *Women in Russia*. Stanford, 1977.

Belkin, M.S. "Russkie zhenshchiny-vrach – pionery vysshego zhenskogo meditsinskogo obrazovaniia." *Sovetskii vrachebnyi sbornik*, 14 (1949): 29–36.

Bemert [Böhmert], Victor. *Universitetskoe obrazovanie zhenshchiny*. St Petersburg, 1873.

Besançon, Alain. *Éducation et société en Russie dans le second tiers du XIXᵉ siècle*. Paris and The Hague, 1974.

Bidelman, Patrick Kay. "The Feminist Movement in France: The Formative Years, 1858–1889." PH D dissertation. Michigan State University, 1975.

Binshtok, V. "Iz istorii zhenskago obrazovaniia v Rossii." Parts 1, 2. *Obrazovanie*, 5 (October, December 1896): 50–67, 11–30.

Black, J.L. *Citizens for the Fatherland. Education, Educators, and Pedagogical Ideals in Eighteenth Century Russia*. Boulder, CO, 1979.

Bobrova, L.A. "Vysshie zhenskie kursy professora Ger'e v Moskve, 1872–1888 gg." In *Trudy Moskovskogo gosudarstvennogo istoriko-arkhivnogo instituta*. Vol. 16. Edited by S.O. Schmidt, 253–65. Moscow, 1961.

Bogdanovich, T.A. *Liubov' liudei shestidesiatykh godov*. Leningrad, 1929.

Bogolepov, I.P. *Gramotnost' sredi detei shkol'nago vozrasta v Moskovskom i Mozhaiskom uezdakh Moskovskoi gubernii*. Moscow, 1894.

Borozdin, I.N. "Universitety v epokhu 60-kh godov." In *Istoriia Rossii v XIX veke*. Russian Bibliographical Institute Granat. Vol. 4., 185–212. St Petersburg, 1907.

Broido, Vera. *Apostles into Terrorists. Women and the Revolutionary Movement in the Russia of Alexander II*. New York, 1977.

Brower, Daniel R. *Training the Nihilists. Education and Radicalism in Tsarist Russia*. Ithaca and London, 1975.

Bulanova-Trubnikova, O.K. *Tri pokoleniia*. Moscow and Leningrad, 1928.

Byrnes, Robert F. *Pobedonostsev: His Life and Thought*. Bloomington and London, 1968.

Chekhov, N.V. *Narodnoe obrazovanie v Rossii s 60-kh godov XIX veka*. Moscow, 1912.

Coquart, Armand. *Dmitri Pisarev (1840–1868) et l'Idéologie du Nihilism Russe*. Paris, 1946.

Curtiss, John Shelton. "Russian Sisters of Mercy in the Crimea, 1854–55." *Slavic Review*, 25, no. 1 (March 1966): 84–100.

Dudgeon, Ruth A. "The Forgotten Minority: Women Students in Imperial Russia, 1872–1917." *Russian History*, 9 (1982): 1–26.

– "Women and Higher Education in Russia, 1855–1905." PH D dissertation. George Washington University, 1975.

Dzhanshiev, G.A. *Epokha velikikh reform: istoricheskiia spravki*. 2nd ed. St Petersburg, 1902.

Edmondson, Linda Harriet. *Feminism in Russia, 1900–1917*. Stanford, 1984.

Eimontova, R.G. "Universitetskaia reforma 1863 g." *Istoricheskie zapiski*, 70 (1961): 163–96.

– "Universitetskii vopros i russkaia obshchestvennost' v 50–60 godakh XIX v." *Istoriia SSSR*, 6 (1971): 144–58.

Eklof, Ben. "Peasant Sloth Reconsidered: Strategies of Education and Learning in Rural Russia before the Revolution." *Journal of Social History*, 14, no. 3 (Spring 1981): 355–85.

Emmons, Terence. *The Russian Landed Gentry and the Peasant Emancipation of 1861*. Cambridge, England, 1968.

Emmons, Terence and Wayne S. Vucinich, eds. *The Zemstvo in Russia. An Experiment in Local Self-Government*. Cambridge, MA, 1982.

Engel, Barbara Alpern. *Mothers and Daughters. Women of the Intelligentsia in Nineteenth-Century Russia*. Cambridge, England, 1983.

Evteeva, Z.A. et al., eds. *Vysshie zhenskii (Bestuzhevskie) kursy. Bibliograficheskii ukazatel'*. Moscow, 1966.

Fedosova, E.P. *Bestuzhevskie kursy – pervyi zhenskie universitet v Rossii (1878–1918 gg.)*. Edited by E.D. Dneprov. Moscow, 1980.

Field, Daniel. *The End of Serfdom: Nobility and Bureaucracy in Russia, 1855–1861*. Cambridge, MA, 1976.

Filippova, L.D. "Iz istorii zhenskogo obrazovaniia v Rossii." *Voprosy istorii*, 14, no. 2 (1963): 209–18.

Fischer, George. *Russian Liberalism: From Gentry to Intelligentsia*. Cambridge, MA, 1958.

Friche, V.M. "Vysshaia shkola v kontse veka." In *Istoriia Rossii v XIX veke*. Russian Bibliographical Institute Granat. Vol. 9, 145–63. St Petersburg, 1911.

Frieden, Nancy Mandelker. *Russian Physicians in an Era of Reform and Revolution, 1856–1905*. Princeton, NJ, 1981.

Gay, Peter. *The Bourgeois Experience: Victoria to Freud*. Vol. 1, *Education of the Senses*. New York and Oxford, 1984.

Gertsenshtein, G.M. "Zhenskie vrachebnye kursy. Statisticheskie materialy k istorii ikh." Parts 1, 2. *Vrach* (August 1880): 553–8, 569–75.

Goldberg, Rochelle Lois. "The Russian Women's Movement: 1859–1917." PH D dissertation. University of Rochester, 1976.

Grebenshchikov, V.I. "Opyt razrabotki resultatov registratsii vrachei Rossii." In *Spravochnaia knigna dlia vrachei*. Vol. 1. Edited by Meditsinskii Departament. Vol. 1, 103–43. St Petersburg, 1890.

Hans, Nicholas. *History of Russian Educational Policy (1701–1917)*. New York, 1964.

Ivanov, I.M. "Statistika obrazovaniia. Uchenyia professii i vysshee zhenskoe obrazovanie." *Obrazovanie*, 10 (January 1901): 83–93.

Ivanov, N. "Zhenskoe obrazovanie." In *Novyi Entsiklopedicheskii slovar'*. Edited by F.A. Brokhaus and I.A. Efron. Vol. 17, cols 786–813. St Petersburg, 1915.

Jarausch, Konrad H. *Students, Society, and Politics in Imperial Germany. The Rise of Academic Illiberalism*. Princeton, NJ, 1982.

Jarausch, Konrad H., ed. *The Transformation of Higher Learning, 1860–1930: Expansion, Diversification, Social Opening and Professionalization in England, Germany, Russia and the United States*. Stuttgart, 1982.

Johanson, Christine. "Autocratic Politics, Public Opinion, and Women's Medical Education during the Reign of Alexander II, 1855–1881." *Slavic Review*, 38, no. 3 (September 1979): 426–43.

Johnson, Paul W. "Taming Student Radicalism: The Educational Policy of I.D. Delianov." *Russian Review*, 33, no. 3 (1974): 259–68.

Johnson, William H.E. *Russia's Educational Heritage*. Pittsburgh, 1950.

Kaidanova, O. *Ocherki po istorii narodnogo obrazovaniia v Rossii i SSSR na osnove lichnogo opyta i nabliudenii*. Brussels, 1938.

Kassow, Samuel David. "The Russian University in Crisis: 1899–1911." PH D dissertation. Princeton University, 1976.

Katz, Martin. *Mikhail N. Katkov: A Political Biography, 1818–1887*. The Hague, 1966.

Korbut, M.K. *Kazanskii gosudarstvennyi universitet imeni V.I. Ul'ianova-Lenina za 125 let (1804/5–1929/30)*. 2 vols. Kazan, 1930.

Kornilov, A.A. *Obshchestvennoe dvizhenie pri Aleksandre II (1855–1881)*. Moscow, 1909.

Lange, Helene. *Higher Education of Women in Europe*. Translated by L.R. Klemm. New York, 1890.

Leary, Daniel Bell. *Education and Autocracy in Russia. From the Origins to the Bolsheviki*. Buffalo, 1919.

Leikina-Svirskaia, V.R. *Intelligentsiia v Rossii vo vtoroi polovine XIX veke*. Moscow, 1971.

Lemke, Mikhail. "Molodost' Ottsa Mitrofana." *Byloe*, 1, no. 13 (January 1907): 188–233.

Likhacheva, E. *Materialy dlia istorii zhenskago obrazovanii v Rossii, 1856–1880*. St Petersburg, 1901.

Lipinska, Mélina. *Les femmes et le progrès des sciences médicales*. Paris, 1930.

L---ia, S.V. "Vysshie zhenskie kursy v Kieve." *Zhenskoe obrazovanie*, 3 (November 1878): 594–601.

McClelland, James C. *Autocrats and Academics: Education, Culture, and Society in Tsarist Russia*. Chicago and London, 1979.

Manning, Roberta Thompson. *The Crisis of the Old Order in Russia: Gentry and Government*. Princeton, NJ, 1982.

Margolin, D.S., ed. *Vademekum po vysshemu zhenskomu obrazovaniiu. Polnyi sbornik pravil priema i programm vsekh vysshikh zhenskikh obshcheobrazovatel'nykh, spetsial'nykh i professional'nykh, pravitel'stvennykh, obshchestvennykh i chastnykh uchebnykh zavedenii v Rossii*. Kiev, 1915.

Mathes, William L. "The Origins of Confrontation Politics in Russian Universities: Student Activism, 1855–1861." *Canadian Slavic Studies*, 2, no. 1 (Spring 1968): 28–45.

– "N.I. Pirogov and the Reform of University Government, 1856–1866." *Slavic Review*, 31, no. 1, (March 1972): 29–51.

Mavrodin, V.V., ed. *Istoriia Leningradskogo universiteta, 1819–1969. Ocherki.* Leningrad, 1969.

Meijer, J.M. *Knowledge and Revolution. The Russian Colony in Zurich (1870–1873). A Contribution to the Study of Russian Populism.* Assen, Netherlands, 1955.

Mikheeva, E.P. "Vysshee zhenskoe obrazovanie v dorevoliutsionnoi Rossii (1872–1917 gg.)." PH D dissertation. Moscow University, 1969.

Miller, Forrestt A. *Dmitrii Miliutin and the Reform Era in Russia.* Charlotte, NC, 1968.

Mills, James Cobb, Jr. "Dmitrii Tolstoi as Minister of Education in Russia." PH D dissertation. Indiana University, 1967.

Moser, Charles A. *Antinihilism in the Russian Novel of the 1860's.* London, The Hague, and Paris, 1964.

*Nikolai Ivanovich Pirogov i ego nasledie. Pirogovskie s'ezdy. Iubileinoe izdanie.* Edited by M.M. Gran, Z.G. Frenkel', and A.I. Shingarev. St Petersburg, 1911.

Orlovsky, Daniel T. *The Limits of Reform: The Ministry of Internal Affairs in Imperial Russia, 1802–1881.* Cambridge, MA, 1981.

Ostrogorskii, M. *The Rights of Women. A Comparative Study in History and Legislation.* London and New York, 1893.

Peskovskii, M.L. "Ocherk istorii vysshago zhenskago obrazovaniia v Rossii za 20 let." Parts 1-3. *Nabliudatel'*, 1 (April, May, June 1882): 74–92, 166–77, 117–36.

Pirumova, N.M. *Zemskoe liberal'noe dvizhenie. Sotsial'nye korni i evoliutsiia do nachala xx veka.* Moscow, 1977.

Polianskii, A., ed. *Russkaia zhenshchina na gosudarstvennoi i obshchestvennoi sluzhbe.* Moscow, 1901.

Raeff, Marc. *Plans for Political Reform in Imperial Russia, 1730–1905.* Englewood Cliffs, NJ, 1966.

Ransel, David L., ed. *The Family in Imperial Russia. New Lines of Historical Research.* Urbana, Chicago, and London, 1978.

Rashin, A.G. "Gramotnost' i narodnoe obrazovanie v Rossii v XIX i nachale XX v." *Istoricheskie zapiski*, 37 (1951): 28–80.

Rieber, Alfred J. "Alexander II: A Revisionist View." *Journal of Modern History*, 43, no. 2 (March 1971): 42–58.

Rieber, Alfred J., ed. *The Politics of Autocracy. Letters of Alexander II to Prince A.I. Bariatinskii, 1857–1864.* Paris and The Hague, 1966.

Rozhdestvenskii, S.V. *Istoricheskii obzor deiatel'nosti Ministerstva Narodnago Prosveshcheniia, 1802–1902.* St Petersburg, 1902.

Ruud, Charles A. "Censorship and the Peasant Question: The Contingencies of Reform under Alexander II (1855–1859)." In *California Slavic Studies*. Vol. 5., 137–67. Berkeley, Los Angeles, and London, 1970.

– *Fighting Words: Imperial Censorship and the Russian Press, 1804–1906*. Toronto, 1982.

*Sankt-Peterburgskie vysshie zhenskie (Bestuzhevskie) kursy (1878–1918 gg.). Sbornik statei*. 2nd ed. Edited by S.N. Valk et al. Leningrad, 1973.

*S-Peterburgskie Vysshie Zhenskie Kursy za 25 let, 1878–1903. Ocherki i materialy*. Edited by Komitet Obshchestva dlia dostavleniia sredstv vysshim zhenskim kursam v S-Peterburge. St Petersburg, 1903.

Satina, Sophie. *Education of Women in Pre-revolutionary Russia*. Translated by Alexandra F. Poustchine. New York, 1966.

Seredonin, S.M. *Istoricheskii obzor deiatel'nosti komiteta ministrov*. Vols 3–4. St Petersburg, 1902.

Shashkov, S.S. *Istoriia russkoi zhenshchiny*. 2nd ed. St Petersburg, 1879.

Shchepkina, E.N. *Iz istorii zhenskoi lichnosti v Rossii. Lektsii i stat'i*. St Petersburg, 1914.

Shchetinina, G.I. *Universitety v Rossii i ustav 1884 goda*. Moscow, 1976.

Sheremetevskaia, A.N. "Stranitsa iz istorii vysshago zhenskago obrazovaniia." *Istoricheskii vestnik*, 65 (July 1896): 171–84.

Shibkov, A.A. *Pervye zhenshchiny-mediki Rossii*. Leningrad, 1961.

Sidorov, N.I. "Statisticheskie svedeniia o propagandistakh 70-kh godov v obrabotke III otdeleniia: Zapiska M.M. Merkulova o propagandistakh 70-kh godov." *Katorga i ssylka*, 38 (1928): 27–56.

Sinel, Allen. *The Classroom and the Chancellery: State Educational Reform under Count Dmitry Tolstoi*. Cambridge, MA, 1973.

Sipovskii, V.D. "Polozhenie u nas voprosa o vysshem zhenskom obrazovanii." *Zhenskoe obrazovanie*, 1 (August 1876): 255–68, 161–8 [sic].

Stanton, Theodore, ed. *The Woman Question in Europe. A Series of Original Essays*. New York, 1884.

Starr, S. Frederick. *Decentralization and Self-Government in Russia, 1830–1870*. Princeton, NJ, 1972.

Stasov, Vladimir V. *Nadezhda Vasil'evna Stasova. Vospominaniia i ocherki*. St Petersburg, 1899.

Stites, Richard. "M.L. Mikhailov and the Emergence of the Woman Question in Russia." *Canadian Slavic Studies*, 3, no. 2 (Summer 1969): 178–99.

– *The Women's Liberation Movement in Russia. Feminism, Nihilism, and Bolshevism, 1860–1930*. Princeton, NJ, 1978.

Stoiunin, V. Ia. "Obrazovanie russkoi zhenshchiny (Po povodu dvadtsatipiatiletiia russkikh zhenskikh gimnazii)." *Istoricheskii vestnik*, 12 (April 1883): 125–53.

Strannoliubskii, A.N. "O zhenskom professional'nom obrazovanii." Parts 1–3. *Obrazovanie*, 5 (February, March, April 1896): 34–50, 8–28, 16–41.

Sushchinskii, P.P. *Zhenshchina-vrach v Rossii. Ocherk desiatiletiia zhenskikh vrachebnykh kursov, 1872–1882 g.* St Petersburg, 1883.

Tatishchev, S.S. *Imperator Aleksandr II: ego zhizn' i tsarstvovanie.* 2 vols. St Petersburg, 1903.

Thiergen, Peter. *Wilhelm Heinrich Riehl in Russland (1856–1886). Studien zur russischen Publizistik und Geistesgeschichte der zweiten Hälfte des 19. Jahrhunderts.* Giessen, 1978.

Tikhomirov, M.N. et al., eds. *Istoriia Moskovskogo universiteta v dvukh tomakh, 1755–1955.* 2 vols. Moscow, 1955.

Timiriazev, K.A. "Probuzhdenie estestvoznaniia v tret'ei chetverti veka." In *Istoriia Rossii v XIX veke.* Russian Bibliographical Institute Granat. Vol. 7, 1–30. St Petersburg, 1909.

"Ukazatel' literatury zhenskago voprosa na russkom iazykh." Parts 1, 2. *Severnyi vestnik*, 7, 8 (July, August 1877): 1–32, 33–55.

Vucinich, Alexander. *Science in Russian Culture, 1861–1917.* Stanford, 1970.

Whelan, Heidi W. *Alexander III & the State Council. Bureaucracy & Counter-Reform in Late Imperial Russia.* New Brunswick, NJ, 1982.

Whittaker, Cynthia H. "The Women's Movement during the Reign of Alexander II: A Case Study in Russian Liberalism." *Journal of Modern History*, 48, no. 2 (June 1976): 35–69.

Yaney, George L. *The Systematization of Russian Government: Social Evolution in the Domestic Administration of Imperial Russia, 1711–1905.* Urbana, Chicago, and London, 1973.

Zabludovskii, P.E. *Istoriia Otechestvennoi Meditsiny.* Moscow, 1961.

Zaionchkovskii, P.A. *Krizis samoderzhaviia na rubezhe 1870–1880-kh godov.* Moscow, 1964.

– *Rossiiskoe samoderzhavie v kontse XIX stoletiia.* Moscow, 1970.

Zeifman, N.V. "'Srednee obrazovanie v sisteme kontrreform 1880-kh godov." PH D dissertation. Moscow University, 1973.

Zelnik, Reginald E. *Labour and Society in Tsarist Russia. The Factory Workers of St Petersburg, 1855–1870.* Stanford, 1971.

# Index

Academic intelligentsia, 21, 27, 36–7
Academy of Science, 61
Advanced midwifery courses, 56, 57, 77–84. *See also* Women's medical courses
Aksakova, Vera S., 95
Alarchinskie Courses, 42–3
Aleksandrova, Varvara, 55
Alexander II, 3, 5, 8, 24, 40, 62, 67, 75, 77, 85; assassination of, 58, 71, 81; attitudes concerning women's education, 7, 81, 87, 102; and ministers, 7, 27, 33, 41, 78, 86; reforms of, 6, 17, 96; and State Council, 27, 97
Alexander III, 72, 76, 88, 93–8 passim, 100; and State Council, 96–7
All-Russian Union for Women's Equality, 102
Andreev, K., 71
Antonovich, P.A., 64

Bakunin, Michael, 53
Bardina, Sofiia, 54–5
Beketov, A.N., 37, 39, 74, 76
Bestuzhev-Riumin, K.N., 37, 39, 74
Bestuzhevskie Courses of St

Petersburg, 63–4, 72–6, 81, 98–100; enrolment, social status, and religious affiliation of auditors, 73, 99–100; and radicalism, 67, 76; Soviet scholars' views on, 6, 74–5
Bokov, P.I., 14
Bokova, Mariia A. (née Obrucheva), 14, 19, 25, 26, 57
Bolsheviks, 101
Borodin, A.P., 87
Boys' secondary education. *See* Gymnasia
Bréa, Léonie [pseud. Andrée Léo], 5–6
Butler, Josephine, 5

Chaikovskii Circle, 42–3, 54
Chemodanova, Larissa V., 54
Chernyshevskii, N.G., 13–15, 54
*Crime and Punishment* (Dostoevskii), 16
Crimean War, 5, 7, 9, 10, 11, 17, 21, 29, 100

*Dead Souls* (Gogol), 4
Decembrists, 35
D'Héricourt, Jenny, 5, 12
Delianov, I.D.: assistant minister of education, 58–

61 passim, 68; minister of education, 49, 66, 71, 74, 76, 88–9 passim
Delianov Commission on women's higher courses, 59–62, 123–4n3
Dolgorukov, Prince V.A., chief of gendarmes and head of Third Department, 20
Dostoevskii, F.M., 16
Dragnevich, Natalia P., 91
Drentel'n, A.R., chief of gendarmes and head of Third Department, 67, 69, 70, 86
Dubovitskii, P.A., 25

Education system, 60–1
Elementary schools, 3, 60, 61
Emancipation of serfs, 6, 17, 20; economic consequences for gentry women, 26

Family: women's position in, 4, 13, 14, 26, 54
*Fathers and Sons* (Turgenev), 16
*Fel'dsher, fel'dsheritsa. See* Paramedics
Feminists: Western, 5–6, 12; Russian organizations of, 102

cholas II, 100–1. *See also* Bestuzhevskie Courses; Guerrier's Courses; Lubianskie Courses
Women's legal training, 100
Women's medical courses, 5, 8, 27, 56, 57, 77–84; enrolment, social status, and religious affiliation of auditors, 81–2; and radicalism, 66, 85–6; closed under Alexander III, 87–8,

94; development under Nicholas II, 100
Women's Progressive Party, 102
Women's theological courses, 100

Zasulich, Vera, 66–7
Zemstvo: educational role, 30–2 passim; liberalism, 24–5; and women's higher courses, 69–70; and

women doctors, 77, 83, 84–5, 89, 91–2
*Zhenskii vopros. See* Woman question
*Zhenskii vrach. See* Women doctors
*Znakharka,* 92
Zurich: Russian revolutionary organizations at, 53. *See also* Russian women in Zurich